THE GREATEST COAST GUARD RESCUE STORIES EVER TOLD

EDITED BY TOM McCARTHY

Guilford, Connecticut

An imprint of Globe Pequot

Distributed by NATIONAL BOOK NETWORK

British Library Cataloguing in Publication Information available

Library of Congress Cataloging-in-Publication Data

Names: McCarthy, Tom, 1952- editor of compilation.
Title: The greatest Coast Guard rescue stories ever told / edited by Tom
  McCarthy.
Description: Guilford, Connecticut : Lyons Press, [2017] | Includes
  bibliographical references.
Identifiers: LCCN 2016059607 (print) | LCCN 2017000141 (ebook) | ISBN
  9781493027026 (pbk.) | ISBN 9781493027033 (e-book)
Subjects: LCSH: United States. Coast Guard—Search and rescue
  Operations—History.
Classification: LCC VG53 .G735 2017 (print) | LCC VG53 (ebook) | DDC
  363.28/60973—dc23
LC record available at https://lccn.loc.gov/2016059607

♾™ The paper used in this publication meets the minimum requirements of American National Standard for Information Sciences—Permanence of Paper for Printed Library Materials, ANSI/NISO Z39.48-1992.

Printed in the United States of America

CONTENTS

Contents

Introduction

THERE IS NOTHING REMOTELY RELAXING ABOUT READING THIS BOOK— in the best way possible of course. There is certainly much to be inspired about, and perhaps even be mesmerized by. Awestruck even. This collection will give you much to reflect on as you sit back in the plush comfort of your favorite chair.

But relax? Forget about it.

Whether it is pulling survivors hanging to life by a fingernail from the frigid waters of midwinter Lake Michigan or jumping from a helicopter that is beyond its fuel limit, the US Coast Guard has always done what it was supposed to do. It has done it without fanfare or hoopla or self-centered celebration. The men and women of the Coast Guard have for decades put their own lives at risk so others might live. Plain and simple: They did it and continue to do it *because* it was what they have been trained to do and what they want to do.

The stories in this collection have two common threads: They are unbelievable yet true, and they are remarkably inspirational. It's important to emphasize the "true" part, because if these stories were fiction, no one would believe them. Too full of adrenaline and heroics, you would say. But they are true, and along the way readers will learn the rich and stunning history of a service branch few people know much about. It is ironic in a way. People should know more about the Coast Guard, but the people on these pages could not care less about fame and celebrity.

They save lives; that is all that matters—all they want to do.

Here are thirteen dynamic stories that will keep you on the edge of your seat, glad you are safe and warm, and thankful there are men and women out there who will put their lives in danger at the drop of a hat to save you. Never give it a second thought, in fact. It's their job. And you will learn their jaw-dropping skills and daring came after arduous training designed to weed out the weak and the undecided. Make no mistake—the men and women of the Coast Guard are heroes.

Snow, ice, surf, monster waves, enemy attacks, hurricanes, raging seas—the settings and the challenges they presented were simply a minor change in the script. The setting really didn't matter. What mattered were the people in danger and saving them. The Coast Guard went out, went unblinking and unaffected, and calmly accomplished their mission.

People who make their living pulling the unfortunate from icy waters and crashing waves don't decide to take it up on a whim. They know what's in store and do it anyway, with great pride and enthusiasm. And they would return and do it again the next day without complaint.

As one of the heroes here says to a colleague as their rescue boat is overwhelmed by waves, referring to the manual by which they train and live:

"The Blue Book says we've got to go *out*," he snapped at the man. "It doesn't say a damn thing about having to come *back*."

The courageous men and women you'll read about here were all active participants in what the bureaucrats euphemistically called "search and rescue" missions. The "search" part actually sounds benign, maybe even boring. But of course the reality is the "rescue" part—the dangerous and sometimes fatal efforts these men and women put forth day in and day out.

The stories here will take you into the Gulf of Alaska to pluck grateful survivors from imminent and certain death to the Atlantic coast looking for German U-boats during World War II. Few people know it, but the Coast Guard's most intense lifesaving activity was in the dark days of early 1942, when Nazi submarines were running rampant along the Atlantic and Gulf Coasts, picking off freighters and tankers even within sight of land.

You'll find yourself in the Gulf of Mexico during Hurricane Katrina and off ship-killing Cape Hatteras during Hurricane Sandy. You'll learn how a Coast Guard crew saved the entire New York Harbor from incineration.

"Two Tankers Down," Robert Frump's account in chapter twelve of what many have called the greatest Coast Guard rescue in history—which is truly saying a lot—was made into the 2016 blockbuster film *The Finest Hours*. I'd assert without going out on a limb that Mr. Frump's account of the sinking oiler tankers off Cape Cod, the ravenous seas, and the unrelenting nor'easter is much better than the film.

But of course you already know that reading is much better than watching. That will only be reinforced by the treasures here.

Just don't expect to relax.

—Tom McCarthy

The Falls

Martha LaGuardia Kotite

"When we would show up on scene for a rescue, you'd never know exactly what you were going to get. There was always that excitement, that anticipation that every day was going to be a little different."

FOR COAST GUARD SECOND CLASS AVIATION SURVIVAL TECHNICIAN Eric Mueller, his first tour as a rescue swimmer was unusual. In just four years at Air Station Detroit, he earned multiple prestigious medals for a variety of harrowing rescues. About that period in his life, the twenty-eight-year-old rescue swimmer recalled, "I was on fire. It just happened to be I was in the right place at the right time."

Being in the right place was fortunate for Mueller, who had discovered the Coast Guard by chance. Pursuing a degree in recreational management at Sierra Nevada College in Lake Tahoe, he spent more time snowboarding than studying. After switching colleges a couple of times and averaging a 3.5 GPA, he decided that he did not want to continue his college education. Sitting in class and trying to take notes made him crazy because he believed he was missing something. He talked with his father, a retired U.S. Army colonel, about his future. Serving in the Marine Corps seemed to be a fine idea and a good fit.

Mueller drove two hours to the joint service recruiting building in Cleveland, Ohio, to meet with the Marine recruiter. As he left the meeting to think things over during lunch, something caught his eye. It was a poster of a Coast Guard rescue swimmer jumping out of a helicopter. Halfway down the hall and almost signed up with the Marines, he turned into the Coast Guard recruiter's office. He told his story. When he finished, Mueller was surprised that the recruiter refused him. He told Mueller to finish college because he had great potential to become an officer. "He wouldn't sign me and told me the rescue swimmer program might be finished by the time I completed boot camp anyway," recalled Mueller. During this period, the Coast Guard was restructuring the aviation workforce.

Mueller returned home to think over his options. The next day he returned to tell the Marine Corps recruiter he wanted to serve in the Coast Guard instead. It took another meeting with the resistant Coast Guard recruiter before Mueller would enlist. One year later, in 1994, he began his active duty service, still convinced he wanted to be a helicopter rescue swimmer.

After finishing boot camp, he was selected to serve in the Presidential Honor Guard for two years in Washington, DC. From this plum assignment as a seaman, he transferred to Air Station Barbers Point in Hawaii in 1996. There, he was encouraged to consider another aviation specialty. It would be a lengthy wait to be accepted into the rescue swimmer school.

"I told them that this is all I want to do and if I can't do this, then I'm not going to stay in the Coast Guard," Mueller said. He chose to wait for his chance to go to rescue swimmer school.

Committed to his dream, he volunteered after hours assisting aircrews with their training requirements, or "minimums," by being the hoist "duck" (volunteer) riding in the rescue basket. Mueller would also come into work early to complete his assignments so he could justify going on the flights. "Being a seaman was a lot different from being in the Presidential Honor Guard. [As a seaman] I was cleaning toilets, picking up, doing lawn care, carpentry, and stuff like that," mused Mueller. He spent as much time as possible working for the rescue swimmers. "I probably did a lot of their work learning about their job."

Three years after signing up with the recruiter, Mueller completed AST school and was officially qualified as a swimmer with his name nationally registered as a certified EMT. Mueller was ready. He had no idea that his vision of a perfect career would be cut short because of a crippling injury. Meanwhile, he would have the time of his life.

The good times started in Detroit. As a third class aviation survival technician assigned to Air Station Detroit, Mueller became known for his first rescue. During the night of December 29, 1998, he recovered eighteen hypothermic fishermen and their "rescuers."

The men were trapped on a fast-sinking ice floe in Lake St. Clair, Michigan. Firemen were first to arrive on scene aboard a hovercraft. They had tried to save the fishermen when a sudden increase in the lake's wave height combined with strong gusts of wind and snow showers capsized it. Everyone was tossed into the icy lake.

"When we were trying to find people in the ice, we hit a whiteout, where you can't see anything but snow," recalled Mueller. "The pilot started losing altitude and the copilot picked up on it, grabbed the controls, and brought us back up to altitude."

The Coast Guard aircrew located the people and quickly deployed Mueller. "They were sticking up from the water, sinking, and coming up again for air," recalled Mueller as he was hoisted down to recover the men. "One of the firemen had shuttled people off the ice when it started to break up," Mueller recalled. "The waves were so big that the hovercraft overturned. The civilian they had rescued fell into the water again. I saw the fireman hold his hands, pull him off the bottom of the upside-down hovercraft. He looked like a crucifix he was so rigid."

After two hoists of survivors using direct deployment, the helicopter experienced mechanical difficulties, which mandated an immediate return to the air station. Mueller transferred from that helicopter to the waiting one, which immediately took him back to the scene.

The Coast Guard had also launched a forty-one-foot utility boat. It had to be pulled out of dry dock and deiced before the coxswain could navigate up the icy Detroit River.

The Coast Guard's work boat was directed in closer to be used as a platform to bring the men into shore. "The small boat coxswain called the helicopter and said 'I'm worried the ice is going to poke a hole in my hull. You've got to come get them,'" Mueller said.

Working together the small boat and second helicopter aircrew sent down Mueller who hoisted the four remaining firemen from the boat's deck out of the arctic-like conditions.

In all, one rescue swimmer and two Coast Guard HH-65 helicopters and aircrews executing thirteen hoists saved the stranded people.

There was one moment Mueller will never forget about that night. When he was coming up from a hoist with a survivor in his arms, he was pulled into the cabin by the flight mechanic, who said, "Let me fix this, your strop is not around you right." Mueller had held the man with his legs and held on supporting himself during hoist, all the while not connected to the D-ring that should have taken the load. If he had let go too soon, Mueller would have fallen.

Mueller was awarded the Coast Guard Air Medal. By nature humble and modest, he credited his fellow men for enabling him to save the lives of many. They were the flight mechanic, and Lieutenant Commander Joe Kelly and Lieutenant Rich Suskey, pilots for the first helicopter. The second aircrew comprised Commander Darrell Nelson and Commander Greg Hack and flight mechanic AMT2 Kevin Bunn.

Five months later, Mueller would be dramatically tested again. During the afternoon of May 12, 1999, while refueling an HH-65 helicopter at Port Clinton Airport in Ohio, the Detroit aircrew was called into action. Several Mayday calls were overheard on Channel 16. Before responding, they immediately dropped off a reserve commissioned officer in the aircraft for area familiarization. This left Lieutenant Rich Suskey to single-handedly fly Mueller and the flight mechanic, AVT1 Tom Carter, to the call.

When they arrived, a boat was sinking from a large hole in the hull. A father, mother, son, and their friend struggled to stay afloat in Lake Erie.

A Coast Guard forty-one-foot utility boat, CG 41487, arrived on scene, and the crew pulled the mother from the wreckage.

Mueller deployed. He swam through the debris and large, five-foot choppy lake waves toward the others.

The first man Mueller reached was in a state of panic from hypothermia and then shock. He became combative and ripped off Mueller's swimmer's mask. Mueller spoke to him to calm him, reason with him before he could have him hoisted by rescue basket into the helicopter's cabin.

Mueller turned to look for another person in the debris zone. "A wave dropped and there he was," said Mueller of the adult man. "He jumped on top of me screaming for his dad." Mueller managed to take control of the situation by repositioning the man for hoisting. Seeing that he was obviously distressed, Mueller tried to reassure the person by rationalizing with him. Mueller explained how he would hoist him into the helicopter and out of the dangerous environment before he could look for his father. Mueller asked, "Where is your dad?" He said, "I think he is under the boat."

Suskey held the helicopter in a low hover once the son was aboard. With Carter watching from above, Mueller looked under and around the boat. There was no sign of the father.

Carter and Suskey pointed Mueller toward a shadow just below the murky surface. The father, who apparently had tried unsuccessfully to put his life vest on, was submerged a few feet below. "I dove as deep as I could with a dry suit on," said Mueller. "He was a big guy and unconscious."

Suskey, from the right seat, continued to single-handedly pilot the helicopter and maintain a steady hover at just fifteen feet above the surface. Mueller prepared to hoist the man.

Carter saw exactly where the helicopter needed to be and aimed to pinpoint the rescue basket location there for the recovery. He gave the pilot instructions to move the helicopter and dangling basket into position.

Out of the corner of his eye, Suskey saw the Put-in-Bay Express Ferry approach. It was trying to help with the rescue but was dangerously close to the helicopter. Suskey, afraid they might collide, instructed Mueller to come off the hook.

Mueller grabbed the basket. It was repositioned within his reach after the danger had passed. His adrenaline was pumping now. It supplied him with needed strength to move the heavy man inside. With the man in the helicopter, the flight mechanic sent the bare hook back down for Mueller to attach to his TRI-SAR harness for his hoist.

With Mueller safely aboard, Suskey began his forward flight. He flew to Port Clinton Airport, where emergency medical crews awaited their arrival.

During the flight, Mueller and Carter began CPR to try and revive the father. "I remember the son was in the back of the helicopter watching me. The father threw up in my mouth, so much so that it went around the one-way CPR pocket mask, into my eyes, and all over the helicopter cabin and Carter, everywhere," recalled Mueller. No matter how much effort Mueller put into reviving the man, he died.

While the aircrew dropped off the father, his son, and the friend, the aircrew received urgent news over the radio. The mother was hypothermic and going into shock aboard the Coast Guard utility boat.

Suskey banked the helicopter around toward the boat. Carter quickly lowered Mueller, a trained EMT, to the small boat. Mueller assessed her situation. He found the patient to be in critical condition and decided it would be an unnecessary risk to hoist her. It was safer and just as expeditious to transfer her in the boat to the medical treatment facility.

Mueller was awarded the Coast Guard Commandant's Letter of Commendation for his meritorious service.

Only eight months later, on February 18, 2000, Mueller was called for another daring ice case. Three people were stranded on ice floes in the vicinity of Marblehead, Ohio. He expertly recovered the survivors. For his superior performance of duty, Mueller was awarded the Coast Guard Achievement Medal.

"As recues go, all of us wanted a case off Niagara Falls. It would be really cool," said the now thirty-one-year old Mueller, promoted to AST2. For Mueller, the chance came quite surprisingly on October 24, 2001. This would be the last rescue for which he would receive a personal medal for his valor. It was also shortly before he would suffer a disabling injury.

Following the September 11 terrorist attacks the previous month, Coast Guard aircrews were given weeklong assignments to the Niagara Falls Air Reserve Station. From there, their mission was to fly Homeland Security patrols over the Great Lakes, Saint Lawrence Seaway, and other high-risk targets or waterways looking for unusual activity.

Mueller was seated in the back of an HH-65 helicopter with Lieutenant Commander Richard Hinchion, Lieutenant Eric Hollinger, and Avionics Technician Second Class Sean Lott.

Having just completed their morning surveillance flight of targets of interest along the lakes, they refueled the HH-65 helicopter, tail number CG 6558. Anticipating another surveillance flight assignment after lunch, the pilots had elected to take on a maximum fuel load, four hundred pounds above normal. This was the first day of their duty week, and they were looking forward to their lunch break.

As Mueller reached for the door of the Chinese restaurant, Hinchion's cell phone rang. Everyone watched as Hinchion listened intently to the call and mouthed to his team, "O-P-S." He motioned with urgency for everyone to turn back to the van; he had just spoken with operations, and they had been assigned a rescue. Hinchion increased his pace to a jog, and the others followed. Jumping into the van, the pilot reported to his team that a man was clinging to a rock at the top of the American Falls.

Lott, who had slipped into the driver's seat, spun the van around like it was a sports car and skidded out of the parking lot. Back on the base, "We were flying through barricades because we knew we had to move fast to save this guy," said Lott. Reportedly, the man had jumped into the whitewater and was carried downstream with the twenty-five-knot current. He clawed at anything with his bare hands and legs to stop his progression toward the falls. In a desperate attempt to stop, he grabbed on to a partially submerged rock.

Local fire departments and police had already tossed lines and a life raft to try and save the man. The lines were swept downstream before ever reaching him, and the life raft toppled over the edge of the falls. "We really thought the park rangers were going to save the guy first," recalled Mueller of his thoughts as he prepared for the rescue. "We were out of our civilian clothes and into our dry suits with the rotor blades of 6558 turning in about five minutes."

Hollinger took the right pilot's seat and was at the flight controls. Next to him in the copilot's position sat Hinchion. He would oversee the mission as aircraft commander. As they taxied the helicopter, each expressed mutual concern about the aircraft's load weight being at its upper limit. Should they take precious time to jettison fuel, time that could be used to save a man exposed now to the frigid waters for over thirty-five minutes?

"They questioned if they would have enough power to pull up into a hover because we had so much fuel," said Mueller. Attempting to hover and rescue the man over the 176-foot falls even without extra fuel was extremely dangerous. According to www.niagarafallsalive.com, the volume of water flow could reach 150,000 U.S. gallons per second. Knowing that every moment was critical, the pilots decided to test the helicopter's power in a fifty-foot hover before they left the airport. Surprisingly, the available power was good. The pilots counted on the falls to provide some airlift too. Relieved that it was not crucial to jettison fuel, they pressed on.

Without a speed restriction, they traveled at airspeeds exceeding one hundred and twenty knots. In just three minutes, they were over the Niagara River executing a slow flyby of the American Falls to search for the man. He was visible from the air only because his presence made a much bigger white spot in the dark green and blue rapids, giving away his location. He appeared as an interruption, a break in the water's rush toward the falls. It slammed into and over him, creating the white water and spray that was larger than anything else nearby. He miraculously clung to a submerged rock near the top of the falls.

The man had been in the fifty-degree water for close to forty minutes. The Coast Guard rescuers guessed he was hypothermic and barely holding on. They could see the water rushing by him with excessive speed on its natural highway.

Hollinger circled the helicopter overhead while Lott and Mueller made preparations in the cabin to deploy the rescue swimmer.

It was Hollinger's first case as "pilot at the controls." Hinchion trusted him and provided guidance as the aircraft commander. In addition to overseeing the mission, he monitored the radios, which were "out of control" with chatter from the other rescue teams working the case.

The aircrew had been trained to use a decision-making process called Crew Resource Management. "We talked about what we wanted to do and how to do it safely. If the swimmer felt it was beyond his capabilities, he could refuse to go in the water," explained Mueller. "I've never heard of anyone doing that. I will admit that I did have a lump in my throat and my heart was pumping as I got my gear ready."

In no time, the team had agreed to rescue the man using a "swift water rescue" method. This direct-deployment technique, taught at the Advanced Rescue Swimmer School, meant that Mueller would stay attached to the hoist cable when he entered the currents.

"He was like a little kid he was so excited," recalled Mueller of Hollinger's first rescue. With great care, Hollinger flew toward the stranded man in an attempt to maintain a twenty-foot hover directly overhead. Aware of the dangerous forces created by the helicopter's own powerful push of air and water from its spinning rotors, he knew the rotors could "wash" the man right off the rock.

Lott, in his first year of flying as a flight mechanic, was working his second case. In a pivotal job, he would control the aircraft's hoist cable, the lifeline for both Mueller and the man, while directing Hollinger into an exact position for the hoist. He would serve as the pilot's eyes in the backseat. The pilots sat too far forward of the hoist area to observe what was happening below and behind them as they attempted to maintain a hover.

Mueller was the glue that made it all stick. He planned to deploy attached to the hoist cable. He would use standard hand signals to communicate with Lott regarding where he wanted to be moved. Mueller's objective was to secure some rescue strops around the man, without knocking him off the rock and before the man's hold weakened.

They were ready to execute the mission.

"Lott put me down in the water far enough upstream so I could use the currents to draw me towards him and straddle the rock he was on," said Mueller. "But the twenty-five-knot rapids were swirling and I shot right around him."

The first attempt failed to get Mueller close enough to carefully grab the man, but Mueller was able to see that he was holding on to the rock with only his bare hands. Water rushed into his face. "I was scared I might knock the guy off the rock or else he would be swept off the rock at any moment!" said Mueller. "The water was only about five feet deep, but it was moving so swiftly that he could not even stand up."

Determined, the aircrew knew without a spoken word to set up, try again. "I told Hollinger that his hover was not steady enough. We were moving around too much," said Lott over the ICS. Hinchion suggested Hollinger use the trees, a fixed object, on shore to give him fixed positions. It would be a tool to help him steady his hover. "The water which moved under the helicopter played tricks on his mind, giving an illusion that he was not holding the helicopter steady," said Mueller. "It had caused him to readjust continually."

Lott guided Hollinger into the "sweet spot" he wanted the helicopter to be in before deploying Mueller. Within a second, the helicopter was over the target and Lott lowered Mueller.

Mueller now fished for the man from the end of the stainless steel hoist cable. Lott released more cable as Mueller advanced. This would enable Mueller to be carried forward using the force of the raging waters instead of fighting it.

"When I finally got to the rock, I straddled it to break the force of the water which rushed around my body and kind of bypassed him, taking the water off of his face," Mueller stated. "Then I immediately stuck one of my hands up through his belt so that if the man did let go, I'd have him around my forearm. With my other hand, I put a 'quick strop,' or horse-collar-like device, around his chest and then grabbed his coat," recalled Mueller. "Then I put a crotch strop between his legs to keep him from sliding out of the quick strop. While I was doing all this, the man wrapped the slacked cable around his forearm!

"The man was panicking—he saw the cable and wanted to get wrapped up into it," exclaimed Mueller. "I didn't want to say anything to him, fearing he might let go. He was very incoherent. He was rigid with hypothermia and had tunnel vision too. He just wanted to get into the helicopter."

The man's action had in an instant created a life-threatening situation for the rescuer too. Lott saw what was happening and remained calm just as he had been trained to do in a justifiable panic situation. He articulated new positioning instructions to Hollinger in a controlled voice, hoping not to alarm him.

Mueller had to clear the cable before he could send Lott a thumbs-up, or ready-for-hoist, signal. He had no other option but to force the man to release. To free their lifeline, Mueller gave a couple of swift blows to the man's forearm hoping he would let go. The man did not release; he had a deathlike grip on it. Mueller opened his nonskid, lined-gloved hand and pounded his palm onto the man's hand. The man must have felt sharp pain, because he let go. Mueller looked up into the sky for Lott, who saw what he was waiting for: a thumbs-up. With that permission, Lott hoisted the men in less than a minute to the safety of the helicopter's cabin.

Ready for forward flight, the pilots prepared to leave the perilous hover. Because of the weight-load limitations of the helicopter, the pilots could not safely climb up and over the trees that provided a natural fence on both banks of the river. The only way out was directly over the falls. At twenty feet and with fifteen-knot airspeed, Hollinger commanded CG 6558 forward over the falls. Using the gorge's drop as a cushion, he had room to increase power and altitude. The helicopter throttled ahead and out. Around seventy knots airspeed and above the gorge, Hollinger banked the helicopter left over the American Falls. They flew toward the park's parking lot, where an ambulance and emergency crews were awaiting their arrival.

During the short flight, Mueller and Lott treated the man for hypothermia in the rear of the cabin. They carefully removed his wet clothing. "While I was taking off his layers of sweatshirts, he reached under the last one and pulled out his Marine Corps pin and demanded that I take it from him. He was expressing his gratitude," said Mueller. "I insisted that I couldn't take it from him before he again became combative, a sign that he was going into shock." Mueller and Lott used blankets and dry clothing to warm up the man's body.

Five minutes later they landed in the parking lot. When Lott opened the cabin door, an excited crowd greeted them. Some of them were rescuers who had attempted to reach the man from shore and others were throngs of tourists who had lined the riverbanks to watch the spectacle.

The ambulance crew made room and helped Mueller and Lott place the man on a stretcher. As he was being wheeled away, he sat up and saluted Mueller with tears in his eyes.

"A lot of people who are in the rescue business told me how cool it was that I got a rescue on the falls," said Mueller. "I later learned that the man was suicidal and apparently had changed his mind about dying that day!"

Aviation Survival Technician Second Class Eric Mueller was awarded his second Coast Guard Air Medal for his extraordinary heroism. The pilots and crew of CG 6558 each received Commendation Medals. In October of 2002, the Coast Guard Foundation in its annual ceremony recognized the crew of CG 6558 as heroes during its New York City Salute to the Coast Guard. Mueller made a point to recognize the aircrew he flew with as enabling him to accomplish the mission.

"Eric Mueller is someone I've flown with a lot. If you're going to pick your best to represent you, or a person that shows the corps' values of honor, respect, and devotion to duty, Eric shows all three," said Lott. "I look up to him. Once we get into a situation, I know he's going to do it right and not make it worse."

The summer of 2003, Mueller, his wife Barbara, and daughter Mikayla moved to Oregon, where he was assigned to Air Station North Bend. His son, Jacob, was born in October of that year. Mueller did not plan to reenlist when his commitment ended in September of 2004.

He had one very unlucky day two months before he would leave the Coast Guard and apply to serve as an Ohio fireman. During a lunch break, Mueller and others at the air station played street hockey. The command-endorsed "sport lunch" included wearing safety gear, no skates, and clearing the helicopters out of the hangar to make room for the sport.

"My foot just grabbed a really clean piece of floor and it stuck," recalled Mueller. "I swung around my leg. At the kneecap, the calf or bottom portion of my leg stuck to the ground and my thigh spun around it. My heel was in the front and my toes were in the back." Being a trained EMT, Mueller took action. "I reached down and realigned the lower half of my leg so that my toes were now facing forward," said Mueller. "The resulting maintenance of blood flow may very well have prevented the need for amputation."

Mueller pushed through his recovery like a rescue swimmer would. Initially, doctors felt if he had lost circulation to the lower part of his leg, they would have to amputate it. He had what he refers to as a "lame leg," or limited use of his right knee.

With his drive and determination, the athletic Mueller progressed a lot further than doctors ever expected he could for the injury he had suffered.

After about a year of rehabilitation and working out in the weight room, he regained strength and movement in his knee. Because nerves in his leg remain irreversibly damaged, he can no longer lift his foot when he walks. He uses a spring-activated brace to assist him. "I'm not complaining, but it is still a pain in the ass. Little kids notice when I'm walking with shorts on."

Recently medically retired, Mueller was credited with eleven years of service. Of all the awards and recognition he received during his career, the one thing that would have meant more would have been to receive a thank-you note from one of the people he saved. "That is the only thing I did not receive."

He is a stay-at-home dad for the couple's two-year-old son and eight-year-old daughter in Bowling Green, Ohio. His wife works as an English teacher at a Penta Career Vocational Center, one of her many different jobs during her career as spouse of a constantly relocating Coast Guard petty officer.

Of caring for his son, he says it is one of the toughest things he's ever done.

In the future, he would like to go back to school to earn a bachelor's degree in construction technology from Bowling Green State University. "I'd like to manage construction sites and finances for large corporations, firms, or even homes." He likens his future goal to being an apprentice for Donald Trump.

Rescuing the Rescuer:
Critical Incident Stress Management

You are able to off-load the information, and that is a part of the healing process. Rescue swimmers or firefighters are usually macho, type-A personalities. The last thing they want to do is admit to someone that they need some help.

—Chief Warrant Officer George Cavallo,
rescue swimmer

During the evening of July 12, 1994, Air Station Humboldt Bay in California responded to a distress call from two people aboard a grounded, forty-foot sailing vessel by sending an HH-65A Dolphin rescue helicopter. "While engaged in a nighttime search for the stranded vessel, the 6541 struck a shoreline cliff in heavy fog just south of Shelter Cove and was lost," wrote rescue swimmer and Chief Warrant Officer George Cavallo.

The rescue swimmer on that search and rescue mission, Senior Chief Petty Officer Peter A. Leeman, perished along with pilots Lieutenant Lawrence B. Williams and Lieutenant Mark E. Koteek and flight mechanic First Class Petty Officer Michael R. Gill.

The two people on the sailboat made their way safely to shore.

Then a first class petty officer, George Cavallo was assigned to lead the Air Station Humboldt Bay ASM shop six weeks after Senior Chief Peter Leeman died. He worked with the men, one of whom was his brother-in-law, to bring them back, help them want to go out to save lives again. By paying attention to them, understanding their grief, and normalizing their emotional stress, they were able to overcome their traumatic experience and return to work.

Cavallo would find himself working as a rescuer in a similar tragic case. He was the Coast Guard rescue swimmer deployed to the crash site of the United States Air Force Reserve HC-130 P aircraft on November 22, 1996.

According to Cavallo's written summary of the accident, the fixed-wing aircraft departed Portland, Oregon, on a routine, over-water navigation training mission to Naval Air Station North Island, California, near San Diego. Two hours after it left that evening, all four engines flamed out and the crew declared an emergency. On its final descent, fifteen minutes later, the aircraft slammed into the Pacific Ocean at two hundred miles per hour. Ten of the eleven men on board died. The sole survivor was the radio operator.

What Cavallo saw during his rescue of the C-130 survivor was haunting. The rescue aircrew arrived on scene aboard a Dolphin helicopter and commenced a search for the C-130 crew. "The problem was we only had seven to ten minutes of fuel before we had to go back," Cavallo said. "The first two guys we really couldn't do much for, with sharks circling and taking hits. They were obviously deceased. Then we saw the third guy was waving; we got him and brought him back," said Cavallo, who was hoisted down to rescue the man. "We sent in Coast Guard small boat crews to pick up the bodies. They had been through a catastrophic crash, so the bodies were not in the best shape, and then the sea creatures were taking their turn on them. So those guys [the rescuers] went through critical incident stress counseling, but not with us."

Cavallo and those affected by the traumatic event were provided assistance dealing with their stress or adverse psychological reactions, which can accompany a disaster response. Counselors helped them normalize their experience as part of a Coast Guard–wide program called Critical Incident Stress Management (CISM).

"They put us through these demobilizations, basically where the aircrews got together and each told a part of the story that we knew to be true. . . . I did this, this is how I felt, I saw this, smelled this," Cavallo said. "We go around the group and everyone does that; you are able to piece a whole story together in your brain and in some ways put it to rest. Or if you have questions or you might always be wondering what happened here or there, you are able to now get some kind of closure."

Immediately following Hurricane Katrina's massive rescue and response, CISM counselors were on scene to help rescuers cope. Cavallo, a trained CISM counselor, was close to retirement, working as a marine inspector in New Orleans. He agreed to go behind the scenes with other CISM-trained rescue swimmers, including Lieutenant Mike Odom, who debriefed Cavallo after he worked on the Pacific Ocean C-130 crash in 1996.

"You are able to off-load the information, and that is a part of the healing process," said Cavallo. "Rescue swimmers or firefighters are usually macho, type-A personalities. The last thing they want to do is admit to someone that they need some help." Cavallo said they've found that peers—folks that have been there, done that, have picked up the bodies—are the best folks to talk to these people. "If you've been around rescue swimmers, you know there is a brotherhood, a kind of tightness. To penetrate that circle as a mental health worker or as a psychologist, it is not going to work. They are not going to want to talk to you," Cavallo said.

Cavallo has found acceptance as a CISM counselor throughout his career by starting off by talking about his own experiences as a rescue swimmer, stationed at five air stations, and as a chief at Air Station Kodiak. "The next thing you know they are telling you their life stories; it's great because you really see it work." The program also works the same way for the flight mechanics, pilots, and copilots.

Right after an event, counselors informally talk with rescuers one on one to hear and understand what they went through, which is called demobilization. "We slip in that it is normal to feel that way;

you went through an abnormal event, you picked up some bodies, saw some gory stuff," Cavallo said. "You try to normalize the situation for them so they don't feel like a wimp or not adequate because they can't sleep at night." Cavallo advises those he talks with to spend some of their time off with family; he also encourages exercise.

"We've been working with Master Chief Scott Dyer, the head rescue swimmer, to come up with a game plan on how we're going to talk with a lot of these swimmers. At one point he had sixty rescue swimmers working for him in New Orleans," said Cavallo.

Counselors try to match their interventions, or debriefs, with people they know would feel comfortable talking with them; for example, setting up senior officers and senior enlisted with senior people and vice versa.

Five months after Katrina, a CISM team of rescue swimmers' counselors returned to New Orleans to debrief, or "defuse," rescuers who still needed assistance processing their experience and were having trouble sleeping. "After that, if they need help, they will probably be referred to an Employee Assistance Program. As a peer, you can only do so much," said Cavallo.

The rescue environment following Hurricane Katrina was diverse and unusual. The sheer volume of cases over an extended period of days caused stress to build up with little room for release. Everyone involved in saving lives was dealing with a catastrophic event, a new environment where people had lost everything; each day was uncommon to behold. The culmination of it all led to instances of posttraumatic stress disorder.

"A lot of rescue swimmers were affected by the kids. [A helicopter] would lower a swimmer down and fly off, which is very unusual; usually the helicopter never leaves," said Cavallo. "They would fly off so the rescue swimmer could hear the yells for help. It was dark and they could not see where the people were, so they'd listen. Then [the swimmers] called the helicopter back, got picked up, and [would] go over to the house they heard the cries coming from. They were able to help some, but they would have to leave when the helicopter was full. That meant there was never closure. Rescuers asked, 'Did all those people get saved?'"

In another case, a flight mechanic aboard one of the first helicopters involved with rescues after Katrina stormed ashore was exhausted. She had been hoisting all day long. "We did a debriefing with her," Cavallo said. "She was very concerned about hurting or putting the rescue swimmer in danger because she was so fatigued."

Cavallo was aware that a lot of pilots were having trouble sleeping. In another situation, a rescue swimmer was lowered to search inside a darkened hospital for survivors. "He came around the corner and was faced with four guys with shotguns," said Cavallo. "Earlier that same day people were firing at helicopters. It turned out they were security guards, but [the swimmer] didn't know that at the time." Swimmers were essentially unarmed during the operation. They did carry an ax to help chop into roofs. "You don't want to bring an ax to a gunfight," Cavallo said. "Some of the people in hospitals were in there trying to get drugs. They had to bring SEAL teams in to storm the Convention Center to take it back. There were gangsters in there with guns who were mad they had not been rescued from there and after a while were shooting at helicopters.

"Of course that's on everybody's mind. That's not the thing you're used to. Usually people are very excited to see us and rescue them, and now you're dealing with the possibility of getting shot at, and that's not good.

"Any rescue swimmer will tell you that it is the whole crew, they can't stress that enough, the whole crew has to be cohesive and work together to adjust and overcome the situations they find themselves in."

Three years after the entire Coast Guard aircrew died in the Air Station Humboldt Bay crash, another tragedy would befall Air

Station Humboldt Bay. Cavallo, still the AST shop supervisor and AST1, was six months away from transferring to another air station.

It was June 8, 1997. ASM3 James G. Caines jumped with excitement aboard the HH-65A Dolphin helicopter, tail number 6549. It was his first search and rescue case. Pilots Lieutenant Jeffrey F. Crane and Lieutenant Junior Grade Charles W. Thigpen, along with Aviation Machinist Mate Third Class Richard L. Hughes, were the other members of the aircrew. They were responding to a floundering thirty-seven-foot sailing vessel's call for help. The disabled vessel, with five people on board, was approximately fifty-seven miles west of Cape Mendocino. Buffeted by high winds and heavy seas, it was hardly afloat.

A Dolphin helicopter aircrew flew out twice to circle the boat. The crew dropped a radio to establish communications with the sailors and convince them to abandon ship. "They wouldn't. Then another aircrew assembled, and I flew out with them," Cavallo said. "We spoke to [the people on the boat] on the radio and tried to convince them to get off during the daylight hours, and they said no." Cavallo and his aircrew returned to the air station, close to being "bagged" with too many hours to continue flying. Phone calls were made to bring in a third team.

Meanwhile, the Coast Guard had dispatched an eighty-two-foot patrol boat to the sailing vessel's location to tow it in. A Coast Guard C-130 was circling overhead to help coordinate communications and monitor the unfolding case.

"I was walking across the hangar deck after cleaning the aircraft and here comes Jamie," said Cavallo. "He said, 'Let me take the duty; in case this goes down, I want to take the rescue.'" ASM3 "Jamie" Caines, twenty-four, had qualified as a rescue swimmer two days before. "He was a sharp kid, really driving hard, and we marveled at how he qualified in record time," Cavallo said.

Cavallo tried to convince him that the case was over and would be handled by the patrol boat. He told the younger man to go home, be with his family and young son. Caines was not deterred, saying to Cavallo, "I've trained so hard, worked so hard over the last five months, and I really want to put it all together."

Cavallo, who believed the case was in fact over, said, "All right, if you really want it that bad, you can have it.

"He reached over and hugged me on the hangar deck and said, 'Thanks, I really want to do this,'" recalled Cavallo, very surprised by the affection. "It was just weird, like he was waiting all his life to have this case."

Cavallo went home and had dinner with his wife before going to bed. His phone rang around 11:20 p.m. that night, waking him out of a deep sleep.

—◦—

It was Keith Young, a flight mechanic performing the duties of the air station watch captain that night.

"He said, in a really monotone, depressed tone I'll never forget, 'I've been trying to call the '49. We lost comms with the '49 for over a half hour.'"

"It still didn't dawn on me. I said, 'The '49? Is it on another rescue?'"

"No, they went back out," said Young. "That sailing boat took a bad wave, and it blew out a couple of windows. They took on a little bit of water. The 82er came in and tried to remove the people off the deck. The seas were too rough. It was determined that a helicopter needed to come out and hoist everybody off the vessel."

Cavallo replied, "I'll be right in." He hung up the phone and told his wife they had lost communication with the Coast Guard helicopter, tail number 6549. "I ran out the door and drove to the air station at light speed and went into the communications center." He was informed that they were launching another helicopter to go look for CG 6549. It was now forty-five minutes to an hour after they had lost communications with their fellow airmen.

Cavallo's wife was very alarmed and called his brother-in-law, another rescue swimmer, who in turn informed other swimmers assigned to the air station, who all raced over.

Cavallo got his gear. "I got all dressed up except for my harness. I went out on the tarmac and laid my harness down to step into it. I was pretty frazzled trying to put on my harness." His brother-in-law, ASM1 Mike Steinbach, and another rescue swimmer, ASM2 Rick Flemming, walked over and helped him get dressed. "We didn't say a word to each other. The pilots came out. We were all professional, talked about where we were going, what we were going to do."

The aircrew got into the helicopter and launched into the darkness. "About that time we knew they didn't have enough fuel to get back, so we were all thinking the worst," said Cavallo. They had been briefed about what had happened on scene. "The eighty-two-foot motor lifeboat had put its small boat [a rigid-hull inflatable] back in the water again. It took them a while, but they were able to get everybody off the vessel. The sailboat was bobbing up and down so badly that it would land on the rigid-hull inflatable and bounce off. It was bad conditions, and they were able to pull it off somehow. They had a really rough time."

Cavallo's helicopter arrived on scene, and the aircrew searched until they exhausted all their fuel and had just enough to make it home and land with their normal reserve.

"That was the hardest thing I've ever done in my whole life, my whole Coast Guard career. It was like searching for family or searching for your own. It was very emotional for all of us," Cavallo said. Inside the helicopter it was silent except for the crew maintaining their professionalism, flying and doing the jobs they had to do. "Everybody was glued to every window, looking for a flare, looking for a guy in the water waving, anything. We could not fathom that the whole crew would be lost."

—◦—

"While maneuvering to pick up the sailors, the 6549 and its four-person crew disappeared from contact and was lost," wrote George Cavallo in his summary of the accident. He believes the aircraft hit the water while making an approach to the sailing vessel.

"By this time, every air station along the Pacific Coast had sent a helicopter and every ship within a thousand miles had been diverted. The Coast Guard is a small service. Everyone and their brother were coming in to look for their fellow Coasties."

The captain of the air station grounded Cavallo and the entire aircrew once they landed because they were too close to the situation. There was an abundance of other aircrews and helicopters to continue the search they had started.

The tail of CG 6549 was located later on that afternoon. It would be months before the helicopter was recovered from the deep. There were no survivors. Only the flight mechanic's body was recovered.

"Three rescue swimmers threw their wings on my desk and said they were never flying again," said Cavallo, who was the one to support and lead the swimmers in the shop through the emotional stress and tragic loss. Other air station swimmers were called in to assist. "I left their wings on my desk, and as soon as I got permission to stand duty, I was the first person to stand duty. Three or four days later, they all started standing duty again. They all went on to fly and have great careers. . . . The initial shock was over."

Cavallo says he has a good support system and credits his wife, a psychiatric nurse, with helping him. She also assisted many Coast Guard families as a CISM counselor in Kodiak. "One month later, for about three days, I could not get off the couch, and my wife said to me, 'You know you are going through depression?'"

The two Air Station Humboldt Bay helicopter crashes and resulting loss of precious life in an attempt to help "so others may live" have a significant place in the history of Coast Guard aviation. Neither rescue swimmer was actively deployed when he died. The loss of each man, each member of the aircrew, resonates throughout the Coast Guard to this day.

—MLK

Superstorm: Inside Hurricane Sandy

Kathryn Miles

11:00 p.m.
140 miles off the coast of Hatteras
62°F
Barometer: 29.93 inches (falling)
Winds: 64 mph (N)
Waves: 40 feet
Precipitation: Heavy rain

SCHOLARS ESTIMATE THAT NEARLY A MILLION PEOPLE DIED IN TROPI-
cal cyclones in the last half of the twentieth century. They have no way
of extrapolating how many people died before that. They have even less
of an idea how many people experienced a hurricane and lived to tell
about it. The eyewitness accounts gathered over the years are intermittent
and uneven at best, but they share the hyperbole needed to attempt to
describe what it is like to be trapped inside a storm. One mariner wrote
in 1831 that the "distant roar of the elements" was enough to make him
go mad. The sound, he said, was like "winds rushing through a hallow
vault." Washington Irving called it "a terrific noise" capable of convincing
many that "the end of the world was at hand."

That's how it felt aboard the *Bounty*. The vessel was in trouble. More
than that, it was in crisis. Adam Prokosh had taken a fall at least as

serious as Walbridge's. Claudene Christian was tending to him as best she could. There'd been an electrical fire in the galley, where the force of the waves had also pulled tables from the hinges. Waves had crashed through the windows of the great cabin. The engine room was so inundated with water that equipment was arcing and sparking. The crew had had to abandon it, lest they be electrocuted. Twice, John Svendsen had asked Walbridge to call the Coast Guard. Twice he had refused. The captain was in obvious pain. A few crewmembers wondered if he was able to think straight with that much discomfort. They doubted they'd be able to. Claudene Christian was frustrated—she still felt like she had been trying to help, but people weren't listening to her.

Laura Groves passed around motion-sickness medication, but not everybody could keep it down. It was just so rough out there. Conditions continued to deteriorate. The engines failed, leaving the ship helpless against the waves and winds. The generators stopped as well. The ship went dark. A few crewmembers donned headlamps, but there weren't enough to go around. "I need a light over here," people kept yelling.

It was time to prepare to abandon ship. John Svendsen went above deck to try [to reach] Tracie Simonin on the satellite phone, but the wind was blowing so fiercely he couldn't tell if she answered or not. He ended up talking to her voice mail. Eventually he sent an e-mail to her instead, and it found its way to Coast Guard Chief Petty Officer Jeremy Johnson, the command duty officer at Sector Wilmington. The *Bounty* needed help, but Johnson didn't know how to get to them. He checked the position of all Navy and Coast Guard vessels, but they had long since cleared out of the area. He dialed up the AIS and found a lone cargo ship in the vicinity. It was too dangerous for them to turn back. Johnson contacted his supervisor, Billy Mitchell, who was at home helping his kids prepare their Halloween costumes. His daughter was going as a geisha girl. His son was dressed up as the Flash. Rain was falling outside. There was a little wind.

"It was like watching a horror movie where the audience knows the hero is in trouble, but he doesn't yet realize it," says Mitchell.

Just how bad things had gotten on the *Bounty* was anyone's guess: Billy Mitchell's team at sector was already engaged in a convoluted game of telephone between the *Bounty*, its home office, and the Coast Guard communications center. He needed to talk to them directly, but the only way to do that was to get a plane in the air.

He called Captain Joseph P. Kelly, commander of the Elizabeth City Air Station. It was almost midnight.

"I need a big metal antenna in the air," said Mitchell.

"You're asking me to send my folks into a hurricane," Kelly shot back. Mitchell asked if he had concerns. That struck Kelly as almost absurd.

"Of course I have concerns," said Kelly. "You're asking me to put my assets and my crews in danger. Ultimately, I'm responsible for their lives."

Kelly is a funny, warm, jovial guy. He likes to laugh and quote country music lyrics. Mitchell is hilarious too, though more in a hipster kind of way. They're both as easy to get along with as anyone you might meet. But things had taken a serious turn. Every Coast Guard mission is rated on what's called the GAR score, based on its predicted dangers. A green rating means the crew can pretty much just notify the operations boss on their way out. An amber score and they need to get clearance from that boss. Only Kelly can authorize a more dangerous mission.

"If it's in the red, nobody goes anywhere until I get briefed and I feel good about it," he insists.

But, he adds, it can be a challenge to persuade his crew as much: "They're go-getters. They want to go out. That's just who they are." Sometimes, he says, it's up to him to hold them back.

It was a decision bigger than either he or Mitchell was capable of making, and they knew it. Within minutes, a conference call had been convened, including a representative from the 5th District admiral. They were trying to weigh the cost-benefit of sending personnel into the storm. What, specifically, was to be gained? What could be lost? *A great deal*, thought both Mitchell and Kelly.

"Look," said Kelly. "We're in a storm the size and power of Katrina. It's ugly out there."

Mitchell was resolute. If asked, he is quick to say he doesn't wear his heart on his sleeve, but he was certain someone or something wanted the Coast Guard out there. He wanted Kelly and the others on the phone to understand that he didn't need a plane on top of the *Bounty*—he just needed them to get close enough to communicate. He had to know what was happening on the ship. "Just let them try," he said. "They can always turn back."

———

As soon as Captain Kelly got off the conference call, he picked up his personal cell phone and called C-130 pilot Wes McIntosh in Raleigh. He and his crew were already prepping for their departure. The *Bounty* crew, Kelly explained to McIntosh, had indicated they could make it until morning. Kelly didn't want anyone risking their lives if the ship was going to be okay.

"Listen, I'm very concerned about this," he said to McIntosh.

The pilot told him they had been looking at the radar.

"Good," said his commander. "Then you know that the bands of heavy weather are stretching from shoreline to ninety miles out."

McIntosh said he did. They wanted to go.

Kelly sighed. It was, he thought, a lot easier to be a pilot than to be a commander sitting at home worrying about one.

"Okay," he conceded. "Get your crew. But you are to go no farther than you need to establish comms. If you can talk to them from the shore, then that's where you stay."

He repeated himself. "Just establish comms. That's all you need to do now."

"Roger," replied McIntosh. "Got it."

The pilot took a deep breath. It was either going to be an exhaustingly long night or a tragically short one. It all depended upon the *Bounty*.

———

MONDAY
2:28 a.m.
Elizabeth City, North Carolina
62°F
Barometer: 29.31 inches (dropping)
Winds: 27 mph (NW)
Precipitation: Rain

Joseph Kelly was pacing around his house, stopping every few minutes to check the weather. Storm surge in Maryland was more than four feet. Waves tore through the pier in Ocean City. Twenty-foot waves were being recorded as far north as Islip, on Long Island, New York. Sandy's predicted change in direction was happening. "The turn toward the coast had begun," tweeted the Weather Channel. Kelly's phone rang just after he read that. It was the Coast Guard base, saying that McIntosh's C-130 crew hadn't been able to drop dewatering pumps for the *Bounty*.

Kelly was incredulous. And a little more than mad. "What do you mean they tried to drop pumps? I said establish comms. That's it."

The operations chief on the other end didn't know what to say to that. He stammered a little. Kelly hung up and got dressed. There was no way he was going to sleep now. He'd always told his pilots that he would support them even if he disagreed with their decisions, so long as they could demonstrate a logical thought process. He was really hoping that McIntosh had one now.

———

3:40 a.m.
130 miles off Cape Hatteras
62°F
Barometer: 29.21 inches (falling)
Winds: 57 mph (N)
Waves: 38 feet
Precipitation: Rain

They were the only two planes in the sky for hundreds of miles. That struck both the crews as eerie. Wes McIntosh and his Coast Guard crew continued to circle over the *Bounty*, ducking down to make radio contact with Svendsen, then returning to a safer cruising pattern. His crew was sick and getting pretty banged up. That worried him. Not far from him, the Hurricane Hunters had their own concerns. Jon Talbot didn't like what the data was telling them. Dropsondes on board found a small surface area where winds were registering above 90 miles per hour. Thunderstorms were continuing to build around the storm center. They flew through a perfectly round eye twenty-eight miles across and made note of that too. "#Sandy is still a fully tropical cyclone at this time," tweeted the Weather Channel. "No doubt about it."

One hundred and fifty miles off of Hatteras, the *Bounty* crew was huddled in the great cabin. Some of the headlamps had started to flicker out. They were waiting, but for what they didn't know. Walbridge had thought they could make it until morning. Now he wasn't so sure. Josh Scornavacchi had snagged a guitar out of the lazarette. He was hoping there'd be time for Claudene Christian to sing one last song. But they didn't get a chance. Their captain told them it was time to go. They struggled to climb into their survival suits. Claudene Christian had never practiced getting into one. Jess Hewitt showed her how and cracked a few jokes. "Remember the number of your suit," she told Christian. "That way you'll know where to put it back." That made her friend smile.

Walbridge always warned his crew never to take anything with them in an emergency. "You can't go back for anything," he would say. "Anything." But he did, somehow. Even injured, he managed to make his way down to his cluttered little cabin. He took Claudia's picture off the wall and stuffed it into his suit. Doug Faunt grabbed his teddy bear. Jess Hewitt took the medallion given to her by the crew of the *Mississippi:* By Valor and Arms, Pride Runs Deep. She also grabbed a hair tie and a cigarette lighter. She planned on having a smoke as soon as they made it back to shore. She went back down for a couple of other things too: Prokosh's captain's license—it was a bitch to get a replacement one, she'd always heard—and his pea coat. He had to be freezing. Claudene asked her to go back again, she really wanted her journal, she said.

An hour later, and they were all up on deck. The ship was listing. The skies were clearing. Every once in a while, they could pick out the lights of the C-130 overhead. McIntosh and his crew had done exactly what their commander had told them not to do: They flew in and tried to help. When conditions there got too bad, they'd fly back to their safe holding space on the side of the storm.

"It was important. We were holding their hands," says Mike Myers. "We were trying to say, 'You're not alone. Keep fighting.'"

Somewhere in the distance, the Hurricane Hunters' C-130 was struggling through its own flight pattern.

~ ~

4:28 a.m.
130 miles off Cape Hatteras

On board the *Bounty*, the crew congregated into two groups, braced against whatever they could find to keep from tumbling down the steeply pitched deck. Jess Hewitt thought about capsizing and tried to reassure herself: *I just need to keep breathing. If I can keep breathing, I'll be okay.* She and Drew Salapatek clipped their climbing harnesses together. "You better not leave me," she told him. Meanwhile, Claudene looked around: Matt wasn't nearby. She caught sight of him up near the mast. She smiled and darted to him. Even in the storm, Anna Sprague remembered thinking it was "a cool move."

Claudene never wanted to be alone. Especially in the dark. She nestled in with Sanders. "It's going to be okay, baby girl," he said. That was his nickname for her: *baby girl.* He kept saying it over and over again: "It's going to be okay. It's going to be okay."

Above them, the C-130 kept circling, ducking down just long enough to check on the status of the ship. Every time they did, the turbulence became unbearable. The crew in the back were vomiting. The cargo bay door was covered in it.

Everything appeared to be in stasis. Until suddenly, it wasn't. A wave—bigger than the rest—struck the side of the ship. The vessel screamed and rolled from a 45-degree angle to a 90-degree angle. They were dangling over the water now. Debris rained down around them. A few crewmembers jumped. Some tried to hold on. Matt Sanders caught his foot—it was pinched and he was stuck. Claudene panicked. "What do I do?" she screamed. "What do I do?"

"Claudene, you just have to go for it," Sanders replied. "You have to make your way aft and get clear of the boat."

So she did. Or tried to, anyway. The last he saw of her, she had worked her way back to the mizzen—back to where her original group had been crouching. She was standing on a rail, looking as if she was trying to decide whether or not she should jump. There was no more singing. He never saw her again.

The human body will do anything to avoid drowning. It begins with an involuntary desire to gasp. *Go ahead*, your cells plead, *take a breath*. The pulse accelerates. Carbon dioxide levels in the blood rise, creating first heightened alertness and then anxiety. Once that carbon dioxide reaches a pressure of 55 mm in your arteries, there is no longer any reasoning with your nonthinking self. It will force you to take a breath. If you are still underwater when this decision is made, that is when you will inhale. And if you do, your larynx will spasm—violently—again and again as it attempts to divert the water to your stomach instead of your lungs. In this process, this spasm will also force you to exhale any last remaining air that you didn't even know you had. Your body will do anything—everything—to keep your lungs safe. And this commitment will work, up until the very last second. No matter what, your nonthinking brain will preserve your lungs, the place where air converts into life. Autopsies of drowning victims reveal gallons of water in their stomachs, bellies distended in a last ditch effort to preserve their lungs. So long as it's conscious, the brain will drink until it can breathe.

In the storm-churned sea, the *Bounty* crew were gulping down gallons of oily seawater as they tried to thrash away from the ship. No matter how hard they tried, they could not find enough air. They flailed against debris, trying to grab anything that might save instead of kill them. Most of them were quickly separated. Not Jess Hewitt and Drew Salapatek. They were still tethered together and now trapped underwater. Jess struggled and writhed and bit at her harness, all too aware of what was happening. But still she was pulled down, down, down. She felt like she had become a giant weight. *I can't fight this*, she thought. She prepared to give up. And just then, she popped to the surface. Somehow, Drew had wriggled out of his harness and saved them both.

For now.

Jess faced the *Bounty*, now lying on its side. Each time a waved rolled by, it would possess the ship, raising its enormous masts and spars high into the air before slamming them down again. One of her crew mates got caught on the mizzen mast and was lifted twenty feet in the air. He thought he heard a voice say *Jump, Jump!* So he did, into the recirculating suction caused by the vessel. John Svendsen was there too. Jess watched in horror as the rigging slammed down again, one of the spars smashing against the first mate's head. She turned away and tried to swim; she didn't want to see any more.

—— ◆ ——

6:10 a.m.
Staten Island, New York
57°F
Barometer: 29.36 inches (dropping)
Winds: 29 mph (NNE)
Precipitation: Light rain

Sandy picked up speed, moving northward. The strange blocking pattern over Greenland was preventing the storm from moving out to sea, and the trough over the United States was only deepening the storm's nor'easter characteristics. Inside, winds were gusting at nearly 100 miles per hour, and an eyewall had reemerged. Inexplicably, Sandy was again becoming a hurricane.

"A meteorologically mind-boggling combination of ingredients is coming together," wrote Stu Ostro of the Weather Channel.

Sandy's new eye was now just 220 miles southeast of Atlantic City. Tropical storm gusts of 40 miles per hour had arrived on parts of Long Island and as far north as Boston. High-wind warnings were in effect in seventeen states, including Georgia, Maine, and Ohio. On the Weather Channel, Con Edison spokesperson Chris Olert was explaining that the company had already disconnected steam customers. Thousands of people were without power in Connecticut and on Long Island. Blackouts continued as far south as Georgia.

On Staten Island, traffic was light. The train stations were dark. Wind rocked signs, scattered leaves and trash. It had been raining for most of the night; Damien Moore finished getting ready for work and began his drive into Brooklyn. His neighborhood in Great Kills wasn't in the evacuation zone. It seemed like everything would be fine.

—◆—

6:41 a.m.
Hatteras Island, North Carolina
53°F
Barometer: 29.24 inches (rising)
Winds: 38 mph (W)
Waves: 23 feet

Water streamed across Highway 12, the single route onto the island, tearing off a section of asphalt as it did. It ripped homes off their foundations, crumpling some as if they were made of gingerbread. Even as the storm began to pass, seas remained above twenty feet and winds were as high as 60 miles per hour. Even above the thundering sound of both, residents could hear the telltale *whompa-whompa* of a Jayhawk helicopter. Someone was in trouble. They didn't know that one of the most dangerous rescues in Coast Guard history was unfolding—that five crews were risking their lives in conditions too dangerous for their superiors to require them to attempt a mission. The crews had chosen to go.

Aaron Cmiel was piloting the C-130 that replaced McIntosh's. The storm cracked his windshield, but he kept flying. The first helicopter launched as soon as its crew got the call. The Jayhawk pitched against the wind as pilots Steve Cerveny and Jane Pena strained to keep it at an altitude of two thousand feet for the flight out. They'd never been in conditions this nasty. None of the crew had. Inside the wall of clouds, everything was pitch-black, and it was easy to get disoriented. Their flight mechanic, Mike Lufkin, scanned the horizon for air traffic like he had been trained to do. And then he laughed a little, thinking there was no way anyone would be stupid enough to be out in this.

As the helicopter neared the *Bounty*, the clouds began to break a little. Lufkin remembers thinking the sea looked more gloomy than anything else—a dark gray-blue marked by a widening debris field. He'd never seen anything like it.

Neither had Pena. She scanned the horizon, trying to make out human forms, a life raft, anything. She pulled her night-vision goggles back on and was blinded by a beacon of light. Attached to it was what looked like a five-gallon tub. And attached to that was one very battered John Svendsen. Cerveny lowered the helicopter so that the swimmer, Randy Haba, could execute a rescue. Pena tried to keep her voice calm as she called out approaching waves. She fought to be heard over the instruments, over the warnings going off in the cockpit—the recorded female voice urging "ALTITUDE! ALTITUDE! ALTITUDE!" every time a wave broke under them. They were coming from everywhere—there was no rhythm to them. Just chaos.

Lufkin lowered Haba for a direct deployment: no basket, just a strap that he could wedge under Svendsen's armpits to raise him up. Haba felt confident he could handle the conditions—until he got down there and encountered his first wave.

"It was pretty much like an airplane hangar barreling down on you," he says. The waves crashed over him. He dove down as far as he could.

Haba says he lost track of time after that. He kicked against waves, felt himself raised and lowered by Lufkin. He lost his mask and snorkel. He checked the raft: empty. He checked another one and saw seven very scared faces staring back at him. The *Bounty* crewmembers had found one another, had made a daisy chain and fought like hell for what seemed like hours to get into the raft, their survival suits so filled with water that they couldn't lift themselves. They had been tumbled and tossed. But they were floating now. And they were together. Nobody wanted to leave. Haba clambered into the raft. The crew was wide-eyed and very, very quiet.

"Just relax," he told them. It didn't help. How could it? He looked around the raft, trying to make quick assessments about everyone's condition. Doug Faunt was hunched over, clutching his belly. He had swallowed so much seawater he was really sick. He was also clearly the oldest in the bunch. Haba picked him to raise first. Lufkin struggled to lower the basket, but the winds were so strong they kept stripping it way from him. He tried weighing it down, but that just made it sink. He tried and tried and tried, eventually getting close enough for Haba to get Faunt inside.

One by one, they packed the *Bounty* crewmembers into the very small cargo hold of the Jayhawk. They tried not to notice the smell of shit and vomit, the rising heat from bodies that had worked too hard for too long.

A second Jayhawk arrived on the scene and found another raft. Another rescue swimmer was lowered.

"Hey, guys," he said. "I heard you need a ride." He became a national hero for that.

Back on base and at sector, coordination was hovering just above controlled chaos. Rescue swimmers were beginning to collect *Bounty* survivors. But how many? And which ones? The phones were ringing nonstop. One of the calls was from the British consulate: They'd heard news that the HMS *Bounty* was in trouble and wanted to know if it was one of their ships. Sector officials divided the lists of crewmembers and began making phone calls. Commander Anthony Popiel says most of the people didn't believe him when he called.

Within minutes, though, the story was all over the news. Jamie Trost had been up all night long, keeping an eye on the *Pride of Baltimore*. He was one of the first people to see the headline. He texted Jan Miles: *They went over.*

The sound of the text awoke the captain. He grabbed his phone. It woke his wife too.

"What's going on?" she asked.

He shook his head. "They went over." There wasn't anything else to say.

In times of natural disaster, it's not uncommon for people to tell stories of visitations from loved ones the moment they died. The night the *Fantome* went down during Hurricane Mitch, relatives of every crewmember who died experienced a kind of vision: Some say they were visited by the overwhelming smell of decay; others say their loved ones come to them in a dream and told them everything would be okay. That proved particularly comforting. But the survivors of the missing on the *Bounty* received no such comfort. And it certainly was a long time coming.

Dina Christian called Brad Leggett to tell him that the first Coast Guard helicopter was on its way back from the shop.

"They've picked up six survivors," she said. "But I don't know which ones."

"It's always women and children first, isn't it?" Leggett asked, "She's got to be one of them."

Ralph McCutcheon, Walbridge's friend and former shipmate, was just waking up then too. It had been decades since he had turned on the morning news: He says he's always been more of a coffee-and-newspaper kind of guy. But that morning, something told him to make a beeline for the television set. He couldn't say why—he still can't say way. Not that it really matters. Because once he turned it on, he learned that all but two of the crew had been recovered. McCutcheon knew that one of them had to be the captain.

"Robin is a traditionalist. And traditionally, the captain always goes down with his ship."

Claudia McCann had no idea the ship had even gone over until a reporter contacted her, saying that two people were missing.

"I knew immediately that it was him," she says. "If the boat was going to go down, he was going to be the last one off." But she also knew that he would have his survival suit on. "He's one tough cookie. I was optimistic that they would find him."

Her phone was ringing off the hook now: Everyone from the *Today* show to CNN to international magazines was calling. She didn't want to talk to any of them. Seventeen years of wondering if her husband was okay had hardened her a little bit, but she still had feelings. She wanted to be alone, in the bungalow Robin had made perfect. She still believed he would be coming home.

Rex Christian held no such belief. When the Coast Guard called him to explain that Claudene was missing, he threatened to go get his gun.

"Apparent suicide threat," the sector communication officer noted in the case file.

8:11 a.m.
Atlanta, New York, Philadelphia, and Virginia

"And so it begins," wrote Bryan Norcross on his blog that morning. "Mega Monster Sandy" was about to smash into the Northeast. "There's no good news from the Hurricane Hunters or the computer forecast models. If anything, the storm is providing more drama in its first act than was expected. Water is coming over seawalls. Flooding and whipping winds have already started. Just from the fringe of Sandy."

He was still fuming over the National Hurricane Center's decision. But it was too late now, he thought. People's lives were in danger. He urged them to stay indoors—away from rooms where trees could fall and crush them. He told them to cover their windows, especially in highrises, where wind would stress the glass, causing it to explode. "Even Wednesday and Thursday we'll know that a giant storm is nearby," he concluded. "That's it. Hunker down, be smart, and stay safe."

By the time his column appeared on the Weather Underground website, the day's first high tide approached, and surge began to overtake the New Jersey coast. LaGuardia Airport was recording gusts of 60 miles per hour. The wind and the tide ripped away eighty feet of the boardwalk in Atlantic City, where it careened down what had once been streets. Officials in North Wildwood reported major flooding as the tide continued "roaring in." In Ocean City, flooding had brought together the ocean and bay in one uninterrupted froth of surf. All roads leading to the town were now submerged. Anyone still there was trapped. Officials told Kathy Orr, meteorologist for the Philadelphia CBS affiliate, that they'd never seen anything like it.

Inside the Upton NWS office, water was streaming inside the ceiling. Mickey Brown had stopped by to check on his staff. He'd never seen anything like this, either. Four thousand feet above him, winds were nearing 100 miles per hour.

At 10:31 a.m., Governor Cuomo sat flanked by a U.S. Army Corps of Engineers colonel and a general from the National Guard, both wearing battle fatigues. They were broadcasting live from the New York State Office of Emergency Management. Cuomo announced that the storm surge in New York City was already rivaling Irene levels. Later that afternoon, he would be closing both the Holland and Brooklyn Battery tunnels. He assured the residents that the state was prepared. "We think we've done everything we need to do."

To his south, NWS offices were issuing blizzard warnings for the Shenandoah region. Even veteran meteorologists were surprised. "History is being written as an extreme weather event continues to unfold, one which will occupy a place in the annals of weather history as one of the most extraordinary to have affected the United States," wrote Stu Ostro. "This is an extraordinary situation, and I am not prone to hyperbole."

WHOA, read the top headline for *Business Insider*, THE WEATHER CHANNEL METEOROLOGIST JUST COMPLETELY FREAKED OUT ABOUT HURRICANE SANDY.

Ostro was beating the drum of storm preparation and evacuation, urging people to get out, regardless of what Sandy was called. But residents across the mid-Atlantic weren't sure. Social scientists from the Wharton School of the University of Pennsylvania had been engaged in telephone polls all morning. Most residents thought they were under a hurricane watch. They told surveyors that they were expecting maybe some hurricane-force winds, "but then displayed limited degree of concern over this prospect," noted the report. Even residents living next to the coast continued to believe that the surge effects would be minimal— despite having seen the destruction brought by the morning tide. Of them, only half had flood insurance policies. But they said they weren't concerned about that, either. That they took the time to answer a phone survey with about seventy questions on it is pretty telling too.

Still, at least people were now paying attention. The National Hurricane Center webpage passed a billion hits. The Weather Channel set a new record for viewing, with an estimated 39 million households tuning in that day. Their website and mobile apps got an additional 450 million visits. Sandy had become the biggest news in the history of the channel.

Nevertheless, residents in the flood zone remained—and only 17 percent of them said they thought they were in any real danger. It didn't matter that this storm had already washed away Highway 12 and stranded residents on Cape Hatteras, or that Route 1 had been swamped in Delaware. A mere 150 people had checked in the three shelters open in Philadelphia. They brought with them "dogs, cats, turtles and a spider," Mayor Michael Nutter told the *New York Times*. The tone of the article was light.

On Staten Island, Angela Dresch was home from school and feeling kind of bored. She scrolled through Twitter and Facebook, looked at some posts by her favorite boy band. Regina George, the fictional character from the film *Mean Girls*, posted a snarky tweet: "Is it raining?" Angela thought that was pretty funny. She retweeted it. Outside, waves had swallowed the beach and were snaking their way through the trees and brush. Her dad was pretty sure they wouldn't get much farther than the first floor of the house.

Across the New York Bay, in the Rockaways, a father of four was being interviewed by his local radio station. "I don't think my safety's at risk," he told the DJ. "We're going to tough it out and play Wii all day until the power goes out."

He wouldn't have long to wait. By 10:00 a.m., the neighborhoods around JFK Airport in Queens were reporting flooded streets and houses. Water was breaching the dunes in Maryland and Delaware. It stranded a police car. A woman in Delaware returned home to find a notice on her door: IF YOU DECIDE TO STAY, DON'T CALL EMERGENCY SERVICES, BECAUSE WE WON'T BE ABLE TO HELP YOU. She turned around and left.

New York Department of Health officials told reporters they remained confident that the impact to hospitals in the flood zone would be minimal. State Health Commissioner Shah speculated that, at most, one might lose power.

"Conditions are deteriorating very rapidly," said [Mayor] Bloomberg at a morning press conference. His voice was uncharacteristically clipped and hurried. He barely paused between sentences. "You're sort of caught between a rock and a hard place," he told residents in the flood zone. "You should have left, but it's also getting too dangerous to do so."

By 3:00 p.m. two feet of water had pooled in sections of Atlantic City. It was as high as eight feet in places. Officials there estimated that

80 percent of the city was flooded, and the storm had not yet made landfall. Those residents who had ignored the evacuation order were now calling for help. The city's 911 system failed after a gasoline tank spilled inside City Hall. They managed to get the system back online, but by then it was too late. Special National Guard flood vehicles attempted to reach the city, but high winds turned them back. The city was on lockdown. One official said it was like being "under siege."

In Far Rockaway, waves were biting at the boardwalk. Gusts of wind pulled apart the roof of the NWS Eastern Region Headquarters. When Mickey Brown went out to investigate, he found entire sections of the roof waving. Drainage pipes were pulled loose. Water began to pour inside.

"It was one of those times you think twice about Mother Nature," he says.

He knew it was going to get worse as the next high tide appeared. Surge was expected to reach eleven feet. Too many people weren't prepared. "There will be people who die," promised Martin O'Malley, Maryland's governor. Dannel Malloy, the governor of Connecticut, agreed.

"The mother is yet to come," he told reporters.

—◆◆—

4:00 p.m.
Elizabeth City, North Carolina
50°F
Barometer: 29.14 inches (steady)
Winds: 24 mph (w)
Precipitation: Rain

Time wasn't doing much to clear up the flurry of misfortune about the *Bounty*. The crew hunkered down in a cheap motel wearing clothes purchased at Walmart by the Red Cross. Calls to the ship's owner were going unanswered. The crew needed help, and the last thing they wanted to do was talk to the media. Facebook posts were mounting by the minute, some saying that Claudene had been found alive, others that she was still missing. As the day progressed and no official word was given, Brad Leggett became increasingly concerned.

Something ain't right, he thought to himself.

Out in California, Claudene's longtime friend, Wendy Sellens, was having similar thoughts. The two had been friends since grade school, and Sellens had always admired her friend's audacity. She hoped it would be enough to get her through. *Claudene is really good in a crisis*, thought Sellens. *I know she can keep a clear head.* But that didn't keep the adrenaline from flowing, or Sellens's mind from setting on the idea that Claudene may very well be experiencing her greatest fear. "I was freaking out," she says. "And we were all so confused."

Rex and Dina Christian didn't want to wait any longer for official news, so they hopped the next plane for North Carolina.

The cutter *Elm* was on the scene now, rolling on thirty-foot seas. The *Gallatin* was on its way from Charleston. At Elizabeth City, Jayhawk copilot Kristen Jaekel had been working desk duty all night and was itching to get on one of the recovery flights. Her aircraft commander tapped her that afternoon.

I'm in, she thought. *I get to play!*

That's a remarkably common response from these flyers. Rescue swimmer Randy Haba had thought the same thing earlier, when he had gone out to pull survivors from the churning seas. *I get to be in the game.*

"We're competitive by nature," says Jaekel. "We all want to be the one to participate. Everybody wants to be the one to help somebody."

Jaekel was just twenty-nine. This was her first SAR case.

They set out to explore the drift patterns established by sector. Below them, they began to see signs of debris: a few disused life rafts, a cooler, some spars, a couple of survival suits. That alarmed Jaekel at first, but her pilot explained to her the way you can tell that they're empty—how they look unnatural, with a leg flipped over backward or tangled in the arms.

Theirs was the last flight of the day. The sun would be setting soon. The *Bounty* had righted itself, regulated by the additional water it had taken on, and Jaekel felt a chill every time they flew over it. There was a survival suit tangled in the rigging. They were sure it was empty, but still.

Fuel levels were getting critical. They decided to leave their search area, just in case. The next survival suit they came upon looked a lot different from the others. The helicopter circled around again. There was nothing distorted about this suit, said Jaekel, and there was something graceful about the way it crested each wave. She looked down again and saw a halo of blond hair.

"It was a dead giveaway," says Jaekel. "I didn't know who it was. I didn't even know her name. But I knew this was the person we were looking for."

Jaekel still gets teary when she recounts the rest of the story: about how they had just twenty minutes to complete the mission, how they expedited their safety checklist to make sure there would be enough time, how the helicopter mechanic lowered the swimmer faster than he'd ever lowered anyone, how he struggled to place his rescue swimmer as close to Christian as possible, how her suit was so filled with water that the flight mechanic had to really struggle to get her inside. Brian Bailey, her senior pilot, says he was doing constant calculations in his head: They'd have very limited places to land.

"We get paid to worry," he explains. "There was no Plan B in this case."

He says the best way to get the helicopter back safely is to compartmentalize between what is happening in the front and the back of the helicopter, and that's what he told Jaekel to do. She tried not to look as the swimmer and mechanic cut away Christian's suit and begin CPR. The rescue swimmer didn't even take off his helmet before beginning to do compressions. Jaekel could tell the woman lying on the floor of the helicopter wasn't responsive. Her jaw was so stiff they could barely intubate her. Her face was covered in bruises and contusions. Still, the crew worked on her for the two full hours it took to return to Elizabeth City. As they flew, sector made the call to the Christians, about to board yet another plane on their way to their daughter. When the helicopter finally landed, the swimmer hopped out too. He didn't want Claudene to be alone at the hospital.

Jaekel was visibly shaken. Bailey tried to comfort her. "If we can't bring them home alive, at least we can bring them home." That helped a little. But she made a point not to turn on the television set when she got home. She didn't want to see the photos of Christian alive and thriving. It just didn't square with what she had witnessed in the back of her helicopter.

When Claudia McCann heard word of Christian's death, she says she deflated a little. *Why can't they find Robin?* She began to wonder if he had gone down with his ship. She thought about Claudene's family and the survivors—about what they all must be feeling. That was the hardest thing of all, she says.

Wendy Sellens tried to avoid the questions that kept running through her mind: *Was Claudene strong? Did she struggle? Just how scared was she?* Instead, she tried to content herself with the knowledge that maybe, just maybe, Claudene's long lost friend Mike was with her at the end. Michelle Wilton said she felt like she could feel Claudene somewhere nearby. She still sees her every time a butterfly lands in her yard. Friends and relatives have told Dina and Rex that they are sure Claudene is looking down on them—taking care of them, even. But they feel no such consolation. "We can't feel her at all, no matter how hard we try," Dina wrote on Facebook. "We just keep seeing her fighting alone for her life in the water, then in the morgue. God hasn't taken those sights away yet. They just get worse. Sorry."

Saving New York Harbor

William H. Thiesen, PhD

THE TERMS "PEARL HARBOR," "9-11," AND "KATRINA" CONJURE UP disastrous images for most Americans. But how many have ever heard the name "El Estero"? To New Yorkers in particular this term should strike a chord. It was the greatest man-made disaster in American history that never happened.

It was spring of 1943, a time when the outcome of World War II was still in doubt and port facilities around New York Harbor and northern New Jersey stowed convoy vessels to capacity with thousands of troops and millions of tons of war material destined for Europe, North Africa, and the Pacific. At 5:30 p.m. on April 24th, the call went out to Jersey City's Coast Guard barracks, "Ammo ship on fire! They want volunteers!" The burning vessel was the S.S. *El Estero*, an antiquated 325-foot Panamanian freighter pressed into service with the urgency of the war effort, and it was moored at Bayonne, New Jersey's Caven Point Pier. Members of the Coast Guard's Explosives Loading Detail had just overseen the last load to top off *El Estero*'s holds with 1,365 tons of ordnance, including huge "blockbuster" bombs, depth charges, incendiary bombs, and antiaircraft and small arms ammunition. At 5:20 p.m., the fire had broken out when a boiler flashback ignited fuel oil floating on bilge water under the engine room. As the heat of the fire grew and smoke billowed into the ship's passageways, the engine room crew, armed only with handheld fire extinguishers, gave up the fight and fled the space.

Everyone at the barracks knew volunteering could result in a fiery death for each of them. Most of them were aware that in 1917 the French ammunition ship *Mont Blanc*, loaded with 5,000 tons of TNT, blew up in the harbor of the small city of Halifax, Nova Scotia, instantly killing 1,500 residents, wounding 9,000 more, and leveling a large part of the city. It was the largest man-made explosion in history prior to the atomic bomb blast witnessed at Hiroshima.

The Coast Guard seamen also knew that the potential for catastrophic devastation around New York Harbor was far greater than Halifax, with an explosion that could obliterate nearby ships, the port, portions of local cities, and thousands of residents. Two nearly full ammunition ships, flying the red Baker flag for "hot," were tied up near *El Estero*, and a line of railroad cars on the pier held a shipment of hundreds of tons of munitions for a total of over 5,000 tons of explosives. Add to this the nearby fuel storage tank farms at Bayonne and Staten Island, and massive destruction appeared likely for the nation's largest population center, including swaths of Jersey City, Bayonne, Staten Island, and New York City.

Soon after the smoke began wafting out of *El Estero*, officer-in-charge Lt. (j.g.) Francis McCausland had arrived on scene. He sent out the call to the Coast Guard barracks and signaled two tugs to move the other munitions ships away from *El Estero*. He also helped organize initial firefighting efforts with over a dozen Coast Guardsmen already working on the pier. Meanwhile, Army soldiers responsible for the railroad shipment moved the ammunition boxcars off the pier. By 5:35 p.m., two ladder trucks and three pumpers from the Jersey City Fire Department arrived, as did two thirty-foot Coast Guard fireboats, which all began pouring water into the smoking vessel. Shortly thereafter, members of the Coast Guard Auxiliary mobilized and lieutenant commanders John Stanley and Arthur Pfister arrived by fast boat from the Coast Guard Captain-of-the-Port office, located near the Battery, and took command of operations. Pfister, a retired battalion fire chief in New York City and officer-in-charge of Coast Guard fireboats, assumed overall responsibility for firefighting activities, while Stanley devoted his attention to activities within *El Estero*. It was Stanley's first day on the job.

The timing of the call to the Coast Guard barracks couldn't have been worse. April 24th was the day before Easter, and members of the Explosives Loading Detail had been anticipating liberty for quite some time. They had donned their dress blues and pea coats, and many had just finished shining their shoes. But when the call came down for volunteers, sixty Coast Guardsmen stepped forward, eager to fight the fire. The men scrambled for the barracks door and two awaiting trucks. Witnesses described the scene in almost comical terms, with twenty dressed-up servicemen climbing into a pickup truck designed for no more than ten while the other forty clutched any open space available on a larger military truck. With men hanging from cabs and riding fenders, while red lights flashed and horns blared, the trucks sped down the eight-mile stretch of road to the waterfront, passing longshoremen and dock workers marching in the opposite direction to escape the fire. The trucks screeched to a halt at the pier, and the men hustled to the burning ship to join their shipmates already fighting the fire.

By 6:30 p.m., New York City fireboat *John J. Harvey* and the City's new mammoth firefighting boat *Fire Fighter* arrived on scene and ran dozens of high-pressure hoses into the ship for the Coast Guardsmen to douse the burning vessel. The New York City fireboats pumped a tremendous volume of water on board, but the oil fire continued to gain ground. Flames could be seen escaping through *El Estero*'s skylights, hatches, and scoop-like ventilators while the heat cooked deck plates, blistered paint, and scorched the soles of the seamen's once-shiny shoes. The fire's intensity spread the conflagration from the bilges to all flammable surfaces, including the extensive wooden framework and staging encasing the ammunition and securing it in the hold.

Lt. Commander Pfister noticed that the fire's black smoke began to show yellowish-white streaks, indicating that water from the hoses, fireboats, and local fire trucks had begun to reach the fire's source. But the danger of catastrophic explosion was far from over and in fact had only just begun, as the smoke returned to its oily black consistency. On Lt. Commander Stanley's recommendation, the Coast Guard Commander of the Third District and New York's Captain of the Port, Rear Admiral Stanley Parker, ordered *El Estero* scuttled. But it was too late for that. The sea cocks and overboard discharge valves necessary to flood the ship were located in the engine room underneath the blaze and remained inaccessible.

El Estero's bombs, explosives, and ammunition grew hotter by the minute. Oil fires have to be fought with chemicals, but the fire's smoke and flames were far too dense to allow the application of chemicals to the source of the conflagration. All the seamen could do was cool the ammunition with water, flood the ship's holds as fast as possible, and try to extinguish the fire later with chemicals if water failed to work. Lt. McCausland had led firefighting efforts inside the ship and suffered injuries, burns, and smoke inhalation after rescuing a man in the hold. He had to be evacuated to the local hospital, where he remained for the next three weeks. As one Coast Guard seaman remarked, "It was one hot fire!"

El Estero's deck cargo proved as dangerous as that stowed in the holds. Antiaircraft ammunition for the ship's deck guns was located perilously close to the blistering decks. The Coast Guard's firefighters broke open the ammunition lockers and slid the hot ammo ready boxes down a greased plank to the pier below. In addition, numerous drums of high-octane fuel sat stacked on the ship's deck. But nothing could be done with the fuel barrels because *El Estero* had to be towed away from the waterfront to prevent the pier, stored ammunition, and local fuel storage tanks from going up in smoke. Lt. Commander Stanley and tugboat skipper Ole Ericksen quickly examined harbor charts and selected an anchorage for the ship in the Upper Harbor.

Once Coast Guard officials made the decision to move *El Estero*, Lt. Commander Stanley asked for twenty volunteers to stay on board with him and Pfister to fight the fire during the transit to the Upper Harbor. Far more men volunteered than the number necessary, and many had to be ordered off. One seaman who was engaged to be married volunteered to stay on board, but the ranking boatswain's mate yelled, "You're getting married in a few weeks. Now get the hell off!" At this stage in fighting the fire, the chances of survival for those remaining on board the ship seemed slim indeed, and the men that stayed passed their watches, wallets, and personal effects to their departing shipmates.

By 7:00 p.m., the seamen on board *El Estero* had managed to secure a steel hawser to the ship's bow, and the tugboats began pulling it out into New York Harbor. Meanwhile, the Coast Guardsmen on board the burning ship pushed the cooking fuel drums off the deck. Fuel leaked from some of the ruptured barrels and ignited the water's surface near the blazing freighter, but the firefighters had averted the threat of igniting a massive fuel explosion on *El Estero*'s top side. As the tugboats towed the burning vessel into the harbor, *El Estero* belched black clouds that could be seen for miles and an orange glow above the boiler room illuminated the smoke. The authorities in New Jersey and New York warned residents by radio and through local air raid wardens to prepare for an explosion and braced for a detonation.

Eventually, the convoy of tugboats, fireboats, and *El Estero* reached the target area and the Coast Guard crew successfully anchored the vessel in forty feet of water half a mile west of the unmanned Robbins Reef Lighthouse. At a little past nine o'clock in the evening *El Estero* finally filled with water and settled to the bottom. The flooded vessel rumbled and belched smoke and steam as it cooled in the cold water of New York Harbor. Meanwhile, floating fuel drums exploded on the water's surface and fires continued to burn on the ship's exposed superstructure. By 9:45 p.m., New York Mayor Fiorello La Guardia arrived by police launch to inspect the freighter and reported that it was still burning. As Lt. Commander Pfister later described the fire, "It was touch and go at all times." But by 10:00 p.m., Rear Admiral Parker broadcast by radio the all-clear announcement, and by 11:30 p.m. the *Fire Fighter* and *John J. Harvey* had finally extinguished the remaining surface fires and returned to their piers.

The next morning, thousands of New Yorkers participated in the annual Easter Day Parade, many never realizing how close they had come to a major disaster. A few months after the fire, the Navy raised *El Estero*, towed her out to sea, and sank the ammunition laden hulk in deeper water. Had the *El Estero* detonated and touched off nearby flammables and ammunition, explosives experts believe that Manhattan's skyscrapers could have suffered severe damage and as many as one million residents would have been affected.

The *El Estero* fire had taught military and civilian authorities the perils of loading live ammunition near a major metropolitan area. Not long after the disaster had been averted, the Navy began construction of a weapons depot on a section of rural waterfront property near Sandy Hook, New Jersey. In December, the Navy commissioned Naval Weapons Station Earle, named for former naval ordnance bureau chief Rear Admiral Ralph Earle, which soon became a hub for the region's explosives loading operations. The Coast Guard moved the Explosives Loading Detail from Jersey City to Earle when operations began at that facility.

Early in the war, Coast Guard personnel serving in the New York area had come to be known rather derisively as "subway sailors" and "bathtub sailors," because many came from the greater New York area. However, the men who fought the *El Estero* fire came to be recognized as the heroes they truly were. For his efforts, Lt. Commander Stanley received the Legion of Merit, while Lt. Commander Pfister received the Navy & Marine Corps Medal for his role in fighting the fire. The City of Bayonne threw a parade and huge ceremony recognizing the Coast Guard Ammunition Loading Detail and the City's firefighters, which included speeches, radio broadcasts, and the presentation of specially struck medals to each member of the Detail. In addition, some of the Detail's personnel received a letter of citation from Rear Admiral Parker.

In an unfortunate epilogue to this story, disaster struck a year later at the U.S. Navy's weapons depot at Port Chicago, California, thirty-five miles northeast of San Francisco. The Navy had located this munitions facility in an isolated area far away from the local population center; however, it failed to implement proper oversight and safety procedures at Port Chicago. In an effort to speed up shipments of munitions to Pacific combat zones, Navy personnel ignored Coast Guard safety guidelines and bypassed the assistance of a Coast Guard Explosives Loading Detail for loading operations. In June 1944, a mishap in the hold of an ammunition ship touched off over 4,600 tons of ammunition, atomizing the ship and a another ammo ship, leveling the loading facility, killing over 300 Navy personnel, and seriously wounding 400 others in the area. While not quite as powerful as the Halifax explosion, it was the worst such disaster in U.S. Navy history.

The Worst Days of a Bad Fall

Eric C. Hartlep

By THE TIME THE GALES OF NOVEMBER 1911 ARRIVED, THE LIFESAVERS of Middle Island (Michigan) had already logged more than their share of trouble. Even before the active season began, Captain Eugene P. Motley found himself shorthanded.

"Surfman W. J. McCaffery telephones that he would not be back," Motley wrote on March 11th, "as he had a position in a lighthouse." Ten days later, Surfman Frank A. Paschke also resigned. With Station 253 set to open on April 12th, the sudden death of Surfman Peter Poirer's father meant the No. 2 surfman would be detained on the mainland. This left a crew consisting only of Keeper Motley and five permanent surfmen: Jack Hauck, Louis Candy, George Cottenham, George Hartlep, and Ernest St. Onge.

Between May and October, the depleted crew—filled out with temporary men and the 16-year-old legal ward of Captain Motley, Fred Scarborough—handled the grounding of the 2,005-ton steamer *City of London* and the disabled 4,795-ton steamer *James S. Durham*. They also rescued those aboard the yachts *Janet* and *Jahana*—the *Janet*'s during what Motley called "the worst storm of the season" on July 24th.

But the worst summer storm would be nothing compared to November's fury. Eugene Motley's log for the first of the month painted a frigid picture: "Practiced with signals and service code. Snowed all day, quite cold. Regular winter weather." Only twenty steamers passed by Middle Island. The following day, Motley decided against having men practice with the beach apparatus, "as ground was covered with snow and frequent squalls. Ice formed along the shore a little last night." Two days later he reported: "The spark plugs of motor in lifeboat are all short-circuited and could not get spark sufficient to operate engine."

By November 5th, with spark plugs bought in town at a 50 percent discount, the lifeboat was operational again, and would soon be needed. Fifty steamers passed the island that day, though all of them survived the increasing winds. It was the 30-year-old schooner *John Mee*—a wooden 199-ton vessel of a type almost extinct on the Great Lakes—that demanded Middle Island's attention. On the morning of November 7th, Captain Motley "received telephone message from Presque Isle light that a schooner with a flag half-masted was coming down the lake. At 8:40 a.m. the schooner came in sight. Called crew, launched lifeboat, which on account of low water (in harbor), caused a little delay . . . had to move around inside of island to head off on south side of island."

The aging vessel, with a five-man crew and no cargo, was on its way from Tobermory, Canada, to Raber, Michigan. Motley stated that "While off 40-mile point, 7 miles north of Roger City [the schooner] was struck by NW gale and big seas, which caused mizzen mast to break off at about 5 feet from the deck, and in its fall struck the boat davits on starboard side, breaking rail of yawl, and then going overboard. They had to cut it loose in order to save the vessel, thereby losing all sails and rigging on the mizzen. Also broke off top of main topmast above the stays, and tearing the mainsail badly."

With so much damage, the ship was lucky to be afloat. Motley secured a towline and ran the vessel down the lake, to an anchorage on the leeward side of Middle Island. "Then went to Turnbull's Mill and requested a tug by telephone to come from Alpena and tow them to harbor. Tug arrived 3:45 p.m., helped to get up anchor and they left for Alpena, and I returned to station at 5 p.m. The schooner's hull was not damaged, but the loss will be about $1,000. The lifeboat engine worked well until high tension wire on forward cylinder burnt and broke off. And not having any spare, we had to return to station on 3 cylinders. It was a rough day, big sea and gale of wind. The captain was well pleased with assistance rendered by this crew, and glad when I told him I had secured a tug for him, as his vessel was unable to come in, stay, or work windward with the little canvas left, only stay sail plus reefed foresail and a piece of mainsail."

The gale that wrecked *John Mee* continued unabated, threatening even more vessels over the coming week. According to several *Argus-Pioneer* stories, "A terrific storm swept over the lakes Saturday night and Sunday, a climax to a week's stormy and disagreeable weather . . . the wind blew 42 miles an hour here and 48 miles at Middle Island. Temperatures started to go down after the thunderstorm about 9 o'clock Saturday evening. Many cellars were flooded with water." Under the headline "Lighter Ashore" the paper reported that "A lighter owned by Captain Gillingham went on the beach at Middle Island Sunday. The lighter was brought to the island Saturday, towed by a gasoline launch. The launch could not get the lighter away on account of the storm, and Captain Gillingham was obliged to return to Presque Isle harbor. Captain Motley found it necessary to scuttle the lighter in order to prevent the lighter from beating the lifeboat dock to pieces." The *Argus* failed to mention that the lighter had grounded, then gone sideways on a reef, or that, by Motley's account, the gasoline tug—not a launch—"was being rapidly drawn on the reef so had to cut tow line as tug was striking bottom."

After months of work put in by his crew building the lifeboat dock, Motley surely was not about to stand by and watch it destroyed. Especially by what was essentially a barge, valued at only $200, with no crew aboard and a cargo of 175 fish net stakes. Captain Gillingham was no stranger to disaster when approaching Middle Island, having run aground with his gasoline scow *Molly Hogan* while attempting to deliver cord wood to the station on July 27th of the previous year. In that incident, the Middle Island crew worked almost until midnight to free the wreck, stopping only when "some of the men were nearly perished by the cold water," according to Motley. This time, being later in the year, conditions were even colder. "The tug had a crew of 3 and they were thankful for the assistance rendered as had to work in the water with ice forming all the time. Neither lifeboat nor surfboat used. A small boat, 16ft skiff, made 6 trips on three days. Vessel saved; damage $50. All cargo saved."

Between mishaps, Captain Motley did his best to secure days off for his crew during the continuing storms that November. It was a chancy proposition, as there was no guarantee a man on leave could return if a ship was in distress. On November 17th, harsh weather trapped temporary Surfman James Starr on the mainland. That left only six of the crew—surfmen Collins, St. Onge, Poirier, Hauck, Cottenham, and Hartlep—to man the boats. Motley had no choice but to employ 16-year-old Fred Scarborough as lookout. The move paid off when Scarborough spotted steamer *Isabel J. Boyce* at 1 p.m., as she "came under the island and hoisted distress flag."

Ever since the sunrise, surf around Middle Island had been very high, with alternating rain and snow as temperatures hovered around freezing. "The steamer *Isabel J. Boyce*," reads the station log, "while coming up lake before a SE gale, with a barge *William A. Young* in tow . . . (when) south of island, towline to barge parted and barge went adrift. The sea was so big that in trying to turn about, decks filled with water and steamer was in danger of foundering. They cut holes in bulwarks and let water out, threw over 50 tons of soft coal they had on deck and ran under island and called us out." Besides a hold filling with water, the crew of the steamer faced a ruptured boiler, which they patched together with a "rolling brace." There was also a steam pipe leak. They found shelter below Middle Island, expecting repairs to take "a few hours." With *Boyce* safely anchored, her captain, Robert C. Pringle, was more concerned with the fate of Captain Alex McLean and the six-man crew aboard *William A. Young*, a 28-year-old partly dismasted schooner now used as a barge. But until reaching *Boyce*, and talking to Pringle, Captain Motley had been unaware another ship was involved. Because of extremely high waves, the only chance of reaching the foundering barge in the station's lifeboat was to be towed there by the steamer.

Once alongside, however, Motley found the old schooner deserted, "the crew having left in yawl boat." Still, Captain Pringle "wished us to try and board barge and get anchor down. Started to go aboard, but could not get on, the steamer not stopping to help or stand by, but she started for shelter as soon as they let go of us." The men of Station 253 were left on their own, far from home in a fierce storm. "As I could do nothing in big sea," wrote Motley, "returned to station, having to pull about 3 miles against the sea and wind, which took us nearly two hours, arriving at station 6 p.m. Big sea, terrible day."

"The barge continued to drift before the gale," the keeper wrote later in his wreck report book. "At 8 p.m. heard over telephone that crew of barge in yawl boat had landed at Nine Mile Point, 4½ miles south of station after a very rough trip and had left for Alpena." Once in town, the crew's story of their ordeal made front-page news in the *Argus-Pioneer*: "After the towline parted, the crew of the *Young* battled as best they could. The foremast was down, had snapped off, leaving about a third standing. The mast and rigging, a useless mass of wreckage, were fouled under the bow. Heavy seas were washing over the barge. Captain McLean and crew undertook to pull in the parted towline and fasten it to the wreckage astern in order to steady the barge. However, this could not be accomplished.

"The *Young* was slowly settling. Her seams were parting. In one place three 12-inch planks were torn from her side. The yawl boat might be washed overboard at any moment, so the crew decided it would be safer to abandon the barge and take the yawl boat. Although this was taking an awful chance."

After a few days to reflect on events, Captain Motley completed his final report. It seems doubtful, from the tone of his account, that Motley agreed with the *Argus-Pioneer* that the steamer's captain had done all he could that day, or indeed the next, to save the barge. "The captain of *Boyce* wanted us to go with him in morning [of November 18th] and look for barge. The gale continued shifting to NW with snow squalls. The steamer did not wait for us, but pulled up under False Presque Isle Point 6 miles NW for shelter and did not call for us."

The next day, November 19th, the steamer left for Alpena. Her captain phoned Middle Island around 10 a.m. to inform Motley he "would not leave to look for the boat until Monday morning, 20th, when [he] would call the crew at Thunder Bay Island, the barge having drifted down the lake before the NW gale." *William A. Young* would now be the worry of Captain Persons, a dozen miles south at Station 252. While Captain Motley certainty wished the Thunder Bay Island men no trouble, he must have been glad to wash his hands of the entire affair.

Persons's crew was to be spared a repeat of Middle Island's trials, though at the cost of a sunken vessel. From Motley's log: "November 21st (Captain Persons) reported that the steamer *Boyce* and Thunder Bay Island crew found some wreckage yesterday that would indicate that the barge had sank." *William A. Young* was a total loss.

Still, there was yet more trouble brewing for the Middle Island crew. On November 24th, "Surfman Candy received word that his father was not expected to live and left 2:30 p.m. for town." Candy would not return. With the season of Great Lakes navigation nearing its end, and his father deathly ill, he decided to end his career on Middle Island. Down again to only six men, Captain Motley reactivated young Fred Scarborough as a substitute. In only three days' time, the boy would find himself alone at the station—except for Elizabeth Motley, the keeper's blind and crippled sister—for nearly two full days, while the lifesavers fought to save a stranded tug. "The steamer *Fairmount*," reported the *Argus-Pioneer*, "bound from Harbor Beach to Muskegon, with a big scow in tow, went aground on a reef near Presque Isle light about 3 o'clock Monday afternoon [November 27th]. The Middle Island lifesavers went to the relief of the tug about 7 o'clock and remained with the crew during the night."

Yet it was not as easy a voyage to *Fairmount*, and the lighter she was towing, as the papers made it sound. Three miles from the station, according to Motley's account, the surfboat "broke eccentric rod to water pump and engine would not run. Put on sail and oars and continued as had fair wind arriving at tug at 10:40 p.m. Tried to tow lighter but could not, worked until 1 a.m."

This rescue would be all manpower, not gasoline horsepower, and the site of the wreck was 16 miles distant from Middle Island. Around 5 a.m. on the 28th, the wind shifted somewhat, and using sail and oar the surfmen succeeded in pulling the lighter to safety, anchoring her nearby. That part settled, the crew ran a line to the tug and, using a winch on the anchored lighter and the tug's working engine, were able to pull *Fairmont* free as well at 10:15 a.m. However, with the weather "blowing a gale from NE, rain turning to snow, and as could not return to station with disabled boat in gale," Motley reported, he and his crew laid up "until 7 a.m. November 29th, when hauled boat alongside tug and by using hot water got ice off boat and outfit, so could handle boat and left 8 a.m. for station."

Even with their work done, getting home again would not be an easy venture for the Middle Island crew. "The wind having hauled to west," wrote Motley, "wind kept freshening and hauling to SW so that did not arrive at station until 12:15 p.m., having been 4 hours making 16 miles. It was one of the most severe gales of the season, rain turning to snow and freezing hard. Lifeboat was covered with ice and everything frozen. The damage to the tug would not exceed $500 while damage to the lifeboat consisted of one starboard light washed overboard and lost one oarlock and two oarlocks busted."

The *Argus-Pioneer* summed up the rescue and the season in an article in their December 6th issue, stating that "It was one of the worst days of a bad fall. The lifesavers had a rough trip going over in the lifeboat, and the return was no pleasure trip. They were absent from the island about 40 hours, the longest they have been absent since the season opened." At least the master of *Fairmount*, Captain Louis Larsen, had done all he could to aid the surfmen helping him, even going so far as to furnish them hot meals over three days.

Considering the sheer number of rescues that November and the severity of the weather, the Middle Island crew probably gave no thought to the possibility that the *Fairmount's* rescue would be their last that year, yet it was. Through the first week of December, winds were light, and even with an average of fifty steamers a day passing their lookouts, not one would need their help.

As it became more certain the active season was drawing to a close, the men began to take steps in preparation for a winter away from the island. First, the crewmen's trunks were taken to town, then the station's cooks—Annie Olson and another local woman—were sent to the mainland. On December 4th, the station's inner harbor froze, forming the first banks around the island. Just three steamers passed by on the 14th, and two days later Motley received the expected telegram: "Harbor Beach December 16. Keeper Middle Island Station. Close Station this day, December 16. Signed, Kiah." The men left at midnight for the mainland and home, glad for the end of their worst fall ever.

A Long Good Night

Gerald R. Hoover

DURING THE EARLIEST STAGES OF MY TRAINING PROGRAM, PROOF THAT it was working and that swimmers would rather die than fail, came on Memorial Day, May 29, 2000. As was my custom, I encouraged rescue swimmers to report what they did to those of us not involved, hoping to glean some lessons for all of us. This story is a melding of what all three swimmers shared in the days following that long night.

Rick Bartlett stands tall and lanky, with creases pinching the corners of his eyes. A consummate professional and experienced pilot, he was the aircraft commander on that Monday morning as he and the rest of the duty section relieved the off-going crew at 8:00 a.m. sharp. Rick Bartlett was a lieutenant commander whose collateral duty, when not flying, was acting as a rotary-wing operations officer. He decided when, where, and how the helicopters assigned to the air station in Elizabeth City, North Carolina, would be used. While doing so, he was to keep the operations officer and commanding officer informed and follow their directions.

When an aircraft commander reports for duty, he or she first checks the weather, as it is of pivotal importance. Bartlett strode with his usual air of purpose around the Operations Center, where a junior officer manned the desk. A metallic console housed the myriad radios, phones, and related equipment. The windowed room overlooked another room with a large chart table and a wall-mounted TV that displayed the weather round the clock for anywhere on the planet. Bartlett checked the marine forecast and was immediately drawn to the picture of a growing low-pressure system plowing through northeast North Carolina. Winds were to reach thirty knots with heavy rain, moderate turbulence, and dropping temperatures. He planned to monitor the situation closely.

Bartlett's swimmer for the twenty-four-hour shift was Doug Hanley. Doug is the life of every party. He looked like an offensive lineman, and I wondered how he moved with so much speed when he swam or ran. He is a family man with the requisite wife, kids, and dog. He loves to drink beer and hug, usually in that order, and it doesn't matter who gets wrapped up by his massive arms; everyone is a target.

A workaholic by nature, Doug spent the early part of the duty wrapping expended trail lines for reuse, inspecting life rafts, and similar jobs. These tasks fill our everyday existence and are the lifeblood of our profession. His self-imposed workday lasted until just before 4:00 p.m.

By late in the afternoon, Bartlett realized the forecast had woefully underestimated the storm's intensity. By then, winds had exceeded forty knots, and slanting, slamming raindrops pelted the closed hangar doors. Around 4:00 p.m., Bartlett was ordered by District Five Operations Center to rescue the crew of a sailing boat, *Irish Mist*, a thirty-six-foot, transatlantic boat with two Australian crewmen and their dog on board. The reportedly anemic storm had turned vicious once it moved offshore, and the crew of the *Irish Mist* had suffered several violent knockdowns. A "knockdown" is the term used when a boat, usually a sailboat, is tossed onto its side so that the mast of the superstructure contacts the water. Those on board were willing to abandon ship despite, or maybe because of, the thirty-foot seas.

Bartlett punched the SAR alarm button and calmly voiced the mission over the public address system: "Now put the ready HH-60J on the line, sailing boat taking on water ninety miles offshore." He then picked up the phone and dialed the helicopter watch captain and ordered extra weight bags and trail lines thrown onto the aircraft. He also requested the aircraft be fueled to maximum capacity.

This rescue started no differently from the hundreds of others in which Doug had played a part. He hurriedly dressed in his dry suit and other swimmer gear before hustling to the helicopter.

Bartlett briefed the crew on what to expect from the wind and waves once they arrived offshore. Lieutenant Junior Grade Randy Meader was the copilot assigned the left seat to provide navigation and communication assistance. Meader was very new, having been at the air station for about thirty days. Being prior enlisted helped ease some of his apprehension, but little, other than experience, can prepare one for those conditions. Words cannot adequately describe being there.

Chris Manes eased up beside Doug at the helicopter for the mission brief. Chris worked on the aircraft's avionics when not standing duty as a flight mechanic. Doug was pleased to have someone he had flown with in the past as his hoist operator. Chris is a stout man with a sharp wit.

"We've got ceilings of one hundred to two hundred feet," Bartlett said. "Visibility is down to about a half mile. The winds are a steady forty-five knots with higher gusts. We don't want to run into anything, so let's be careful. Call out obstacles; don't assume we see something. Randy, I filed a Special VFR." He was referring to Visual Flight Rules, which allow us to take off in those conditions. "I want you to plot a course down the Pasquotank River. This should keep us from flying into something we can't see."

Within minutes of the initial alarm, the crew was taxiing to the large painted "H" on the tarmac.

"Tower, this is Rescue six zero three one, ready for takeoff and river departure to the east," Meader transmitted.

"Rescue three one, clear for takeoff; good hunting," the air traffic controller responded.

Bartlett lifted the collective and the heavy aircraft rose from the ground. He tilted the nose over, causing the helicopter to shudder against the wind as it clawed forward toward the river. Meader manned the radios with flight controllers, the radar, and navigation computer. Doug keyed the radio mike from his computer console in the rear to set up a guard with the Coast Guard Communication Unit in Chesapeake, Virginia, known as CAMSLANT (Communication Area Master Station for the Atlantic). Doug did this automatically and with the understanding he was to call in the aircraft position every fifteen minutes. If he missed a call, the CAMSLANT radioman made a concerted effort to reestablish contact. Two missed calls and the "cavalry," in the form of every available Coast Guard asset, would be alerted.

The crew crossed the Outer Banks of North Carolina before dark. The winds increased to a steady fifty knots, and the helicopter jolted roughly along the charted course. The wave tops were being ripped from the water; brown silt was stirred to the surface. The conditions reminded Bartlett of the numerous hurricanes into which he had flown.

Helicopter SAR cases occurring farther than fifty miles offshore are required, by policy, to be escorted by a fixed-wing aircraft: In this case, a four-engine C-130 Hercules was to fly cover for the HH-60J. ("Cover" is the term used to describe the duties of the escort airplane.)

"One five zero four, this is six zero three one on point eight," Meader called to establish a communication link.

"Three one from the O-four, we have divert information on a more pressing case when you're ready to copy," the radioman on the C-130 responded.

"Roger, send your traffic."

"The sailing boat *Cariad* has suffered an explosive knockdown." (An explosive knockdown is described as a roll greater than 120 degrees.) "The rigging was ripped from the mast and the main hatch was washed overboard. A female crewman was injured and is bleeding profusely. An immediate divert is requested by District Operations."

While the crew of the *Irish Mist* was in dire straits, the crew of the *Cariad* was in even greater need. The C-130 radioman transmitted the position of the *Cariad*, and Meader plotted it into the helicopter computer. Only fifteen miles from the scene, Bartlett banked the helicopter on the appropriate intercept course to the new target.

"We have a new mission and we are only about five minutes from the scene. Doug, why don't you get dressed out, if you haven't already?" Doug was prepared.

"Chris, complete rescue check list part one."

"Randy, try to raise the *Cariad* on the radio and find out as much as you can."

Each crew member had his duties clearly defined. The response was immediate.

The helicopter crew communicated through the C-130 with the *Cariad* crew and learned that a two-hundred-pound stove had landed on the female crewmember. She was bleeding from her head and was semi-conscious. The boat had no power and was dragging its mainsail to slow its momentum. Although sailboats are designed to move forward even without the aid of sails, the *Cariad* had enough freeboard on for the wind and waves to push it through the water at about five knots.

The captain was reported as saying, "I'm afraid another knockdown like that last one will cause her to sink. We're ready to abandon ship."

Once within radio range, Meader had activated the radio direction finder and locked onto their transmission. This gave the aircraft commander a course he compared to the position passed by the C-130 radioman. Sometimes information that has gone through several sources before reaching the rescue aircraft is unintentionally incorrect or old, and pilots must constantly update data to ensure a prompt response. Even with all the information they had, the pilots had trouble finding the white hull of the *Cariad* in the frothy white wave tops and spray.

The captain reiterated, "We have three people on board, and we are ready to go."

After the helicopter crew spotted the boat, Bartlett flew in a tight circle to evaluate the seas and contemplate the logistics of the rescue. He estimated the waves to be running about twenty feet when compared to the forty-six-foot hull of the *Cariad*. Each member of the crew provided valuable insight, and Bartlett made quick decisions based upon his own vast experience and input from his team.

"Look at the lines and rigging dragging behind the boat. Do you think you can grab them and pull yourself aboard?" Bartlett asked Doug, despite the nagging underlying question of whether he could deploy a swimmer into those seas and recover him.

"No problem."

"Complete part two for a sling deployment of the swimmer just aft of the boat," he ordered.

"Roger," Chris said. Seconds later he stated, "Part two complete, ready aft for sling deployment of rescue swimmer."

Doug slid toward the open door, dangled his feet outside the airframe, and sensed Chris's hand on the webbing of his harness. The whooshing of wind and scream of helicopter machinery replaced the static of the ICS.

One solid tap on his chest and Doug removed the gunner's belt. He quickly followed the motion with a thumb up then lowered his mask and bit down on the snorkel, tasting the dry acid bitterness that signaled the rush of adrenaline. The harness lifted his heavy body from the deck, and he swung to his right. Chris was facing him, waiting for the second signal that indicated Doug was ready to continue. Doug gave it and was immediately lowered below the aircraft. The aircraft faced the steady wind, pushing the rotor wash aft. The swirling air and choppy seas normally accompanying a hovering helicopter were forced back. Doug squinted upwards one last time, his vision filled with the hover lights illuminating the storm-darkened skies. He turned his attention back to the boat as he approached the water, then abruptly splashed into the water and disconnected from the hoist hook. Without a backward glance he gave the "I'm all right" signal and without interrupting his swim stroke powered his way up one hill of water and slid down the face of the next.

Despite the aircraft's buffeted hover, Chris had done his job extremely well and deposited Doug within a few feet of the line trailing the boat. But the *Cariad* was moving too fast and escaped Doug's reach within seconds of his entering the water. He signaled for a pickup. They had learned the first lesson of the night.

Chris expertly dropped the hook, with an open sling attached, into the water next to Doug, who snapped his harness to it and was yanked from the sea.

With Doug safely inside the airframe and hooked up to the ICS again, they discussed a new approach. Bartlett settled on a course of action and repeated it to ensure that everyone understood.

"We will deploy Doug on his harness and have all three survivors enter the water simultaneously. Doug will retrieve them one at a time until we have hoisted all three."

The plan was understood, and Meader spoke to the crew of the boat while Doug and Chris prepared to do another deployment.

Bartlett was concerned about the injured woman's ability to stay afloat, until the captain of the *Cariad* assured him she could.

The aircraft has a radar altimeter that shoots a signal to the surface, where it is bounced back to a receiver. The time it takes to make the round-trip is calculated into altitude. The system can usually be programmed to hold a desired height, but in this instance, with the seas running greater than twenty feet, it was impossible. Bartlett had to continuously raise and lower the collective to stay at his desired altitude. Chris would have been unable to pay out and take up cable fast enough to keep pace with the up-and-down movement of the airframe. This made it vital for Bartlett to hold the correct altitude and position. Meader monitored the altitude gauge and called out varying disparities over the ICS.

This was not their only flying challenge. Based upon the weather report, Bartlett should have been able to nose the aircraft into the wind, obtain forty-five knots of forward airspeed, and program the computer to hold it on that heading. He knew this was not the case. The wind swirled, pushed, pulled, gusted, slacked, and generally created an uncooperative frenzy. To control the helicopter, Bartlett made constant adjustments of the cyclic, as if he were holding the handle of a spoon and stirring some unseen goo in the bottom of a bowl. Yet, having repeatedly flown in these conditions, Bartlett gave the impression there was nothing to do.

Doug was in hand-to-hand combat with Mother Nature. Together, the three-person crew of the *Cariad*, with life jackets on, had plunged into the sea. Doug powered through the waves like a freight train.

Calmly, but loudly, he yelled, "I'll put you one at a time into the basket."

Doug clamped a beefy arm across the chest of the female survivor and swam away from the two men; swimmers must gain clearance from multiple survivors to be sure the basket does not smack someone else, or more than one person at a time does not attempt to enter it. This gives the swimmer a measure of control and allows for the safe rescue of all.

With blood still spilling from the woman's head, Doug wondered, not for the first time, if creatures higher on the food chain than the two of them would soon show up. Salt water spilled into his snorkel, and he swallowed it. Short choppy waves atop the rollers punched him as he swam. He gave the "ready-for-pickup" signal and waited for the basket.

At that point, Chris was lying on the deck of the helicopter with the hoist-control handle in his left hand and the hoist cable in the other. He thumb-rolled the small wheel on the control handle and paid out slack while observing Doug and said, "Forward and right fifty feet."

Bartlett edged the aircraft closer to Doug while Chris tensed his muscles with every jerk of the cable and pushed the cable in the opposite direction to the basket's swing. This action counteracted the pendulum motion and gave Chris a measure of control. The basket slapped at the water to be pushed back, rolled on its side, and moved to a position under the tail. Doug, with leg muscles burning, kicked his finned feet uphill toward the rescue device, grabbed the rail of the basket with his left hand, and slid his charge inside its protective metal frame. He then released the woman from his left hand and reached around to grab the collar of her life jacket. Holding her in place, he shoved the rest of her body into the bottom of the basket with his chest. He had practiced this maneuver to polished quickness, so that hundredths of seconds after he had the basket in his hand, he gave the thumbs-up signal.

"Keep your hands inside the basket," Doug screamed over the helicopter noise, a lesson survivors have learned the hard way. Unless they do so, a hand can slam into some portion of the airframe, and any limbs or digits extending beyond the protective metal of the basket are fair game.

"Ready for pickup. Taking up slack. Prepare to take the load," Chris announced over the ICS.

The cable rolled onto the drum above Chris's head as he retrieved it. As the basket cleared the water, Doug held it with viselike fingers until it was as vertical as possible. This swimmer procedure is referred to as plumb and helps the flight mechanic control the swing. Once straight under the helicopter, Doug released and swam on his back away from the aircraft.

"Basket coming up, swimmer heading back toward the other survivors; clear back and left thirty," Chris said. By conning back and left, Bartlett could visually reacquire Doug and maintain correct position over the target, although most of his flying was done "lost target."

"Cease commands," Bartlett said, telling Chris to take his eyes off the swimmer and concentrate on getting the basket inside.

"Roger, ceasing commands."

The basket bounced off the plastic skid plate mounted on the open door of the helicopter as the first of three survivors was pulled to safety.

Doug spun away from the hovering machine and met more walls of water. He did not see the two men, but he knew where he had left them and swam in that direction. On the crest of the next wave he spotted them and slightly altered his course for an intercept.

"Woman is out of basket, ready for another hoist," Chris said.

"Roger, begin the hoist."

The basket was outside the door and on its way down before Doug had reached the second man. "Who's next?" Doug asked the two remaining survivors like a drill sergeant addressing wayward recruits. The captain pointed toward the other man. "OK, let's go."

One at a time, both men were plucked from the raging seas. Chris was about to go after Doug when he noticed something odd about the hoist hook.

"The hook clasp is bent," Chris explained to Bartlett.

"It won't lock closed. It must have happened when the seas were batting the basket around."

The hook has a hardened metal spring-loaded clasp that automatically closes and holds rescue devices on the cable. Now the twisting of the basket had bent the clasp and prevented it from functioning, with Doug still in the water.

Doug watched and waited as cold fingers of water crept inside his hood. He was tired and ready to go home.

After contemplating the risks of more hoists with a bent hook, Bartlett said, "Let's pick up Doug and take these survivors back to Elizabeth City instead of continuing on to the *Irish Mist*."

Chris let the thin steel cable slide through his hand as they moved to a position over Doug. "Swimmer approaching cable, swimmer has cable, prepare to take the load, taking the load." Chris hoisted Doug to the aircraft. "Swimmer's in the cabin, hoist complete."

"Randy, pass to the C-130 we will be returning to the air station. Let them know about the bent hoist hook and see if they have another part or another aircraft ready to go."

Thirty-eight minutes had elapsed from the first aborted hoist until Doug's final ride. The crew had saved three lives and had expended some of their available rescue energies, but not all. The physically demanding rescue of the crew of the *Cariad* had been straightforward and simple.

The final hoist of any rescue allows the aircrew to breathe a collective sigh of relief. Doug sat in the aircraft seat with water dripping from his dry suit and harness and visually checked the survivors. After a short rest, he covered them with wool blankets and gathered personal information. Chris moved about the cabin and removed the leather hoist glove, stowed the rescue basket, and secured the cabin. Bartlett wrestled the weather for control of the aircraft as he turned toward shore. He noticed the rains had increased and were pounding the airframe.

It took them forty-five minutes to reach the safety of the air station, and seconds before the wheels touched solid ground Meader received a call from the C-130.

"Three one from the O-four."

"O-four, this is the three one, go ahead."

"Roger, we have information on another boat in need of immediate assistance when you're ready to copy."

"Roger, send your traffic," Meader said as he pulled the pen from its slot on his kneeboard.

"The crew of the sailing boat *Hakuna Matata* is preparing to abandon ship. They are taking on water and are located sixty-three miles offshore."

"Roger, we are on short final approach to E-City. We'll be airborne shortly and reestablish contact." After a moment he asked Bartlett, "Did you hear?"

"Yes, let's hurry."

When the crew radioed the Operation Center at the air station to advise that the hoist hook was bent, the duty watch officer immediately phoned the watch captain. The watch captain mustered the duty section, and they set about trying to solve the dilemma. Initially they tried to acquire a new hoist hook. As a backup plan, they pulled a second helicopter from the hangar and fueled it to maximum capacity. Also, they filled the cabin with extra weight bags and trail lines, just as they had with the first airframe.

The duty officer on the desk was in the middle of recalling a second crew, as it appeared that otherwise the crew of the *Irish Mist* might have to wait too long for a rescue.

Troy Lundgren, another rescue swimmer who lived just two minutes from the front gate of the air station, was first to respond to the order to report. He strode into the hangar shortly after the HH-60J had landed.

Troy, who has been described as a gladiator, possesses chiseled features, a muscular frame, and extraordinary athletic ability. He even played college football before choosing to become a rescue swimmer. His intimidating presence has served him well; he eventually became a renowned instructor at the AST School in Elizabeth City.

By the time Troy met Doug on the hangar, the crew of the *Cariad* had been moved from the helicopter to the waiting ambulance.

"How was it?" Troy asked Doug.

"Rough as shit."

"You guys want another swimmer on this next case?"

"I don't know about Bartlett, but I do. Let's ask him."

Bartlett was more than pleased to have two swimmers on board. His crew now numbered five.

The duty officer on the desk needed to call a third swimmer for the next set of pilots and flight mechanic to go after the *Irish Mist*.

Within thirty minutes, Bartlett and his crew were airborne. Meader immediately established radio contact with the C-130. "One five zero four, this is the six zero two six."

"Two six from the O-four."

"Roger O-four, please pass updated position and condition of the *Hakuna Matata*."

"The *Hakuna Matata* is in close proximity to another boat also requesting assistance. The *Miss Manhattan* has a crew of five, and they are preparing to abandon ship. They are about five miles from the *Hakuna Matata*."

Frustration might be a normal response for anyone not in this line of work. For the crew of Bartlett's HH-60J, the circumstances required quick and correct action. "Triage" is a term used by the emergency medical service community to determine lifesaving priorities. On this day, that task fell to Bartlett's shoulders, and he continued toward the *Hakuna Matata*.

"Plot a course to the *Hakuna Matata*, and let's go on NVGs when we get the chance."

Meanwhile, back at the air station, Lieutenant Commander Randy Watson had arrived to hunker over the chart table, making plans to go out to the *Irish Mist*. Not assigned duty, he had raced to the station when he received the call from the desk officer. Watson was tall, unflappable under pressure, and a soft-spoken pilot with a quiet passion for fast cars. With the rest of his crew on their way, he planned to launch as soon as they arrived.

The maintenance personnel hurriedly repaired the broken hoist hook on the 6031. This would be Watson's chariot.

In the HH-60J, tail number 6026, Meader received an update from the C-130. "Two six from the O-four. The *Hakuna Matata* is crewed by a French father-son team. They do not speak very clear English, but the crew of the *Miss Manhattan* has been able to translate for us. They reported the *Matata* has experienced several knockdowns, which cracked their keel. They are taking on water and need immediate evacuation. We attempted to drop them a pump, but they were unable to get it started in these conditions."

The two sailboats were only miles apart, communicating and providing critical, invaluable information that was assisting in both their rescues.

"Randy, have the O-four drop a smoke pattern for our approach," Bartlett ordered. He was asking for a drop of three or more pyrotechnic flares into the water, upwind and angled off to one side of a hover target. These flares are saltwater activated and provide a small white flame and plume of smoke to alert the helicopter crew to the direction and strength of the surface winds, while also providing a solid hover reference. On a dark and stormy night, the sky and sea can appear to melt into one black curtain so that the pilot's eyes play tricks.

"Smokes are in the water," Meader reported in a moment.

"Roger that, Chris; complete part one."

Troy was strapped into the troop seat next to Doug. Bartlett had to decide which swimmer to use. He ordered Doug to prepare, assuming Troy would be fresh for later. Doug and Troy instinctively looked each other over, checking clasps for security to ensure that neither had forgotten a vital piece of gear. They shared excited smiles as adrenaline pumped through their veins.

By the time Bartlett was overhead of the *Hakuna Matata*, Watson and his crew were airborne and en route to the *Irish Mist*. This lifted some of the burden from Bartlett's shoulders and let him concentrate on the two boats in trouble directly below his helicopter as he continued to communicate with the team.

"I'm going to pull into a hover just aft of the *Hakuna Matata* and plan on completing another rescue like before. Randy, relay through the translator on the *Miss Manhattan* that we want the crew of the *Matata* to jump overboard when they see us deploy our swimmer into the water. Doug, you ready?"

"Oh, yeah!"

Bartlett peered out the right window at his shoulder. The hover light illuminated the rolling seas. The stage was dark; the sun had set. He could only see the area lit by the helicopter's hover lights but felt sure the well-rehearsed rescue would go as planned.

"Complete rescue checklist part two."

"Roger, bringing swimmer aft."

Chris looked Doug over to be sure he had his fins and hadn't forgotten some vital piece of equipment, then rapped Doug's chest with a solid slap, at which point Doug gave the ready-for-hoist signal.

"Swimmer's ready."

"Roger, begin the hoist."

"Swimmer is going up and out the door," Chris said. "Swimmer holding, waiting on load check," he watched for Doug's second thumbs-up signal.

"Load check good, swimmer going down." Chris rolled the thumb wheel on the hoist control pendant, and the tightly woven steel cable peeled off the drum.

The steady howl of the wind mixed with the scream of the helicopter. The *Hakuna Matata* was closer to the center of the low-pressure system. The winds blew a steady fifty knots and created seas in excess of thirty feet, blue-black rollers the height of three-story buildings, unforgiving and powerful.

"Swimmer's in the water, paying out slack."

"Here comes a big one." Meader was looking toward the lit horizon, and Bartlett pulled power to lift the aircraft above the crest of the wave.

"Swimmer's away." Several seconds passed. "Swimmer's OK."

Bartlett backed the helicopter rearward to watch Doug as the survivors hurled themselves into the sea from the floundering *Hakuna Matata*.

Doug's muscles screamed with effort as he battled a ceaseless onslaught from the waves. The helicopter's spotlight bounced around so that it gave only split-second warnings on any advancing wave, and each time Doug saw a wave it was almost upon him. Water slammed his torso and filled his mouth and snorkel, forcing him to swallow it. Pounding Doug's body like a punching bag, the sea dealt him one blow after another.

The crew of the *Hakuna Matata* struggled to survive themselves, wide-eyed and terrified as they watched Doug swim over the crest of wave after wave to inch toward them.

Undaunted, Doug twisted his head to the side to vomit, then brought his eyes forward in one smooth motion. The queasiness did not deter him.

"Swimmer has first survivor," Chris said.

"I have ready-for-pickup signal."

"Roger that, conn me in."

"Forward and right twenty feet."

Bartlett flicked the trim tap on the cyclic up and to the right. Each single push of the small moon-shaped button normally moved the hovering aircraft five feet in the direction indicated. Bartlett was still stirring the bowl and had to constantly adjust the flight controls to move the airframe in the desired heading. The winds remained steady at fifty knots, with occasional gusts to sixty.

Bartlett concentrated on the bobbing flares visible now and then atop the passing waves.

"Up, up," Meader said as a rogue wave approached.

Bartlett lifted the collective, causing the helicopter to ascend.

Doug struggled toward the basket, only to be attacked from behind. The cresting, breaking wave rolled Doug and his survivor underwater. When he looked for light to swim toward, he saw none. The air in his lungs burned to exit, yet he knew that to breathe was to drown, not an option. Instead, Doug kept his powerful arm locked across the chest of the man who was trusting him with his very life. Doug's throat started to constrict and convulse as his body responded to the desire to gasp. Still underwater, he had to wait for relief of the wave's release. At last, as the sea spit the two men to the surface like a mouthful of rancid milk, they sucked oxygen and reclaimed their hold on life. Doug looked around and, for the first time in his life, felt his own mortality.

"Need a little help down here, God," Doug silently prayed as he looked around to gain his bearings. He needed to finish this hoist before another wave sucker-punched him.

Chris spotted Doug popping to the surface and dropped the basket within five feet of him. Doug was still a little dazed when he realized the basket was merely a few feet from his grasp.

"Swimmer has the basket."

"Survivor's in the basket, taking up slack. Prepare to take the load, taking the load. Basket is clear of the water, clear back and left." Chris's steady stream of information painted a clear picture of all that Bartlett could not see.

Bartlett backed away until Doug's stroking arms came into view; Doug was already flying through the water toward the second man.

"Uuuurrraa!" Doug vomited again and then took a mouthful of salt water to wash the taste away.

The second hoist was smoother than the first. Thirty-three minutes had elapsed by the time the second survivor was inside the helicopter and Doug had joined them—two more lives saved.

"Good job everybody," Bartlett said. "Now let's finish this. Troy, you ready?" Bartlett was watching the lights on the horizon where the *Miss Manhattan* and her crew of five waited.

"Randy, have the fifteen O-four drop some more smokes in the vicinity of the *Miss Manhattan*."

"They are running low on fuel and will have to depart scene soon," Meader reported. "They said they would drop the flares before heading to the barn. And Rick, the crew of the *Manhattan* is still trying to decide whether to abandon ship."

Bartlett continued flying toward the *Manhattan*. "I've got two cold, wet survivors and a C-one-thirty departing scene. They need to decide now or wait on the six zero two six to return from the rescue of the crew of the *Irish Mist*."

As the crew of the *Manhattan* digested Bartlett's words, a wall of water higher than thirty feet heaved the sailboat toward the heavens, then rolled and stabbed its mast into the Atlantic. For several seconds that seemed like a lifetime, the mast remained buried in the churning blue-black water, and when the *Manhattan* finally righted herself, thousands of gallons of water poured from the cockpit.

An unidentified female voice screamed over the radio: "We're ready to come off—right now!"

"Complete part one for sling deployment of the swimmer," Bartlett ordered. "Randy, call the crew; let's continue to use what's been working. Have them jump from the boat when they see our swimmer enter the water."

Meader was talking on the radio while Troy spit into his mask to keep it from fogging and climbed onto the deck. He attached the gunner's belt around his waist, then Chris handed Troy the hoist hook and motioned him to slide toward the open door.

"Swimmer's in the door, ready for sling deployment."

Troy had been a spectator until now. The wind had gathered strength during the passing minutes until it sounded like the steady blast of a train whistle. Bucketfuls of rain sloshed sideways in front of his eyes in what seemed like a solid wall of water. The airframe was jolted roughly while he looked down at the *Miss Manhattan*.

Troy, like every other adrenalin-charged rescue swimmer, relished the sensation of the solid open-palm slap on his chest and removed the gunner's belt.

"Swimmer's ready."

Chris sharply eyed Troy's equipment before pushing the thumb wheel upward, taking slack from the cable and hefting Troy from the deck as he made adjustments to the harness. He automatically gave the second thumbs-up as he concentrated on the seas below him. They appeared to be rising, but he knew he was being lowered toward them to be tacked the moment he hit the water. When he released the hook, the next wave pushed and rolled him over. Nausea seized over him as he swam; still he gave the "I'm all right" signal.

Black and gray in the light of the helicopter, the water seemed alive with vicious intent. Small rain-driven bullets of water sprang from the surface as the wave tops burst to skirt just above the water.

The force he faced at that moment would call on every ounce of Troy's strength. Belching as he swam, he knew this was only the beginning of his body's reaction to the motion of the sea, and soon he vomited with force. "Just getting started, can't quit now," he thought.

The crew of the *Miss Manhattan* splashed haplessly into the ocean, but not all at once and not together. Troy swam toward the closest one.

"Just relax," he said. "We do this all the time. We'll have you out of here in a second."

Troy locked his arm across the chest of the woman and turned toward the lights of the helicopter. It seemed a greater swim back than it had been on the way out. The chopper bounced wildly, and occasionally he lost sight of it below the wave tops, but he could hear the scream of the engines and continued to swim closer to the pickup point.

From the door of the helicopter, Chris watched Troy give the ready-for-pickup signal.

"Basket holding ten feet off the water, forward and right fifteen feet,"

Bartlett gave no response, but the airframe inched closer and Chris lowered the basket to splash into the water.

"Swimmer has the basket; he's throwing up, but is giving the ready-for-pickup signal."

The flight mechanic is required to provide both conning commands and advisories, information vital to the aircraft commander's flying decisions. How tired is the swimmer? Is the rescue equipment functioning normally? If over a boat, is the cable in danger of becoming entangled? In this instance, Bartlett worried about Troy becoming dehydrated, particularly in view of the long distances needed to reach and recover each survivor. It was a hell of a swim in such conditions.

Troy hung onto the basket until it was yanked from the waves, then turned back to continue his effort. His vomiting became regular and violent, yet he ignored it and swam toward survivor number two.

By the time he had number three on the way up, Bartlett had decided to pull Troy from the water. The two remaining survivors had drifted farther apart, and Troy's seasickness had not let up. Unable to talk directly to Troy to ask about his physical condition, he called on his other swimmer.

"Doug, are you rested and ready to give Troy a break?"

"Yes, sir."

"Chris, let's complete a bare-hook recovery of the swimmer, then prepare to deploy Doug."

"Roger, bare hook going down."

Grateful for the reprieve, Troy climbed inside the helicopter and tilted his head against the windowsill. Even then, his dizziness and queasiness did not subside.

For Doug, the sight of Troy's sickness and the motion of the water quickly brought back the knot in his stomach. "Only two left, then we can go home," he thought.

"Randy, have the O-four contact the six zero two three one," Bartlett directed. "If they have finished with their rescue of the crew of the *Irish Mist*, I am requesting they stand by as our backup. If we can't finish this, I want them here to help."

Meader began talking on the radio, while Bartlett and Chris returned their attention to the water and Doug. By now Doug had fought his way to the last two survivors, who clutched desperately to an uninflated, but still floating, life raft.

"I'll take one at a time, just like the others. Keep your hands and feet inside the basket," Doug explained as he always did, but got no response from either man. As EMTs, we are trained to recognize and treat hypothermia in our patients, and it appeared to Doug that these two had been in the water long enough to reach that lethargic and confused state. He needed to act quickly, as they were close to death.

Doug pried the cold stiff fingers of one of the men from the raft and turned toward the basket. It was coming into view as soon as he hustled toward the helicopter. As Doug swam, the waves attacked again.

"I can't see those damn things coming," he thought as he and his survivor were rolled underwater. "Come on, God, air please," he prayed.

They found the surface immediately, and the basket was within reach. Doug slung the heavy man inside the bails of the rescue device but had to wrestle with the man's lethargic legs to force them to follow. He then spun around to return for the last man. The sounds of the sea were overwhelming. Seeing the waves coming his way was bad enough; hearing them coming was worse.

"I got you," Doug screamed into the unresponsive man's ear upon reaching him. With renewed energy, Doug kicked his finned feet as his leg muscles screamed for relief. He tried to outswim the next wave, to no avail. It caught him just as he reached for the basket.

"Oh shit!" he thought as he gasped for air while he and the survivor were dragged under the white foamy expanse. This wave was the worst, and it carried them deep. He spit the snorkel mouthpiece from his lips and gritted his teeth against the urge to breathe.

"Hold on," he thought toward the man still wrapped in his arm. This will be over soon, one way or the other. Doug was about to give up and take a deep gulp of water when they popped to the surface. He turned and powered back toward the basket.

Onboard the aircraft Chris said, "Swimmer is at the six o'clock, back twenty feet."

Doug contorted the near-frozen man's body and forced him inside the basket then rolled onto his stomach and looked for the next wave, determined not to be surprised again. Within seconds, Chris had tipped the basket over and dropped the survivor to the deck of the airframe. Troy then dragged the man from the device, and Chris swung it back outside the door.

Chris reported, "Basket outside the cabin door, going down. Hold your position, swimmer at three o'clock, zero feet."

Doug smiled. "I'm outta here," he said to no one, then clambered into the basket before it was fully immersed. The ocean threw one last rogue wave at him, slamming into the metal device and spinning it upside down. Doug clamped onto the rails and took a deep breath as the feeling of being yanked skyward erased his sensation of being upside down.

Chris was smiling. "Swimmer's clear of the water, basket is coming up."

Bartlett, Meader, Chris, Doug, and Troy were done. Chris closed the door of their helicopter at 11:11 p.m. They had been flying for five and a half hours; three of them were in a hover in nasty winter storm conditions. They had saved a total of ten lives.

❧

Yet another account of what happened that night was shared by Shannon Scaff, a rescue swimmer assigned to my shop. His aircraft commander was Lieutenant Commander Watson.

Watson assembled his crew at the door of the HH-60J, and, as always, his highly polished boots, seamlessly smooth flight suit, and above-average preparedness elicited respect from those privileged to know him.

Before they crawled into the belly of the fish-shaped aircraft with its distinctive red and blue stripes, Watson addressed his crew. "The weather is worse offshore than it is here. Bartlett and his men have their hands full. We're going after a boat called the *Irish Mist*. It has two crew and a dog and has taken a pounding for the past several hours. From what I've heard, we will be unable to hoist from the deck of the boat; it's too rough out there. We will adhere to standard procedures throughout, and you are required to speak up if something is not going as you think it should. We'll stop and talk about it at that point."

Watson's requirement to voice an opinion was a radical departure from the mind-set of aircraft commanders of the past. The earlier ones had almost been revered as demigods, whose word was never questioned, a notion Watson threw out the window. Doing so enabled him to reach a level of expertise that those before him had not been able to obtain.

Shannon Scaff was the third rescue swimmer to be called in that night. Shannon knew Troy and Doug were in the middle of a difficult rescue, and he felt the initial surge of adrenaline as he listened to Watson. Shannon oozed confidence from every pore, a man who never imagined he might fail to complete a rescue. Anyone hoping to navigate the modern-day rescue swimmer school must possess a determined spirit, and I tell those on the waiting list they must be willing to die rather than give up. If they lack this trait, they will not make it through the training.

Watson's crew gathered in front of Maintenance Control, a small office close to the large hanger doors that is the nerve center for the watch captain and the rest of the duty section.

Adam Sustachek adjusted the survival vest he had taken from the wood locker on the hangar deck as Watson spoke. An exceptionally good mechanic, Adam had worked on every airframe system, with the exception of avionics, when not performing the duties of flight mechanic. He kept his blond hair as long and wavy as regulations allowed and ditched the thick, black-rimmed Coast Guard–issued eyeglasses for a more modern pair. Adam smiled nervously as he waited to board the helicopter.

The other member of the crew was Lieutenant Nick Koester. Dark haired with a straightforward demeanor, he was a capable aircraft commander in his own right. All Coast Guard HH-60J aircraft have a minimum of two pilots.

Before I became immersed in the world of Coast Guard aviation, the question of how pilots became proficient at flying in horrific conditions never occurred to me. I learned they become excellent stick jockeys because of the leadership of those flying with them. In this case Watson asked, "Nick, do you want the right seat?" This seemingly benign question revealed how pilots are transformed into seasoned veterans. Watson was relinquishing the coveted right pilot seat to Koester. Although Koester was already an aircraft commander, he had never faced the conditions they flew into that night. By sitting in the right seat, Koester became the pilot in control, the decision maker, in essence—The Man. "Sure," he said.

The crew had no questions at the end of the brief. They stormed from the hangar and hustled toward the helicopter that the line crew had already towed onto the ramp.

By 10:53 p.m. Koester had the HH-60J, tail number 6031, bouncing along the same course Bartlett had attempted earlier. Unlike Bartlett's crew, they were not ordered to change course. By 11:25 p.m. they circled above the much-maligned *Irish Mist*.

"What's your on-scene weather," the radioman from the 1504 asked. One of the benefits of having a high-flying eye in the sky is the ability to assist with communications when we might otherwise be out of range.

Watson said, "Ceiling is about three hundred feet. Visibility is two and a half and winds are from zero two zero degrees at steady fifty knots with gusts to sixty. Seas are running," he paused to look outside the window, "a steady thirty feet."

Koester asked, "Shannon, if we deploy you in the water behind the boat, do you think you can grab the line trailing behind the boat and pull yourself on?"

"No problem," Shannon said. Neither man realized Bartlett and his crew had attempted the same thing without success. If they had, it might have swayed their decision. They followed the same steps as Bartlett's crew and ended with the same results. Shannon had to be recovered after several fruitless minutes of powerful swimming effort.

Koester said, "Well, that didn't work. Let's have the crew enter the water once we place Shannon in. Sound good?"

"Works for me." Shannon bent close to the window glass next to his radio console on the left side of the aircraft. Even at three hundred feet, he could see the seas rolling beneath the aircraft like giant killers, indifferent to their victims. Mother Nature has many children; that night, she let some of her nastiest come out to play.

Shannon signaled Adam with a thumbs-up before he slid to the deck and attached the gunner's belt. He was then lifted from the dark gray deck of the helicopter into a black-gray night. He adjusted the lifting straps of the Tri-SAR harness and gave Adam the second required thumbs-up. Once he was lowered below the bottom of the airframe, the wind assaulted Shannon almost immediately. He felt the pressure and power Troy and Doug had surely experienced themselves, miles away.

Shannon entered the water to the sensation of stepping in front of a runaway freight train. As a towering wave slapped his skin and stung his face with its cold power, he reached up and released his harness from the hoist hook. The freedom was a relief, the responsibility heavy. He turned toward the *Irish Mist* and watched the male crewmember jump with the family dog in his arms. Dogs are not our problem, but we will rescue them given the chance if it does not interfere with saving human lives, and a dog alone in the middle of a storm like this is surely a dead dog. The female crewman stayed on the boat to provide steerage and keep the boat away from the hoisting site. In the water, man and dog faced Shannon and squinted against the stabbing rain and oxygen-sucking waves.

Shannon's training and adrenaline kicked in simultaneously. He sprinted through the water hard and fast. Years earlier he had lost the pinky of his left hand in an accident on a Coast Guard cutter, and sometimes the flopping picky finger of his glove will serve to distract survivors from panic long enough for Shannon to approach without that complication. He can see the thought process in their eyes: "Did he break his finger? Is he ignoring the pain to come after us?"

On this night, though, there were too many distractions to worry about, and Shannon grabbed the man as soon as he reached him.

"Does the dog bite?" he asked the man in the water. If so he had no intention of allowing it in the aircraft. A really angry dog could conceivably cause the aircraft to crash, or at least cause bodily harm to the crew in the back, and that he would not allow.

"No . . . no . . . he won't bite," the man gasped in a thick Australian accent.

"OK, hold onto him tight. I'm going to take both of you to the basket. And don't worry; we do this all the time." Shannon had noticed the concerned look on the man's face.

Adam was already rocketing the basket downward when Shannon turned to give the ready-for-pickup signal. A split second later the basket bounced across the wave top and settled calmly in the water. Shannon wrenched the rescue device from the sliding face of the wave and brought it close to man and dog, awkwardly struggling to push both of them into the basket at once. The smooth practiced effort swimmers normally use did not work. It took too long. As Shannon wrestled with the basket and man and dog, an unexpected wave pushed them all under.

As in the attacks on Doug and Troy, Shannon was hit from behind. The wave curled and broke across the surface, rolling the water back onto itself. Close to the beach, surfers might have rushed a curl like this for a ride of a lifetime. For Shannon, it flipped the three of them over and, for a second, sent them sailing through the air. Then the water-saturated air exploded back into the sea and finally slammed them into the wave's trough. The powerful impact shot all three in different directions. Twisted and turned underwater by the surge of pure power, Shannon screamed inwardly, "Damn it, damn it! Where are they?" He turned and saw nothing but moving blackness. He kicked and kicked, swimming in no particular direction, confident that the buoyancy of his equipment would eventually bring him to the surface, where he needed to be. He had to find the man. It was his job.

At last the floodlight of the aircraft illuminated the man's flailing arms in the foamy seas. Shannon saw him immediately and powered toward the survivor, realizing that the dog was swimming in circles out of reach. After regaining control of his first survivor he leaned onto his back and gave Adam the ready for pickup signal. The basket was already below the aircraft and coming toward them as Lieutenant Koester coaxed the aircraft in Shannon's direction.

"MY DOG!" the man screamed.

"I'll get him," Shannon promised, not sure he could carry through.

The basket landed with a splash next to them, and Shannon loosened his grip across the man's chest, rolled the man inside the bails of the basket, and held him there to give Adam a thumbs-up signal. He felt the cable go tight and prayed it would clear the water before another wave hit them. Adam rolled the thumb wheel on the hoist-control handle to its full up position, causing the hoist to suck cable into the drum at a rate of 250 feet per minute. This maneuver, called two blocking, can be a rough ride, but it also can be effective.

As soon as the man was above the waves, Shannon spun around, feeling queasy from swallowing salt water. Ignoring the churning in the pit of his stomach, he searched for the *Irish Mist* through 360 degrees without finding the boat and his last survivor. The boat had disappeared, but still swimming in circles just 25 yards away, he spotted the dog.

"They will be a minute before they pick me up, so I might as well see if I can catch this mutt," Shannon thought, approaching cautiously, not knowing what to expect. Even the tamest of dogs might become violent in such circumstances. This dog was a healthy-size yellow Lab with terror-filled eyes, but once Shannon moved to face it, the dog settled its paws on his shoulders and relaxed to let Shannon hold its weight in the water.

"It's OK, boy, we'll get you out of here," he said.

"Shannon has the dog," Adam said as the survivor crawled from the basket.

"I see that, let's pick him up," Koester ordered.

"Conn me in."

"Forward and right, fifty feet, basket's going down."

"See, here it comes," Shannon explained to the dog as the basket came into view of the hover lights. The metal rescue device landed with a gentle splash. Adam paid out enough slack to allow the basket to ride the backside of the wave, and Shannon settled the dog feet first in the bottom of the basket. The Lab seemed to know not to climb out and crouched low, shaking but still, as it waited. Shannon gave the ready-for-pickup signal. Adam rolled the cable up until the basket shot from the sea.

"Basket is clear of the water, clear to move back and left thirty."

"Roger, once that dog is inside, leave it in the basket and send the bare hook down for Shannon. We need to reposition to pick up our final survivor."

Watson had monitored the forward progress of the *Irish Mist* and knew they would have to move Shannon closer. He let Koester know the boat was in forward motion, and they agreed they needed to reposition Shannon. Adam lowered the bare hoist hook to Shannon, who knew he was to be hoisted and, most likely, moved closer to the boat.

"Swimmer attaching the hook; prepare to take the load."

Shannon was hoisted into the cabin, and Koester hover-taxied the aircraft aft of the sailboat. They followed the same steps they had used earlier, and Shannon again found himself in the maelstrom of the Atlantic. Gratefully, the woman abandoned the wounded sailboat's wheel.

Shannon told her, "That last hoist was a little rough, so I'm going to lock my hands around you. If we go for a ride underwater, just hold your breath and relax, we will come back to the surface in short order." He was relieved to be rid of the dog, having almost lost a human being while trying to save it.

Shannon gave the signal and swam toward the downward spiral of light coming from the underside of the helicopter, looking up to watch the gleaming black letters USCG on its white underbelly grow larger.

"Forward and right ten feet," Adam conned.

"Roger, lost target."

"Swimmer approaching basket, swimmer has the basket, waiting for ready-for-pickup signal."

"Have ready for pickup, taking up slack, prepare to take the load, taking the load," Adam said as he hoisted the basket from the water.

"I've got to get out of here," Shannon thought as his seasickness returned with a vengeance. The bare hook descending was a welcome sight.

"Swimmer has the hook, is connecting the hook. Have the ready-for-pickup signal. Swimmer's inside the cabin, hoist complete."

Watson, monitoring the radios, said, "The six zero two six has requested we cover them in case they can't retrieve everyone from the two boats they are hoisting from." There was no time to celebrate. If another crew was requesting assistance, they needed to hurry.

"One five O-four, advise the two six we are en route to their position," Koester reported.

"Nice job, gentlemen; now let's give our brothers whatever help they need," Watson said over the ICS.

At 12:40 a.m. on May 30, Koester added power, tilted the nose over, and headed toward Bartlett and the crew of the crew of the 6026.

As it turned out, Bartlett and crew needed no assistance. Later, both aircrews assembled at the hangar to discuss the events of the past few hours in detail, with many congratulations passed out. They had saved the lives of twelve sailors and one dog. All aircrews had returned safely, and no aircraft were damaged.

Bartlett thought Chris, his flight mechanic, summed the whole thing up well: "It was a good night."

The U.S. Coast Guard in World War II

Malcolm F. Willoughby

THE COAST GUARD'S MOST INTENSE LIFESAVING ACTIVITY WAS IN THE dark days of early 1942, when Nazi submarines were running rampant along the Atlantic and Gulf Coasts, picking off freighters and tankers even within sight of land. Offshore patrol cutters and craft from lifeboat stations rescued survivors from ships of all leading maritime nations. During the period of the war, 647 United States merchant ships (total gross tonnage 4,156,849) were lost on all oceans. Of this total tonnage, only one-fourth, or 1,081,417, were being escorted or in convoy when sunk.

The following accounts of certain rescues form some of the most thrilling pages in the history of the Coast Guard.

Six months before the Unites States entered the war, cutter *Duane*, while on the weather observation patrol in the North Atlantic, picked up an SOS radio call from the British steamship *Tresillian*. This vessel was being shelled by a German submarine. Reaching the reported position by daylight of 14 June 1941, the cutter began searching for survivors, working to eastward. Three U.S. Navy flying boats soon signaled that assistance was needed, and the cutter proceeded 20 miles farther eastward, as indicated by the planes. There, two drifting lifeboats filled with survivors were sighted, and the victims were taken on board. These proved to be the *Tresillian's* entire crew. Had it not been for the cooperation of the Navy

97

planes, however, *Duane* might never have found the lifeboats, as they had drifted 20 miles from the scene of the sinking.

On 7 December 1941, the day of Pearl Harbor, the 6,256-ton American freighter *Mauna Ala* was ordered back to port after having started for Australia. She was groping her way along our darkened Pacific Coast during a blackout test on 10 December 1941, unaware that all lighted aids to navigation had been blacked out. Mistaking her position, she ran aground on Clatsop Beach, Oregon, and lay in moderately heavy ground swells. Cutter *Onondaga*, patrolling north of Columbia River Lightship, was directed to the scene by radio direction finder bearings, and by a searchlight at Fort Stevens. At *Onondaga's* request, *Mauna Ala's* lights were relighted and the cutter closed in. Repeated efforts by *Onondaga* and other craft to float the vessel failed. The stranded ship began to take water and break up. Thirty-six persons on board were removed, and the million-dollar vessel, with its $100,000 cargo, became another victim of the sea.

An early indication of enemy barbarism with no concern for human life was recognized on 14 January 1942. An enemy submarine torpedoed Panamanian tanker *Norness*, which was carrying fuel oil from New York to Halifax. Cutter *Argo*, then at Newport, Rhode Island, was ordered to the scene, about 150 miles distant. After several hours at full speed, she reached the unfortunate tanker, a grim sight with stern submerged and bow still projecting 40 feet above water. *Argo* sighted a capsized motor launch, and three rafts, on one of which (under the hovering Navy Blimp K6) were huddled 6 frightened survivors, their drawn faces reflecting the ordeal through which they had passed. These 6, who were rescued, were all that remained of a crew of 40.

Four days later, an enemy submarine torpedoed and then shelled an American tanker, but failed to sink her. The tanker eventually escaped. After what appeared to be a lethal torpedoing off the North Carolina coast on 19 January 1942, three crewmembers of the tanker *Malay* left the vessel in a lifeboat. No others abandoned ship. When boats from the Oregon Inlet and other Coast Guard stations arrived, the master, who had remained on board with 34 crewmembers, reported that his vessel had been unmercifully shelled subsequent to the torpedoing.

Malay then got under way and headed for port. Later, the enemy again appeared and began a further bombardment of the already badly crippled vessel. *Malay* was struck amidships, leaving a gaping hole and flooding No. 7 tank. She remained afloat, however. Eluding the enemy, she raced with all the speed she could make and limped into Norfolk under her own power. One crewmember was killed during the shelling; three were seriously injured. The injured were taken on board a motor lifeboat from the Oregon Inlet Lifeboat Station.

On 23 January 1942, when 12 miles south of Hatteras, the British tanker *Empire Gem* was torpedoed and burst into flames. Motor Lifeboat No. 4464 of the Hatteras Inlet Lifeboat Station was sent to the scene and, after arrival, maneuvered around the burning tanker and stood by as close as possible until midnight. As there were no signs of life, she left to search for lifeboats which might have been launched. As if the danger of drowning was not enough when a ship was sinking, an added hazard was often thrown in for good measure, and both fire and water raced to claim lives. Motor Lifeboat No. 5426 from the Ocracoke Lifeboat Station was proceeding to the assistance of steamship *Venore* at 2030 that same night when she received orders to change her course and proceed to *Empire Gem*. She arrived at the scene at 0300 the next morning. The crew sighted three men on the tanker's bow, away from the fire which extended from amidships to the stern.

Finding it impossible, in the heavy seas, to get near enough to take men off, this lifeboat stood by to await dawn. At 0700 the lifeboat got close to the tanker, and three imperiled men jumped overboard. The lifeboat crew picked up two of them and barely missed the third man, who was swept into the burning oil and sank.

After a fruitless search, the Hatteras boat returned to the burning tanker and contacted the Ocracoke lifeboat. The two survivors, who were *Empire Gem*'s master and radioman, were transferred from the Ocracoke boat to that from Hatteras and departed for Hatteras Inlet. The Ocracoke lifeboat remained to search for life rafts which might have put out from the ship. A third motor lifeboat was ordered out from Oregon Inlet Lifeboat Station, 75 miles away, but arrived too late to assist effectively.

Three days later, on 27 January 1942, a dual role of bombing the enemy from the air and bringing aid to survivors was played by Coast Guard airplane V-175, piloted by Lieutenant Commander R. L. Burke from the Elizabeth City (North Carolina) Air Station. The plane received a distress call from the 7,096-ton American tanker *Frances E. Powell* that she was being overhauled by a submarine, 8 miles off Currituck Light, south of Virginia Beach. The tanker was sunk soon afterward. A Coast Guard–piloted J2F-5 plan first sighted the submarine and dropped two depth charges within 100 feet of the submerged marauder. Then Commander Burke in the V-175 dropped a grapnel with 100 feet of line and two life jackets to buoy the spot so that destroyers could later depth charge the area. It seemed likely that the enemy had been damaged, because Burke later saw and photographed what appeared to be a distress buoy from a submarine. All but four of the tanker's crew of 32 were eventually saved by surface craft brought to the scene by the two planes.

The Coast Guard performed another rescue on 3 February 1942, this time off Lewes, Delaware. The sinking Panamanian (United Fruit) freighter *San Gil*, from Marta, Colombia, to Philadelphia with bananas, sent an SOS which was intercepted by cutter *Nike* at 2400. *Nike* immediately proceeded to the scene and took on board the 39 crewmembers and one passenger. A surfboat from Ocean City (New Jersey) Lifeboat Station also arrived and towed *San Gil*'s two empty lifeboats to the station.

The American tanker *China Arrow* (8,403 tons) was torpedoed on 5 February 1942 just southeast of Ocean City, Maryland. She was en route to New York from Beaumont, Texas. Her crew of 37 escaped unscathed in their three lifeboats, but were adrift two days before being picked up by *Nike* with the assistance of Coast Guard aircraft. The cutter took them to Lewes, Delaware; they were unaffected, except by exposure.

The 5,000-ton Brazilian steamship *Buarque*, carrying a general cargo, 11 passengers, and a crew of 74, fell victim to an enemy submarine 10 days later. En route from Rio de Janeiro to New York, 34 crew members and 8 passengers lost their lives. Cutter *Calypso*, with a Coast Guard plane as spotter, located two of her lifeboats carrying 42 survivors, and took them on board. Insufficiently clad the victims were suffering severely from exposure and cold.

On the following day, 16 February 1942, Coast Guardsmen on board cutter *Woodbury*, patrolling off the Chesapeake Bay entrance, heard a deafening explosion and immediately proceeded to the locality. They found a lifeboat with 11 survivors, and after further search, three more lifeboats containing the rest of the crew of 40 of the United States tanker *E. H. Blum*. The latter had been traveling in ballast from Philadelphia to Port Arthur, Texas, when she was either torpedoed or struck by a mine. The survivors were taken to the Navy Section Base, Little Creek, Virginia, and two injured men were hospitalized at Norfolk. Eventually, *Blum* was salvaged; her two halves, which remained afloat, were towed to Philadelphia and rejoined, and the ship later returned into service.

From Cape Canaveral, the Florida eastern shore forms one side of the Florida Straits, which stretch about 40 miles east to the Bahama Banks. Here deep water flows close to the Florida coast. Thousands of ships annually travel the Gulf Stream, funneling through the Straits, and wartime traffic became heavy. These narrow waters were a neutral "happy hunting ground" for enemy submarines. Before sufficient naval strength became available to ward off undersea attacks, 24 ships had sunk there. From these ships, 504 men were saved. Coast Guard lifeboat stations and their crews were often the sole hope of submarine victims. They proved themselves worthy, time and again.

On the night of 19 February 1942, the American tanker *Pan Massachusetts* was torpedoed by a submarine in a storm-swept sea at the north end of the Florida Straits. "Flames sighted 20 miles, 142 degrees from Cape Canaveral," a calm voice reported from the lighthouse at that cape. Cutter *Forward*, sent to investigate, found that the process of abandoning ship on board the burning tanker had been complicated by the swiftly spreading blaze. The flaming lifeboats were useless. The 38 crewmen had leaped overboard into a sea of fire. A British passenger vessel, *Elizabeth Massey*, only a short distance away when the torpedo struck, had put over a lifeboat.

Forward took a lifeboat in tow and moved slowly through the wreckage. As a survivor was spotted, the British seamen in the lifeboat cast loose from the cutter, picked their way to the struggling victim—usually thickly caked with oil—and took him on board. Then, avoiding the flaming oil, they would maneuver back to the cutter. All bodies recovered were placed on board *Forward* and all 18 survivors on board *Elizabeth Massey*, which then proceeded to Jacksonville.

Three more ships went down two nights later, two off Jupiter Inlet and one southeast of Cape Canaveral. The first was the 5,287-ton American tanker *Republic*, which was hit late on the night of 21 February. Twenty-two of her crew made shore in a lifeboat just south of Jupiter Inlet. Seven others were picked up by a passing steamer and taken to Port Everglades, where they were turned over to the Coast Guard.

During efforts to save *Republic*, a second tanker, *Cities Service Empire* (8,103 tons) was torpedoed farther offshore early in the morning of the 22nd. Cutter *Vigilant* was the first vessel to reach her, arriving at 0800. Passing 36 survivors, who had taken life rafts and could be attended to later, Lieutenant L. R. Daniels, commanding officer of *Vigilant*, nosed his ship up to the blazing *Empire's* bow, where he had seen three men fouled in the lifeboat falls. Crawling on board the lifeboat, Coast Guardsmen battled flames as they labored to work the victims free. Two were brought on board, but as rescue crews started back for the third, the tanker exploded and sank, spraying *Vigilant* from stem to stern with unignited oil. Lifeboats from Fort Pierce Lifeboat Station assisted in the search for bodies; seven were recovered, including that of the man Lieutenant Daniels and his crew had almost saved. Meanwhile, the U.S. Navy destroyer *Biddle* had taken the 36 crewmembers from their life rafts about a mile away.

Finally, while details from the Palm Beach Auxiliary and the Lake Worth Lifeboat Station were taking soundings at the scene of the *Republic* disaster, tanker *W. D. Anderson*, 10,227 tons, was attacked nearby. It took Auxiliary less than 40 minutes to organize a search of the area. Only one crewman escaped from this sinking. The search was finally abandoned after rescuing the lone survivor, who had seen the torpedo track and leaped to safety before the explosion.

A six-week lull ensued along the east coast of Florida due partly to measures taken by a handful of ships and 18 Coast Guard planes. Nine planes from the air station at St. Petersburg and nine from that at Miami were divided into three squadrons. Based at Banana River, they patrolled day and night in conjunction with the Navy.

Meanwhile, elsewhere along the Atlantic Coast, enemy submarines were raising havoc with our shipping, much of which was still unescorted in convoy. The American freighter *Marore*, 8,215 tons, with a cargo of precious iron ore, had sent out from Chile and, eluding the enemy, had reached a position off Big Kinnakeet (North Carolina) Lifeboat Station on 26 February 1942 when a torpedo blasted her and sent her to the bottom. Shortly afterward, the lifeboat station lookout saw a small boat rigged with a sail endeavoring to make shore. A motor surfboat from the station went to meet it and, finding on board the master and 13 crewmembers of *Marore*, helped them to land in safety. Three or four of the crew were lost.

The lookout of the Shark River Lifeboat Station on the New Jersey coast, while scanning the ocean from his lookout tower on 28 February 1942, sighted what appeared to be a ship afire. A picket boat and motor lifeboat from Shark River and Manasquan were immediately sent out at top speed toward the burning vessel. On arrival at 0200, the picket boat found the Standard Oil Company tanker *R. P. Resor*, 7,451 tons, afire from bow to stern. Apparently the ship had been hit above the waterline with one or more shells, which exploded, setting oil on fire. Oil seemed to be pouring from the ship faster than the fire could burn it. Blazing oil had spread from the bow toward the south for a distance of 500 feet.

The Coast Guard boat cruised as closely as possible to the burning vessel, when voices were heard crying for help. The smoke that arose was, at times, blinding; the heat was so intense that the Coast Guardsmen were almost overcome. Nevertheless, they brought their boat close to the inferno in an effort to reach the victims, who were threatened with envelopment by the flames. Suddenly there bobbed up before the Coast Guard boat a man so thickly covered with oil as to be almost unrecognizable as a human being. He must have been three times his normal weight, making it difficult to gain a firm hold on his slippery, oil-soaked clothing. The crew were unable to pull him up on board.

The heat was growing more and more intense with the passing seconds, and the strength of the lifesavers was taxed to the limit. After much effort, the men succeeded in tying a line under the armpits of the helpless victim and towed him from the white-hot sides of the burning vessel.

Paint on the side of the Coast Guard boat had begun to blister. The man, with his extra weight, towed under; the boat was stopped, and the four Coast Guardsmen finally pulled him on board. The lifeboat headed again toward the burning tanker to rescue additional victims. Another oil-soaked man was found, clinging desperately to a life raft. Two crewmembers went over the side into the sea into oil to rescue this man, who was too exhausted to get on board without help. Both survivors were stripped of their oil-soaked clothing, wrapped in blankets, given coffee, and otherwise made comfortable in the cabin. Although the station boat searched the rest of the night, no other members of the 49-man crew were found.

The sinkings continued. At least 30 vessels, aggregating 166,578 tons of American merchant shipping, were lost in February of 1942, compared with 23 vessels of 127,642 tons sunk in January. March 1942 came in like a lion in the battle against subs. During the month, 30 more American merchant vessels totaling 193,987 tons were sunk, of which only two (11,533 tons) were in convoy.

The Coast Guard cutter *Calypso* performed a splendid piece of rescue work when she rushed to the aid of the 7,000-ton Brazilian freighter *Arabutan*, torpedoed without warning well off the Virginia Capes on 7 March 1942 while bound from Norfolk to Trinidad with coal and coke. The freighter sank in 20 minutes. The 54 crewmembers, drifting in their lifeboats, were constantly endangered by continued enemy fire. When *Calypso* arrived shortly after midnight, she began searching for survivors in total darkness and heavy wind. The crew of the cutter, in great danger from enemy torpedoes, scanned the heavy seas all night in their determination to find survivors. Next day, an assisting Coast Guard plane, V-183, sighted them and directed the cutter to the spot about two hours distant. Within 15 minutes of her arrival, *Calypso* had taken on board all 54 survivors from four lifeboats and was on her way out of the danger zone and headed for Norfolk. One man of the freighter's crew had been killed in the torpedoing.

Three more sinkings followed off the Atlantic Coast within the next five days. The 6,676-ton American tanker *Gulftrade*, from Port Arthur, Texas, to Philadelphia with oil, was broken in two by an enemy torpedo on 9 March 1942, a half mile off Barnegat Light. While cutter *Antietam* was picking up the 16 survivors of the crew of 34, the submarine fired a torpedo at the cutter which passed within 20 feet of her bow. Two days later, the Norwegian steamship *Hvosleff* was torpedoed off Fenwick Island Light Station near Cape Henlopen. The survivors, in a lifeboat, landed on the beach nearby. Coast Guardsmen assisted and transported them to the Lewes Lifeboat Station.

The next day the American tanker *John D. Gill*, 11,641 tons, was torpedoed while bound from Philadelphia to Texas with a cargo of gasoline and oil. She was found early in the morning by a Coast Guard motor lifeboat from Oak Island (South Carolina) Lifeboat Station. The tanker was afire and sinking, about 25 miles east of Cape Fear. Any survivors had apparently already taken to lifeboats and rafts. The motor lifeboat CG-186 and cutter *Agassiz* began their search. Through fire, smoke, and oil, the Coast Guardsmen combed the area in every direction and were rewarded at daybreak by a red flare. Upon investigation it was found to have come from a life raft with 11 survivors. The exhausted men clinging to the raft were taken aboard and rushed to Southport, South Carolina, by CG-186; the motor lifeboat and the cutter continued the search for many hours. *Agassiz* found 14 bodies and took them to Southport. Later it was learned that 15 more survivors had been picked up by a passing tanker and taken to Charleston, South Carolina. Altogether, 26 of the tanker's 49-man crew were saved.

Two other March sinkings were noteworthy. On the night of 16 March, the 7,118-ton tanker *Olean* was torpedoed 15 miles south of Cape Lookout, North Carolina, while en route from Norfolk to Houston. A motor lifeboat from the Cape Lookout Lifeboat Station arrived at the scene about 0330, and later one arrived from Fort Macon Lifeboat Station. After a careful search, the Coast Guardsmen saw a dim light flicker for only two or three seconds, but that was enough. In a few moments, 20 survivors were found in a lifeboat. Ten of the most seriously injured were placed in the Fort Macon boat together with five from another life raft, and these proceeded to Beaufort, North Carolina, the nearest point where medical aid was available. Later, three more survivors and one body were located by a plane. In all, 6 persons lost their lives and 36 were saved.

The tug *Menomenee* and three barges were attacked simultaneously and shelled by an enemy submarine off Metompkin Inlet Lifeboat Station, 50 miles north of Cape Charles, Virginia, on 31 March 1942. A lookout there reported a small boat drifting two miles offshore that night, and two motor lifeboats rushed to the scene. They found one of the barges belching smoke and fire, with shells from the submarine still bursting about her. The tug, and the barges *Allegheny* and *Barnegat*, sank soon after the attack, and only the barge *Ontario* remained afloat. The crew of the tug had been picked up by *Northern Sun*, a passing tanker. The crew of *Ontario*, those seen by the lookout, were found and saved. Then a motor lifeboat set out at top speed to search for the survivors of the two sunken barges. The intrepid Coast Guardsmen went into the thick of the enemy shelling attack on the now-waterlogged *Ontario*. Here they found crews of the other barges and took them on board. Thus, all nine of the barge crews were saved by the Coast Guardsmen while one barge was still under attack.

In April, American merchant ship losses reached 38 ships totaling 203,303 tons. None of those sunk was in the convoy. There simply were not enough vessels at that time to handle all coastal shipping. On 11 April 1942, the thirteenth day after the 8,272-ton motorship *City of New York* had been torpedoed off North Carolina, a lifeboat with 11 of her survivors came within sight of *CG-455*. Cold, hunger, thirst, and mental torture had racked these unfortunate victims as they had drifted hopelessly day after day. But, contrary to the superstitions, rescue came on the thirteenth day. One saved was Miriam Etter, age three, whose mother had died in the boat; a sailor had also succumbed to the harrowing experience. Another boatload of survivors from the same vessel reached Norfolk after a similar ordeal, during which the wife of a Yugoslav consular official had given birth to a child in the open lifeboat.

Events following the torpedoing and sinking of the Panamanian freighter *Chenango* on 20 April, 55 miles southeast of Oregon Inlet, North Carolina, brought home the horrors of submarine warfare. There were only two survivors. *Chenango* sank in two minutes, so quickly that no boats could be launched. After shelling the stricken vessel, the submarine deliberately cruised through the 15 or 20 survivors struggling in the water, drowning many and leaving all but two to the sharks. The two managed to reach an impoverished life raft, but there were no oars, and the raft drifted away from the other victims.

Twelve days later, on 2 May 1942, these two starving, blistering, sunburned, semiconscious, and emaciated men were sighted by an Army bomber. The Coast Guard's Elizabeth City Air Station was notified, and Lieutenant Commander R. L. Burke then flew from that station and searched the reported location offshore. He finally sighted the raft and made a successful sea landing. Incipient thunderstorms were evident, and there were confused cross seas with waves four to six feet high.

Burke taxied the plane up the wind beyond the bouncing, heaving raft and cut both engines, then drifted downward close to the raft. Burke had to start his engines to get the plane close enough to the raft to heave a line to it. One man was delirious and thought the plane was starting up to take off and was going to leave him behind. He screamed and jumped overboard into the shark-infested waters but was recovered. A line was tossed to the raft, which acted as a sea drogue for the drifting plane, and Burke was able to pull the two close and get them on board. A pharmacist's mate on the plane dressed their wounds and administered sedatives while the plane flew to Naval Air Station Norfolk, Virginia, turning the survivors over to Navy doctors and intelligence officers there.

Such cases of drifting for days and weeks brought inconceivable hardships on the hapless victims, and their rescues were true acts of mercy. Cooperation between Coast Guard and Navy units, both air and surface, led to saving 13 men who had been adrift in the Atlantic for 17 days. Their ship, *Pipestone County*, from Trinidad to Boston, had been torpedoed without warning far to the east of the Virginia Capes on 21 April 1942. She sank in two minutes. A Coast Guard plane from Elizabeth City was scouting far offshore on 7 May. The radioman intercepted a message saying survivors in a lifeboat had been spotted from another Coast Guard plane 30 miles east of Oregon Inlet. The first plane, sighting cutter *Calypso* on the horizon, flew over her and at 1010 reported the situation by message block dropped on board.

Fifteen minutes later *Calypso* picked up a message from the plane pilot stating that he was circling over the lifeboat and giving its exact position. The cutter changed course and steered for the plane; she was further directed by a Navy blimp, which had taken station over the lifeboat. Meanwhile, the 13 men received their first fresh provisions in 17 days from another Elizabeth City plane.

Three hours after receiving the first message, and 33 miles from her original position, *Calypso* reached the lifeboat and picked up the boatload of *Pipestone County* survivors. These said that the rest of the crew had put off in three other lifeboats, which had become separated the first day. The cutter sank the lifeboat by gunfire and took the survivors to the Naval Operating Base, Norfolk. Passing craft farther at sea had rescued some of the others and taken them to Boston The vessel's master, who was in the latter group, reported that 46 men had been on board; most were saved. One of the four lifeboats was never found.

On 26 April 1942, Andrew J. Cupples, AAM 1c, attached to the St. Petersburg Coast Guard Air Station, was returning from patrol in his plane to Key West. He sighted an oil slick nine miles from Marquesa Key, which proved to be a U.S. destroyer, *Sturtevant*, sinking stern first with only a bit of her bow still above water. One lifeboat was afloat picking up survivors. The vessel was inside a recently laid minefield. No ships were in the vicinity, and Cupples, without a radioman, proceeded 20 miles to Key West and made his report. Refueling and taking on a radioman, he took off again and sighted a rescue boat five or six miles from the scene. He directed it to the lifeboat and the rafts containing survivors. Small craft took 137 survivors to Key West. Three were dead and 12 missing in this mishap. Cupples was recommended for commendation by his commanding officer.

At about this time, German submarine commanders again centered their attention on Cape Canaveral, Florida. Fifty miles from the nearest lifeboat station at Ponce de Leon Inlet, and well isolated from any village or town, Canaveral was truly the wolf pack's heaven. Lying offshore, U-boats picked up silhouettes of ships in the flashing light from Cape Canaveral Lighthouse and sent torpedoes crashing into them. Within a two-week period, 151 survivors from torpedoed vessels received first aid, medical assistance, food, and clothing at that lighthouse, which had become a veritable house of refuge. To reduce silhouettes, Cape Canaveral Light was dimmed; shortly afterward, on 9 May 1942, the power of all lights along the coast was reduced.

Lieutenant Commander W. B. Scheibel departed Elizabeth City on 1 May in a Coast Guard plane to search for a lifeboat containing starving survivors of an unknown torpedoed vessel. A heavy smoke pall from swamp fires, carried seaward by a moderate westerly wind, cut visibility to three or four miles. A grid search was begun, and at 1332 a lifeboat from the British *Empire Drum* with 13 survivors was sighted. The exhausted men had been adrift for a week. The plane notified the station and dropped emergency rations, medical supplies, and blankets. One injured, delirious man was on board. The plane landed and took him and one other survivor to Norfolk. Surface vessels rescued the others.

Two cargo vessels and a tanker were torpedoed on the 4th and 5th of May, this time off the southern Florida coast. First time was the steamship *Eclipse*, of Boynton Inlet. She was loaded with essential war supplies worth millions of dollars. Her master had become suspicious and had deliberately run her aground in an attempt to dodge what he thought was a submarine. He was right. However, the Nazis did not fire a torpedo until *Eclipse* had pulled herself off and was again gaining headway. Just after the torpedo struck her side, the vessel went aground again, still off Boynton Inlet and in full view of spectators on shore. Coast Guard Auxiliary members were alerted and reached the scene within a few minutes.

The commercial tug *Ontario* was in the vicinity with a tow. The commanding officer of Base Six at Fort Lauderdale, on orders from his District Coast Guard officer, went on board this tug while still at sea with her tow. Because of the grounded vessel's cargo, it was essential that *Eclipse* was pulled from the shoal; those supplies were needed by the fighting men on the other side of the world. The Coast Guardsmen explained this to the tug's captain and asked that *Ontario* release her tow and hurry to the aid of *Eclipse*. Under strong persuasion coupled with a threat to commandeer the tug, *Ontario* secured her tow, put about, and steamed for Boynton Inlet. *Eclipse* was finally pulled off the bar. *Ontario* and another tug, *Bafshe*, took her to Port Everglades.

While the tugs and escorts were en route, the 8,327-ton American *Java Arrow*, a straggler behind its convoy all the way from New York, was torpedoed off Bethel Shoals, presumably by the same raider that had blasted *Eclipse*. Also, word was received of a torpedoed steamship, *Delisle* (3,478 tons), aground of Jupiter Inlet Light. The tugs and their escorts were ordered to proceed to *Java Arrow*, which was loaded with war supplies, with the report that she could be salvaged. The master and her crew had been removed. Lieutenant Maurice G. Field went on board from Fort Pierce Lifeboat Station and directed the initial preparations for salvaging while awaiting the arrival of the two tugs. The crew were returned to the ship.

Field's plan was to cut the anchor chain at a 6-fathom shackle, linking the shackle to a towline. A Fort Pierce acetylene torch operator was rousted out of bed at midnight, rushed to the scene, and cut the chain. The eerie light of the blue-flamed acetylene torch, with no other illumination except flashlights, was too much for the *Java Arrow* crew, most of them veterans of one or more torpedoings. They demanded to be returned to the beach. Lieutenant Field went ashore, where, from West Palm Beach, he directed *Java Arrow*, her tow, and escort during the four-day trip to Port Everglades. Two other vessels were sunk in that vicinity while *Java Arrow* was making port.

Still another tanker, *Lubra Foil*, was hit on its way into Port Everglades *in full view* of the salvage fleet. One of *Java Arrow*'s escorts, together with Auxiliary and Coast Guard vessels from Lake Worth Inlet Lifeboat Station, managed to pull 31 survivors from flaming wreckage in a debris-littered sea, leaving *Lubra Foil* to drift northward for two days before she sank. The escort then returned to *Java Arrow*, and the salvage party proceeded to Port Everglades. Other sinkings kept things lively.

Lifeboat stations and District Headquarters during this time worked around the clock. Officers and men barely had time to eat; sleep was out of the question. One assignment had scarcely been completed before another took its place. Late in May, two Mexican tankers were attacked, one off Miami and the other off the Florida Keys; three survived from *Porter de Llano*'s crew of 35, and seven days latter cutter *Nemesis* brought in 28 survivors from the other, *Faja de Oro*. A few days after this, Mexico formally declared war on the Axis.

The United States tanker *David McKelvey*, 6,821 tons, was torpedoed and sunk off the Mississippi River Delta on 14 May 1942. A Coast Guard plane from Biloxi Air Station proceeded to its reported position, located an oil slick 15 miles to the eastward, and discovered the tanker afloat on fire. Tanker *Norsol* was approaching and was told that some of the crew were still on the burning vessel. Twenty-five of the 42 crew members were saved. Two days later the plane proceeded to almost the same position, where the American tanker *William C. McTarnaham*, 7,305 tons, had been struck by two torpedoes. Two lifeboats and four rafts with 28 persons on board were three miles away. The plane flew five miles to inform some fishing boats, which then effected the rescue. This tanker stayed afloat, was salvaged, and reconditioned.

There was another similar rescue five days later. Another plane from Biloxi Air Station proceeded to the position of the sunken American freighter *Heredia*, 4,732 tons. Her masts showed above water, well south of Atchafalaya Bay, Louisiana. About a mile to the west, eight men and a small boy were on a raft made from a hatch cover; four more men as well as a small girl were near the mast; and five were clinging to the wreckage. There was also one body supported by a life preserver. The pilot requested his station to send aid and dropped message blocks to the survivors, telling them aid was coming. He then proceeded to six fishing boats, five miles northwestward, which went to the scene and took all survivors on board.

The British steamship *Peisander* was torpedoed on 17 May 1942, about 300 miles off Bermuda. All 61 members of the crew got away in three lifeboats. Two of these boats, with 43 survivors, were found and towed in by *CGR-37* and a motor lifeboat of the Maddaket (Nantucket) Lifeboat Station, but the third boat, with 18 survivors, was still missing. This was sighted by a Navy plane, and word was relayed through Boston to cutter *General Greene*. The latter was ordered, on 24 May, to search for this boat. Fog hampered this operation, but at 0945 on the 25th, the cutter found the third lifeboat near Nantucket Shoals. At the same moment, the lookout sighted a submarine, which was crash diving across the cutter's bow. *General Greene* tried to ram, but the sub was too deep; she then closed in on a sound contact and dropped three depth charges.

An oil slick 400 feet in diameter appeared. Unable to pick up the sound again during the next 25 minutes, the cutter broke off the attack and took on board the 18 occupants of the lifeboat.

These survivors explained that the submarine had been tagging the lifeboat and had sent two torpedoes into the American freighter *Plow City*, 3,282 tons, when that vessel had attempted a rescue on 21 May. One crewmember had been killed. The other 30 crewmen were picked up five days later by USS *Sapphire*, a converted yacht.

General Greene took the 18 survivors and their lifeboats to Nantucket Harbor. Here she collected the other 43 survivors of *Peisander* and carried them to Newport, Rhode Island.

The Panamanian tanker *Persephone*, traveling in convoy from the Dutch West Indies to New York, was torpedoed in daylight on 25 May 1942, two and a half miles from Barnegat, New Jersey. First on the spot was patrol boat *CG-159*, an escort. Those on board *CG-159* had seen the tanker hit when about four miles from Barnegat Lightship Gas Buoy. This Coast Guard boat proceeded at full speed toward the stricken vessel and, arriving within 10 minutes, immediately began circling, looking for survivors.

Meanwhile, four picket boats were ordered out from Barnegat Lifeboat Station and arrived at the scene about 20 minutes after *CG-159*. The first took on board 14 crewmembers from a life raft; the second rescued a man in the water; the third picked up 12 men from a partly submerged life raft. These two vessels returned promptly to Barnegat Lifeboat Station while the other boats stayed for further search. The master of *Persephone* was taken off soon after by *CG-159*, which then searched two hours for the submarine. Meanwhile, two boats had returned to the search for nine missing men, but without success. Following this, *CG-159* sent men on board the damaged tanker to salvage the ship's papers and mail, 23 bags of which were turned over to the Barnegat Station. On shore, all survivors were cleaned of oil, fed, and given medical attention; six were hospitalized.

And so it went.

Ordeal in the Ice

Geoffrey D. Reynolds

ON SATURDAY, FEBRUARY 8, 1936, BOATSWAIN'S MATE EARL CUNNINGham interrupted his day off to come to the aid of fishermen Claude Beardsley and Beardsley's son-in-law, Clayton Brown, after the ice they were fishing from broke loose and moved out into a Lake Michigan blizzard. Little did Cunningham know that he would lose his life in the rescue. Cunningham's death was the only loss of personnel from the Charlevoix, Michigan, station in over 100 years.

Earl Cunningham was born December 18, 1895, in Kinde, Huron County, Michigan. He was one of five children born to George and Annie Cunningham. He spent his childhood on the family farm in Afton, Michigan.

When war in Europe erupted, Cunningham enlisted on June 24, 1918, as a private in the American Expeditionary Forces of the United States Army, seeing action in France and Germany. He was mustered out of the service as a corporal in August 1919 and returned to Afton to work at the Campbell Stone Company, eventually learning to operate the Vulcan locomotive and the steam shovel for the company. After marrying his sweetheart, Miss Helen Teatro, in 1921, Cunningham settled into married life. The couple's family began in 1925 with their first son, Richard, followed by two more boys, Hubert and Wayne, born in 1929 and 1930, respectively.

While he enjoyed his work in the quarry, Cunningham worried about the dangers involved in working with steam and stone. In addition, he had a wife and a young son to think about and needed to find a "safer" profession. So the 5'11", 165-pound war veteran joined the United States Coast Guard in July 1928 as a surfman, earning about $60 per month. The first of his two assignments was at the Hammond Bay station, near Ocqueoc, Michigan, on Lake Huron. There the children attended the Coast Guard School in the Presque Isle county school system and Helen kept house. The remote community was made up entirely of Coast Guard families. Cunningham continued his education, earning certificates along the way, the last one only a day before his death.

In September 1935 Cunningham was assigned to the United States Coast Guard Station at Charlevoix, Michigan, located about 79 miles away from Hammond Bay on Lake Michigan. He arrived on September 22nd to find a house and get acquainted with his new surroundings. After learning that a Charlevoix station member was being assigned to Hammond Bay, he quickly switched houses with the man and solved the housing problem for both of them. While he described Charlevoix as "different" in a letter to Helen and the boys, he promised them they would enjoy the vast differences in the community and life, if only for a short time.

Saturday, February 8, 1936, began with a strong easterly wind and temperatures in the teens for fishing partners Cleo LaPeer and son Lloyd, Eugene Bearss, Claude Beardsley, and his son-in-law, Clayton Brown, as they made their way on the ice near South Point. By early afternoon the outing turned into a life-threatening situation when a southerly wind broke loose the ice they stood on. Soon United States Coast Guard Surfman William Woods spotted their predicament from the Charlevoix Station's lookout tower, and the push was on to rescue the stranded anglers.

Acting Captain George Kelderhouse assembled his men and rushed with a small skiff to South Point. Once there, Surfman Quinton Duhn started out onto the ice with the rescue craft and into the water. Soon he was able to reach the flow and secure Bearss and LaPeer and his son, leaving Beardsley and Brown behind for another attempt. Boatswain's

Mate Earl Cunningham volunteered to take a boat and rescue the remaining two men, even though he was off duty at the time. Unfortunately, blinding snowfall and rising waves forced Cunningham, Beardsley, and Brown to forfeit to the wind and let their oars rest in the boat as they awaited rescue.

While the stranded men drifted, Captain Kelderhouse and the other members of his crew rushed back to the station to retrieve a small, 1,000-pound motorized dinghy. Soon they were rushing back to South Point with the new rescue craft on a horse-drawn sleigh, towing it across rough ice to open water. As they proceeded, the first sled broke and another had to be located. With a new sled, they once again attempted to reach open water, but crashed through weak ice up to their waists. Finally they had reached open water and launched the small open boat and searched throughout the night, but to no avail, as the missing men had steadily drifted to the north in the subzero temperatures and blinding snow.

When the searchers returned at 5:30 a.m. on Sunday, their clothing was frozen. They found that the channel was still blocked and getting worse, with the northwesterly wind blowing at force 5. While Kelderhouse purchased dynamite to clear the channel and attempt a launch of the eight-ton motor lifeboat *Big Bertha*, the crew returned the ice-coated dinghy to the station by sleigh. Surfman Woods was taken to the hospital with frozen feet.

With assistance of crewmembers and local citizens, the motor lifeboat and its crew made it to open water and spent the rest of the day looking for the lost trio, but again they could find no sign of life. The missing men drifted farther up the lake, growing colder and less hopeful for rescue. While the local crew desperately searched for the lost trio, assistance from the Sault Sainte Marie Coast Guard Station steamed toward Charlevoix in the form of a cutter and two airplanes, one from the *Detroit News* and the other from the Coast Guard, but no one could find the missing men.

Around 6:00 p.m. on Sunday, Cunningham succumbed to the cold and died in Brown's arms. Conversation between Beardsley and Brown now turned to their families as they struggled to keep their blood flowing by pacing around the icebound boat. At 10:00 p.m., after moving toward the shore with Brown, Beardsley fell waist deep into the lake and was retrieved with Brown's pike pole. Soon after that Beardsley lay down on the ice and died. Knowing that he would also perish if he did not reach shore soon, Brown steadily, sometimes crawling, moved toward Good Hart, Michigan, almost nine miles away. By Monday afternoon Native Americans on the shore had sighted Brown and went to rescue the delirious and incoherent man. Authorities and friends learned of his survival by telephone and rushed by ambulance to Good Hart. There they listened to his ordeal and learned of his companions' deaths.

Now the task of recovering the bodies of Cunningham and Beardsley began. After the Coast Guard–chartered search plane spotted the bodies and the skiff on Tuesday, the Charlevoix crew set out to retrieve them, but poor visibility and a force 4 wind forced them to turn back. The next day fellow Coast Guardsmen and local Native Americans returned, pulling a boat the nine miles out onto the ice. Later that day, after eight hours on the ice, they returned with the two bodies. "Two Dead, Third Survives Floe Ordeal" read the headline in the *Charlevoix Courier*, February 12, 1936, as U.S. Congressman John Lesinksi read "A Tribute to Heroism" in honor of Earl Cunningham on the floor of the House of Representatives in Washington, DC.

So marked the end of an event still unmatched in the people of Charlevoix's long and tenacious relationship with Lake Michigan. Later that week, Cunningham was laid to rest at Silver Lake Cemetery in Wolverine, near Afton, and Beardsley at Charlevoix's Brookside Cemetery, while Brown lay recovering from frostbitten feet. Both men left grieving families and a shocked community that marked this as the worst ice tragedy in the history of the village.

In late March, Brown lost both his feet to gangrene, brought on by cold and the bruises from beating them with an ax handle to keep the blood flowing. According to the newspaper, members of the U.S. Coast Guard received commendations for their "highest type of courage," a phrase that definitely described Cunningham's actions that day. A chapter about this event, entitled "Greater Love Hath No Man," was also published in a 1937 book by Karl Baarslag titled *Coast Guard to the Rescue*, and in August 1940 a plaque in tribute to Cunningham and all who have perished in the history of the United States Coast Guard was dedicated in Grand Haven, Michigan.

━━

Postscript: After writing an article for the *Charlevoix Courier* in February 2000 about this incident, I became curious about what had happened to Helen and the three boys, then ages four, six, and ten. I knew from the newspapers that she had returned to Afton with the boys, but nothing more. After getting nowhere with the National Personnel Records Center, I turned to the Internet for help finding Cunningham's three boys and possibly more about their father. There I discovered that all three had passed away, the last in 2000.

So I turned to Earl's grandsons. I wrote letters to men with matching first names of the boys, explaining my interest in their grandfather. After many weeks of waiting, I received a phone call from Penny Helmer of Hudsonville, Michigan, granddaughter of Earl Cunningham and daughter of Wayne, saying that her mother had received my letter and that she, Penny, wanted to visit me in Holland.

Upon her arrival, she opened a box containing a family scrapbook and the medals received by Earl Cunningham during his service in the Coast Guard. It was there I discovered that he had been nominated for a Carnegie Hero Fund Commission medal, but turned it down because of his employment with the service at the time. I also discovered Coast Guardsman Cunningham's coveted Gold Life Saving Medal and other service awards, including a letter from the U.S. Treasury Department to Helen, awarding her late husband the Gold Life Saving Medal "in recognition of the heroic daring displayed by him in attempting to rescue two men from drowning on February 8, 1936."

Man Down

Kalee Thompson

As the giant *Munro* lurched through the waves, the tiny 65 Dolphin helicopter clung to the flight deck on the ship's stern. The helo resembled an unwieldy piece of furniture cinched to the roof of a car on a potholed road. It was perfectly secure—but still looked precarious.

Pilots TJ Schmitz and Greg Gedemer zipped up their orange dry suits and pulled on their visored helmets. Bracing against the 35-knot winds, they ran from the hangar out to the aircraft. The flight deck netting whipped violently in the wind, as the men walked around the helicopter, making sure the aircraft hadn't built up too much excess ice. Then the pilots climbed into the cockpit and started her up; rescue swimmer Abe Heller and flight mechanic Al Musgrave buckled up in the back.

"The limit light is on," Gedemer told Schmitz. "It's flashing on and off."

An indicator panel warned that the conditions outside the aircraft were out of limits for takeoff.

"Yeah, that's because the blades are flopping all over the place," Schmitz said.

The wind across the *Munro*'s flight deck was so strong that the helicopter's computers had determined the aircraft was already at limits. They'd have to do a high-wind start.

The *Munro* had turned to secure the best launch course. In the engine room, the ship's engineers had stopped the vessel's high-speed turbines and were back on the diesel engines. They slowed the ship to about 10 knots and pointed the bow straight into the swells. Once the pilots were in the helicopter and hooked up to the ICS, they could communicate with Erin Lopez and the crew in Combat, who were in direct communication with the engine room. Up on the bridge, Captain Craig Lloyd was also looped in.

When their landing signal officer (LSO) gave the okay, four tie-down crew ran out onto the flight deck, hunched down against the powerful blow of the 65's rotors, and unhitched the wide canvas straps that held the helicopter tight to the deck. Bundled up in bulky, insulated blue jumpsuits, matching helmets, and vest-style PFDs, the tie-down crew was easy to distinguish from the aircrew. The *Munro's* officers had taken to calling them the "blueberries." The captain and crew could watch the action on a series of black-and-white video screens on the bridge. The sequence looked like a well-choreographed dance, the 65 helicopter the prima ballerina among a troupe of little scurrying mice.

Everyone knew that the conditions were right on the edge of limits. Or, more accurately, every few minutes there was a minute or so that was in limits. If this had been a training exercise, it'd have been canceled. But in life-or-death situations, the call is up to the commanding officer, and Captain Lloyd trusted his pilots. From the moment Schmitz arrived in Combat and heard the details of the case, he'd felt confident they would be able to launch. Now Schmitz was in the right seat, with Gedemer at his left. He studied the incoming swells through his night vision goggles. They were close to twenty-footers, but rolling in at a pretty steady pace.

Schmitz had already briefed the crew on the takeoff conditions: "This is the deal," he told them. "We're going to over-torque the airframe when we take off. As long as we don't pull more than eleven point eight, we can continue on in the mission."

Coast Guard regulations lay out stricter operating standards at night than for daytime flights. In the dark, anything over 4-degree pitch, 5-degree roll is considered out of limits. But when a mission involves the opportunity to save a life, the men are authorized to go beyond those limits—even at the risk of damaging the aircraft. "Warranted effort," the regulations call it.

Back in Combat, Schmitz had briefed Captain Lloyd on his plan. He would load on 1,750 pounds of fuel, several hundred pounds more than normal. Though the 65 has a powerful engine, its gearbox is relatively weak, which means that the weight of a full load of fuel makes it difficult, if not impossible, for the helo to maintain a stable hover—a more power-consuming maneuver than forward flight. In any case, they'd most likely burn off a good quarter of their fuel load just to reach the scene of the sinking. Schmitz told Captain Lloyd that he was expecting to over-torque, or stress, the main rotor head on takeoff, but wouldn't push it so far that he'd sacrifice the ability to keep flying. "In other words, I'm gonna break it, but I'm not gonna break it so bad that I have to land right away," the pilot told the captain.

Now Schmitz watched the waves. A set of big swells was rolling perpendicular to the cutter's bow. Under normal conditions, a pilot would launch at a lull between waves, waiting for the calmest moment to lift from the deck. Not tonight.

"Six five six six, ready to take off," the crew heard up on the bridge. Schmitz waited until the next wave pitched the bow into the air, and just as it began the sharp fall that would buck up the stern, Schmitz pulled the 9,000-pound bird off the deck, using the momentum of the lurching ship to catapult the helo into the air.

Gedemer called out the torque as Schmitz slid the aircraft to the ship's left side. The helo's official torque limit at takeoff is 10.3; Gedemer's highest number was 9.9. They were golden—they hadn't over-torqued after all.

Schmitz's unconventional maneuver had worked.

It was just a couple minutes before 6:00 a.m. as the crew marked the *Munro*'s position and set off toward the last known coordinates of the *Alaska Ranger*.

Jim Madruga had to pee—bad. He'd been in the water for what seemed to him like three or four hours. What else could he do? When he finally let go, the warm stream felt so good. He was cold but, except for the urine inside his Gumby suit, dry.

His suit fit, the seals had held, and he felt alert. He was clearly doing better than the fisherman who had been floating with him for the past couple hours. The guy was out of his mind with fear. Jim tried to calm him down, but hadn't been able to help much. Every time they heard an aircraft overhead, the guy started screaming.

"Save your strength," Jim told the younger man. "They'll be coming for us, but they have to get the other people first."

Jim was the *Ranger*'s second assistant engineer. He was fifty-nine years old, and, like many other men of his generation, he was a former San Diego tuna fisherman who had made a second fishing career for himself up north. He'd headed straight to the wheelhouse after being woken up that morning. His chief, Dan Cook, was up there and had already concluded that the ship wasn't salvageable.

"Abandon ship" was all Dan had said to him.

Jim and Dan went way back. They'd both started fishing in Alaska more than a decade before. For a few years, both men worked for Trident, one of the biggest fishing companies in Alaska. One year they'd sailed one of the Trident's old ships to India to be scrapped. It was a skeleton crew on an adventure, and Jim and Dan had gotten to know each other well. When they reached India, they drove the boat right up onto the beach at full steam. The carcasses of other ships littered the sandy expanse, and they watched as the Indian Scrap crew went at it. They looked so poor; those skinny little guys wear only sandals and skirts to crawl around on a heap of rusty metal like that.

A few years later, both men found themselves working for the same company again. Dan's brother Ed had been with FCA for a few years, as had David Silveira, a cousin of Jim's from San Diego. That's the way it worked in the fishing—the same guys again and again over the years.

A handful of men had been in the wheelhouse when the last call was made to the Coast Guard, and then everyone got out. By that time, the water was almost to the wheelhouse door. Jim hadn't seen where everyone else entered the water. He was alone with Dan. The chief engineer had been in poor health. They were both nudging sixty years old, but to Jim, Dan seemed like he could be a decade older.

Dan wanted to wait until the very last moment to get off the ship. Jim figured his friend was thinking that if they waited longer, they wouldn't be in the water as long before help arrived. He wanted to stay to make sure Dan got off safely.

The two men waited until there was literally no choice. Then they jumped off the boat together.

"Dan, try to stay with me!" Jim yelled. The wind seemed to be blowing 50 knots, and the waves were at least twenty feet, and breaking. Jim watched helplessly as Dan was pushed away by the waves.

After a few minutes, Jim drifted up next to some fishing net and buoys—debris from the ship's deck. He grabbed on. He'd been floating there for about half an hour before he saw Byron, one of the new kids, a Hispanic guy who'd been on the boat just a few days. Jim hadn't talked to him too much, but he'd sat next to him at lunch a few days before. He remembered Byron's name. Jim also remembered this was his first time on a fishing boat.

The engineer grabbed the younger man and pulled him into the net. They hadn't been on the water that long, but already the kid seemed to be going into shock. "What's the matter, Byron?"

"I'm so cold," Byron cried. "I'm so cold."

Jim pulled Byron closer and put his arm around him. He tried to keep him talking to get his mind off things. The younger man spoke a little about his family, a wife and two young daughters back in California. But mostly he just kept mumbling about how cold he was, and about all the water that had filled his Gumby suit.

Jim just held on to him, and they stayed with the net. It gave them a little buoyancy, and Jim figured it might be easier to see from the air.

"Help me! Help me!" In the distance, Jim thought he heard Dan Cook yelling. At least an hour had passed since they'd abandoned ship, and Jim could barely make out his friend's screams over the wind. He scanned the waves. For a moment he thought he saw Dan floating on his back about fifty feet away. But there was no way he could get to him. Before long, Dan had drifted out of sight again.

Eventually, Jim saw what looked like a Coast Guard plane overhead. Byron must have seen it too, because he began to yell.

"Just save your breath, man," Jim told him. "They can't hear you."

Jim's strobe light was out. It had worked on the ship, but after he'd been in the water for a while, he noticed it had gone dark. Byron's was working fine, though, so Jim knew they were visible.

Was there a boat in the distance? Jim could see a bright light right on the horizon. At first it seemed to be getting closer, but then it stopped. *Maybe they're getting people out of the water,* Jim thought.

Awhile later he saw a helicopter in the distance.

Again Byron started yelling, but Jim pleaded with him.

"They know we're here," he said. "They will come eventually."

Aircraft Commander TJ Schmitz pulled the 65 Dolphin up to about five hundred feet and started south toward the last known coordinates of the *Alaska Ranger*. Even with the tailwind, the seventy-mile journey would take them about forty-five minutes. They'd heard some chatter over the radio from the Coast Guard rescuers already on scene. It sounded like the larger aircraft was at capacity, and had left quite a few people behind in the water.

Schmitz started talking strategy. He was expecting the worst. By the time they got there, some of these people would have already been in the water for close to three hours. He knew from experience that, even in survival suits, many people couldn't make it in cold water for more than two.

Do we pick up people who might be dead? Schmitz thought. *Or do we pick up people who seem the most responsive.* He posed the question to the rest of the crew. In Schmitz's opinion, the best course would be to focus on the most responsive people first.

"Even though they're not responsive, they may not be dead," rescue swimmer Abe Heller noted from the back of the helo.

"Yeah, but we only have so much room," Schmitz said. "Depending on how many people are in the water, you know, who do you go for first?"

When the 65 Dolphin was about fifteen miles north of the site, Gedemer spotted the larger 60 Jayhawk helicopter to their west.

He picked up the radio: "6007, this is rescue 6566."

Brian McLaughlin told the Dolphin's crew that there were two rafts holding survivors—and that at least a dozen or more people were still in the water.

"The survivors are getting less and less responsive," McLaughlin reported.

Based on the inflection in McLaughlin's voice, Schmitz anticipated a grim scene. He knew their tiny helicopter couldn't possibly get even half the people out of there in one load.

"Okay, we're going to need to do this as fast as we can," Schmitz told the rest of the men.

Schmitz had spent his previous four-year tour in the Great Lakes, where he had plenty of experience with hypothermic victims. The rescue crews had often used a procedure called the "hypothermic double lift." In the later stages of hypothermia, a person's blood collects near the heart and vital organs. If the victim is suddenly lifted upright from the water, there's a risk that his blood will rush from the torso into the legs, causing heart failure. Because of that risk, professional rescuers are taught to keep hypothermic victims in a horizontal position. Coast Guard helicopter rescuers are trained to use a double-harness system. The regular quick strop is fastened around the victim's knees, while a second strop—a larger, older model sometimes called the "horse collar"—is secured under their armpits and then tightened around their chest. Ideally, the hypothermic victim will be raised with knees and chest at about the same level, like a bride being carried over the threshold.

The crews had been trained that the two-strop method was the best for someone with hypothermia, but they knew that it was an inconvenient lift. It was time-consuming to get the victim settled securely into the two-strap setup, even in calm conditions when the survivor was later warm and cooperative. With severely hypothermic survivors? In high seas? In the dark? It might eat off fifteen to twenty minutes a person.

We don't have that much time, Schmitz thought.

In the back of the helo, Musgrave and Heller were thinking the same thing: *the basket*. With the metal rescue basket, they'd be able to raise the hypothermic fishermen in a seated position and minimize the risk of heart failure. The basket would also be faster because there were no straps to secure. With his dry gloves on, Heller knew he wouldn't have much mobility in his fingers. It'd be tough to fiddle with the buckles on the straps and the clip on the hoist. With the basket, none of that would be a problem.

Heller had been on two long patrols since his arrival in Kodiak's ALPAT shop two years before, but he'd never launched in conditions like this. Back on the shift, Aircraft Commander Schmitz had pulled the swimmer aside. This would be a "load and go" mission. It was clear people were in the water. Hopefully most were in life rafts, and it was likely they'd be lifting people from rafts up to the helo. There'd almost certainly be more people than they could take in one trip.

"If it's all right, I may want to leave you in a raft out there," the veteran pilot had said to the twenty-three-year-old swimmer.

Heller was ready to do whatever was necessary. He went back to his rack and bundled up in everything he had. He knew the more layers he wore under his dry suit, the less dexterity he'd have in the water. But it was cold, and there was a good chance he could be in the Bering for hours. The trade-off was clear. His first layer was long underwear made of Nomex fleece, similar to Polar fleece, but with fire retardant built in. Over the long johns, the swimmer wore another pair of fleece pants, two more shirts, a fleece unitard—a "uni" the Coasties called it—and then a heavy coat and wool socks. Last, he layered on his orange dry suit and his neoprene and rubber boots. Depending on the situation, he might have chosen wet gloves. Those form-fitting gloves offer more dexterity—but less warmth. But this morning he couldn't risk frozen fingers. He grabbed the dry gloves. Limited mobility would be better than none.

Like rescue swimmer O'Brien Starr-Hollow, Heller had landed in Kodiak on his first assignment as a rescue swimmer. Historically it was rare to end up in Kodiak for your first billet as a swimmer, and even rarer to end up in Alaska Patrol, the ALPAT shop. Heller figured maybe the guy doing assigning that month didn't know the guidelines. In any case, it'd worked out well for him. He liked Alaska. He'd grown up in Wyoming in a Navy family, graduated high school in 2003, and joined the Coast Guard the following December. All his life, Heller had been interested in aviation. His dad worked for the Wyoming Bureau of Land Management as a range conservationist. He dealt with a lot of helicopters, helping to manage the aviation side of wildland firefighting. Heller researched the Coast Guard's three aviation rates, and Aviation Survival Technician—AST, or rescue swimmer—sounded like the most fun.

He went through boot camp, made it to A School in a couple years, and failed out two weeks later. It was the "rear release" test that got him. Its drill meant to prepare the swimmer for managing a panicking survivor. An instructor grabs hold of the swimmer from behind, and the swimmer has to take him underwater, wrestle him off, and come up with the instructor in tow.

Heller didn't know why he failed. He'd done rear release perfectly in training several times. But each time it counted, he couldn't pull it off. He was one of the five of ten in his original class who didn't make it through the course. If Heller had raised his hand and said, "I quit," there would've been no second chance. But if a student is injured or just has trouble with a specific skill, he or she may be permitted to try again.

Heller spent the rest of the fall of 2005 in the airman program in Elizabeth City. He prepared for two more months—more physical training ("PT" as the military calls exercise programs), more pool time. His next class started with nine students. Four months later, seven graduated, Heller among them. After A School, Heller spent three weeks at EMT school in Petaluma, California, and then went up to Kodiak. He'd been there since the spring of 2006 and had a little apartment in town. He'd made lots of friends and gotten in tons of snowboarding on Pyramid Mountain. He'd been involved in a couple of SAR cases.

His first was a medevac—a slip-and-fall victim off an 850 foot container ship. They flew out; Heller was hoisted down to the ship and put the injured crewman on a litter. They hoisted him up and flew him to Dutch Harbor. The whole mission took about an hour. A piece of cake. The next summer, Heller was deployed to Cordova and ended up on another medevac. It was a four-wheeler accident on a remote beach. Kid was getting towed on a sled behind an ATV (all-terrain vehicle) and was tossed off. The Coasties airlifted the kid and brought him back to Cordova for medical treatment.

Heller had only been in the water on a real case one time. Schmitz had been one of the pilots on that case too. It was a small fishing boat, just around thirty feet. The vessel got too close to the shore, got caught in the breakers, and ended up capsizing. The helicopter crew found it at around midnight, lying on its side inside the surf zone, getting knocked around by the waves. The pilots landed the help on the beach and Heller waded out to the boat. He swam around, looking, but there was no one there to save. The fisherman's body eventually washed up on a nearby island. Investigators guessed he'd fallen off the boat before it even got caught up in the surf. The Coast Guard had been too late; there hadn't even been a chance to help him.

Schmitz and his crew were about three miles out from the scene when they spotted the strobes. There were about ten of them, flashing on and off across almost a square mile of ocean. As they got close, Gedemer saw that the two brightest lights came from the life rafts.

"Let's concentrate on the people as far away from the others as we can," Schmitz said.

He could see three lights to the northwest that were off on their own. Those are probably the people who've been in the water the longest, Schmitz thought. That's where we'll begin. The pilots brought the 65 into a hover over a single strobe while flight mechanic Al Musgrave attached the basket to the hoist's talon hook and motioned for Heller to climb in.

"Basket at the door," Musgrave said as he contracted the cable to pull the basket from the floor of the aircraft up and out of the helo. "Basket going down." Within seconds, the compartment hit the swells below. Heller climbed out and swam toward the fisherman alone in the ocean.

"How're you doing?" Heller yelled as he grabbed on to the man.

"Cold as fuck!" the fisherman screamed back.

All right, Heller thought. *This one was probably going to be okay.*

The swimmer had a small green chemical light attached to his mask, similar to the glow sticks sold to kids at county fairs. In dark conditions it was common to use the light in place of simple hand signals to indicate ready for pickup. Heller pulled the light off his mask and waved it above his head to signal to Musgrave to drop the basket. It took just a couple of minutes for Heller to load the fisherman in and to give Musgrave the thumbs-up to raise the compartment.

As the flight mech began the hoist, Heller hung on the bottom of the metal basket, helping to steady it and center it under the aircraft as the lift began. Once he'd been pulled a few feet clear of the water, Heller dropped back to the sea and watched the basket rise another fifty feet to the open door. Musgrave pulled it inside and dumped it sideways so the fisherman could crawl out. Then he sent the basket back down for Heller.

The rescue swimmer climbed in, the flight mech raised him up, and they moved on to the next light, with the basket steadied right outside the open helo door. It was just a few hundred or so yards away. That pick up went smoothly, as did the next rescue, but already the helo's cabin seemed packed.

"I think I only have room for one more," Musgrave reported to the pilots.

"You're gonna have to stack 'em up," Schmitz said. "We're going to have to stay on scene until we run out of gas and we have to go back."

The first man who'd been pulled into the helo had inexplicably started stripping off his survival suit. The second survivor followed his lead buy got stuck. He was kicking, motioning for Musgrave to help him pull the suit off the lower half of his body. The flight mech thought it would be better if the fishermen just left their suits on, but there was no time to argue. He grabbed a webbing cutter from inside the doorframe and pulled it right through the zipper of the man's suit. Musgrave sliced from the fisherman's chest all the way down one leg, like he was opening up a fish. Then he threw the guy a wool blanket and directed both him and his buddy to the back of the cabin, where the rescue basket is normally stored.

The nose of the helo suddenly jerked upward.

"Holy shit! What's going on back there?" Schmitz asked through the ICS.

" The guys are climbing in the back," Musgrave answered.

"All right, put the next guy behind Greg, against the door," Schmitz replied.

The men's movement affected the helo's center of gravity, but at least they'd made room for more survivors. Heller was still in the basket against the open aircraft door as Schmitz circled around to the south toward a clump of lights in the water. The rescuers saw four men locked arm in arm, like a human chain. The two on the ends were waving their free hands. They looked like they were in pretty good shape. Then Schmitz saw another strobe about a hundred yards away.

"There's another survivor off the nose. Let's go get him first," the pilot said.

They only had room for a couple more people in the helicopter. Better to get those who were off on their own, Schmitz thought.

When they got closer, though, the pilot could see that it was two men tangled up in a bunch of netting and buoys, with one strobe light between them. Jim Madruga was waving his arms; Byron Carrillo was just floating.

They came into a hover beside the net, and Musgrave placed Heller a good hundred feet from the debris pile. As the flight mech drew the empty basket back to the aircraft, Heller swam up to the net. Byron was lying limp in the water with the webbing all around him, his strobe light flickering in the darkness.

"Take him first," Jim yelled. "He's in really bad shape."

Byron was reaching for Heller, but the rescue swimmer swam around behind him to get a safe grip. Heller wanted to avoid any struggle with the fisherman; controlling him from behind was the best way to avoid any problem. He asked Byron how he was doing.

With the rotor noise and the fisherman's delirium, Heller couldn't make out what he was saying. But the fact that he was speaking meant something.

Byron had his hand jammed under the net, and Heller struggled to pry open his fingers.

"You gotta let go!" Jim yelled. "You've got to let go!"

Finally, Heller broke Byron free and began to drag him back out of the debris to a safe hoisting location.

In A School, Heller had been drilled in a method to clear rope, netting, or any other refuse from a submerged survivor. The swimmers were taught to go underwater, put their hands on the survivor's spine, and then walk their hands all the way down the victim's body, looking for and feeling for debris. The technique was called a "spinal highway."

Byron was clear, but as Heller dragged him away from the debris, he could feel a piece of line snagged on his own fin. Heller used one hand to steady Byron as he reached down to clear off the debris. As the swimmer was working himself free, a wave knocked the fisherman facedown in the water. Heller looked up to see Byron wasn't righting himself.

Crap, Heller thought. This guy is so far gone he's not even capable of keeping his own face out of the water.

He grabbed onto Byron again, pulled him upright, and swam with him away from the wreckage.

When Heller had the fisherman away from the debris, he signaled for the basket, which was brought down in seconds.

At the sight of it, Byron seemed to snap to attention.

He knows what the basket is, Heller thought. The basket is life. He tried to maneuver Byron inside. He pushed him into the basket, but then Byron would change his position and end up crossways, with feet coming out one end and head coming out the other. Heller yanked him out and tried again. When he got Byron out of the basket, though, the fisherman wouldn't let go of the metal bars. Heller was struggling to get the compartment upright while Byron was pulling it sideways into the waves, flailing in a panic. Heller fought with the man for at least ten minutes.

Heller knew that a hypothermic person often becomes irrational and can have symptoms similar to being drunk—loss of bodily control, slurred words, inability to focus or pay attention to instructions. It wasn't this man's fault, but it was till frustrating. Every second it took to wrestle this person was a second the rescuers could have used to pull someone else out of the water.

Up in the cabin, Musgrave was watching Heller struggle with the fisherman. Since he'd dropped the swimmer into the water fifteen minutes earlier, the flight mech had lost sight of Heller three times. It was called "losing target," and it was something the aircrew never wanted to happen. Disorienting snow squalls were blowing through the area, and the waves were big and irregular. The swells kept pushing the swimmer and fisherman underneath the helicopter, which meant that Musgrave would have to instruct Schmitz to reposition the helo just so he could see what was going on.

Musgrave could hear the pilots talking about fuel. They were getting low, burning through their gas faster than usual. Hovering used up fuel a lot faster than forward flight did, especially with a full cabin like the one they had now.

Musgrave didn't want to let out too much slack on the cable. He couldn't risk it getting wrapped around someone's leg or neck. He let out what he thought was necessary, but still the basket was jerked out of the water a few times. They'd been at it for so long.

Finally, Musgrave looked down to see Heller and Byron centered between swells. The basket was plumb beneath the helo. It looked like if he pulled the basket out of the water, the fisherman would drop down to the basket floor where he needed to be. Musgrave began the hoist.

Down below, Heller was still working to get Byron seated properly when, all of a sudden, the basket lifted above the surface and started rising. Heller didn't give the signal to lift the basket, but now it looked like Byron was in there pretty good. The swimmer felt relieved as he watched the basket rise toward the helo and saw Byron seem to slump down into the compartment.

The basket was fifteen feet above the waves when Heller turned and began to swim back toward the debris field, where Jim Madruga was waiting.

The older fisherman was still floating alongside the net.

Finally, he thought, as Byron was pulled out of the waves. Jim watched the basket rise about twenty feet above the surface, then spotted the rescue swimmer coming back toward him. It had felt like it had been a long time since the Coast Guard swimmer pried Byron from the net. Now it was Jim's turn.

From the open door of the helicopter, Musgrave saw Byron drop down a little bit inside the metal basket. Everything looked good. The flight mech watched his swimmer turn and start moving toward the next survivor.

He continued with the hoist.

"The survivor is in the basket," Musgrave reported into the ICS. "The basket is out of the water. The basket is above the water."

Halfway up, Musgrave saw that Byron seemed to have lifted himself onto the rail. He looked like he was actually sitting on the shorter edge of the rectangular basket; his butt was on one corner and his feet were hanging over the adjacent side. Byron had his arms wrapped around the bales. He wasn't where he should be, but he still looked relatively stable.

But with the basket moving up, more than halfway there, Byron slipped. From above, it looked like the lower port of his body was now outside the compartment.

"The survivor is hanging from the basket," Musgrave announced.

"What?" Schmitz said.

"What did he say?" Gedemer asked.

Schmitz was confused, but from the right seat, he couldn't see what was going on in back. The hoist was Musgrave's show, and he was the only one to see the basket reach the cabin door—with Byron hanging by his armpits from its side.

He seemed huge, as if he were seven and a half feet tall. Most of his body was outside the basket, with his legs hanging straight down below the bottom of the basket floor—and between the bottom of the basket and the helicopter. Byron's position made it impossible for Musgrave to pull the basket into the cabin.

Instead, he brought the hoisting as far as he could without getting Byron wedged up against the aircraft. He started trying to haul Byron into the helicopter.

Musgrave had never been in a situation where he couldn't man-handle someone into the cabin, but he could barely budge Byron's legs. Kneeling in the doorway he was just about at eye level with him. Byron's red neoprene hood was up, but quite a bit of his black hair was hanging out. With the suit's mouth flap fastened, all Musgrave could see of the fisherman was his eyes and the bridge of his nose. There was no point in trying to say anything over the roar of the rotors.

Musgrave looked into Byron's eyes and saw that his face was frozen in terror.

All Byron had to do was move his legs a little, but he wasn't helping at all. His suit is full of water, Musgrave realized. He probably weighs 500 pounds. Musgrave reached back for a knife that was attached to the side of the cabin. He'd slice open the neoprene legs and get the water out of the suit. Then he'd be able to pull the guy in.

The knife was just a couple of feet away, but in the moment that Musgrave moved to grab it, Byron slipped again. When Musgrave turned back to the open door, the fisherman was hanging by his elbows from the edge of the basket. Musgrave grabbed him, and pulled as hard as he could. But it was only two or three seconds before Byron let go.

He slipped out of Musgrave's arms, plunging into the sea forty feet below.

Moments later, Schmitz heard the mechanic's voice.

"We lost him. We lost him." Musgrave repeated.

"We lost who?" At first, Schmitz thought that Musgrave had said, "We lost them."

Though Schmitz and Gedemer couldn't see what was going on back in the cabin, they'd known Musgrave's silence when the basket reached the helicopter that something wasn't going right.

"The survivor," Musgrave said. "He's gone."

Schmitz could see the man's blinking light in the water below. For an instant he thought he saw him move his arms in the waves.

"He's okay! He's moving," the pilot said.

But seconds later a heart-wrenching reality set in: "Never mind. He's facedown."

With the U.S. Life-savers:
Rescue by Moonlight

Francis Rolt-Wheeler

"Help! Help!"

The cry rang out despairingly over the almost-deserted beach at Golden Gate Park.

Jumping up so suddenly that the checkerboard went in one direction, the table in another, while the checkers rolled to every corner of the little volunteer lifesaving station-house, Eric Swift made a leap for the door. Quick as he was to reach the boat, he was none too soon, for the coxswain and two other men were tumbling over the gunwale at the same time.

Before the echoes of the cry had ceased, the boat was through the surf and was heading out to sea like an arrow shot from a Sioux war-bow.

Although this was the second summer that Eric had been with the Volunteers, it had never chanced to him before to be called out on a rescue at night. The sensation was eerie in the extreme. The night was still, with a tang of approaching autumn in the air to set the nerves a-tingle. Straight in the golden path of moonlight the boat sped. The snap that comes from exerting every muscle to the full quickened the boy's eagerness, and the tense excitement made everything seem unreal.

The coxswain, with an intuition which was his peculiar gift, steered an undeviating course. Some of the lifesavers used to joke with him and declare that he could smell a drowning man a mile away, for his instinct was almost always right.

For once, Eric thought, the coxswain must have been at fault, for nothing was visible, when, after a burst of speed which seemed to last minutes—though in reality it was but seconds—the coxswain held up his hand. The men stopped rowing.

The boy had slipped off his shoes while still at his oar, working off first one shoe and then the other with his foot. It was so late in the evening that not a single man in the crew was in the regulation bathing suit; all were more or less dressed. Eric's chum, a chap nicknamed the "Eel" because of his curious way of swimming, with one motion slipped off all his clothing and passed from his thwart to the bow of the boat.

A ripple showed on the surface of the water. Eric could not have told it from the roughness of a breaking wave, but before even the outlines of a rising head were seen, the Eel sprang into the sea. Two of those long, sinuous strokes of his brought him almost within reach of the drowning man. Blindly the half-strangled sufferer threw up his arms, the action sending him underwater again, a gurgled "Help!" being heard by those in the boat as he went down.

The Eel dived.

Eric, who had followed his chum headforemost into the water hardly half a second later, swam around waiting for the other to come up. In three quarters of a minute the Eel rose to the surface with his living burden. Suddenly, with a twist, almost entirely unconscious, the drowning man grappled his rescuer. Eric knew that his chum was an adept at all the various ways of "breaking away" from these grips, a necessary part of the training of every lifesaver, but he swam close up in case he might be able to help.

"Got him all right?" he asked.

"He's got me!" grunted the Eel, disgustedly.

"P'raps I'd better give you a hand to break," suggested the boy, reaching over with the intention of helping his friend, for the struggling swimmer had secured a tight grip around the Eel's neck. The lifesaver, however, covering the nose and mouth of the half-drowned man with one hand, pulled him close with the other, and kneed him vigorously.

"Now he'll be good," said the Eel, grinning as well as he could with a mouth full of water. He spat out the brine, shook the water out of his eyes, and putting his hands on either side of the drowning man's head, started for the shore. Using a powerful "scissors" stroke, the Eel made quick time, though he seemed to be taking it in leisurely fashion. Eric, although a good swimmer, had all he could do to keep up.

"How do you think he is?" the lad asked.

"Oh, he'll come around all right," the Eel replied. "I don't believe he's swallowed such an awful lot of water. I guess he's been able to swim a bit."

The rescued man was a good weight and not fat, so that he floated deep. The sea was choppy, too, with a nasty little surf on the beach. But the Eel brought the sufferer in with the utmost ease.

As soon as they reached shore, Eric grabbed the drowning man's feet while the Eel took him by the shoulders and lifted him on a stretcher which two other members of the Volunteer Corps had brought. As soon as the rescued man was placed on this, the bearers started at a quick pace for the lifesaving station, and artificial respiration was begun.

In spite of the fact that the boy had seen dozens of half-drowned persons brought back to consciousness, the process never lost to him its half-terrible fascination. He always felt the lurking danger, and he had been well trained never to forget how much hung in the balance. Always it was a human life, flickering like a candle-flame in a gusty wind. Always the outcome was unknown.

Once Eric had worked for a solid hour over a man who had been brought in from the beach before he had been rewarded by any sign of life. The U.S. Volunteer Corps had drilled into him very thoroughly the knowledge that tireless patience and grim persistence will almost work miracles. Accordingly, when it came his turn, he joined readily in the work of restoration. The swim had tired him a little, and he was glad to quit when another member of the station took his place over the half-drowned man's body.

"Why do we use the Schaefer method, Doctor?" Eric asked.

"It's the best system for our work," was the reply, "because it can be done by one person. Quite often, a fellow may make a rescue and bring someone to shore so that he will have to work alone. You're not going to be right at a station always."

"That's true," the boy said meditatively.

"Watch, now," continued the doctor, pointing to the lifesaver, who was at work and who was kneeling astride the prone figure of the unconscious man. "You see Johnson's hands are pressing right between the short ribs, aren't they?"

"Yes, that's the base of the lungs, isn't it?" Eric queried.

"It is," the doctor answered. "Now when a man brings down the weight of the upper part of his body on his hands—the way Johnson is doing there—it means that about one hundred pounds of pressure is applied to those lungs, doesn't it?"

"Sure; fifty pounds on each lung," agreed the boy.

"You can see how that forces out nearly every bit of air in the lungs. Then, as soon as he leans backwards again, and takes off the pressure, the air rushes in to fill the lungs. That makes artificial breathing, doesn't it?"

"Of course."

"That's the whole secret of restoration; that, and keeping everlastingly at it."

"But if the Schaefer method is the best way," protested Eric, "I don't see why everybody doesn't use it."

"Such as—"

"Well, the Life-saving end of the Coast Guard doesn't!"

"I don't say the Schaefer is the only good method," answered the doctor; "nothing of the kind. It's the one that suits us best." He stepped over to the prostrate man, never relaxing his vigilant watch for the first sign of life. Then, returning to Eric, he continued, "The Coast Guard uses the Sylvester method, doesn't it?"

"One of the forms of it, Father told me," the boy answered. "He showed me how. It's quite different from what we do here."

"How did he show you?" asked the doctor interestedly; "there are so many different ways."

"Father told me to stand or kneel at the head of the chap who had been rescued, then, grabbing hold of the arms above the elbows, to draw them up over the head, keep them there a couple of seconds, then force them down and press them against the sides of the chest. I suppose the principle is about the same."

"Exactly the same," the doctor said, "but of course everyone has his preference. I like the Schaefer method best, myself, because in it the tongue hangs out and the water runs from the mouth naturally, while in the Sylvester method, the tongue has to be tied."

"But which is the better?" persisted Eric.

"There really doesn't seem to be much difference in the result," was the reply; "it's the man behind the gun, not the system. The Coast Guard so far holds the record for the most wonderful cases of recovery, and theirs is the older method. The important thing is to know exactly what you're doing, and to do it with everlasting perseverance. Never give up! I've seen some wonderful examples of fellows just snatched back to life long after we thought they had gone. There was one, I remember—"

"Doctor!" called Johnson, "I think he's coming to!"

The rescued man gave a gasp and his eyelids fluttered. The doctor was beside him in an instant, but instead of seeming satisfied by his examination, he shook his head doubtfully as he rose from the side of his patient.

"Going all right?" queried Eric.

"No," was the answer, "he's not. I think he's got smokers' heart. You'd better watch him a bit closely, boys! One can't ever tell in these cases."

"You mean he's not out of the woods yet, Doctor?" the lad asked.

"Not by a long shot," was the reply. "You can't play any monkeyshines with the heart. Judging by the shape that fellow's heart is in, I should be inclined to say he's been smoking for nearly ten years, smoking pretty heavily too. And he can't be a day over twenty-three!"

"Do you suppose that had anything to do with his drowning?"

"Of course it had," the doctor answered. "Swimming is a real athletic exercise, and you've got to keep in shape to swim well. What's more, you've got to have a decent heart to start with. But if a youngster piles into cigarettes, it's a safe bet that he's going to cripple himself for athletics in manhood."

"But you smoke, Doctor!"

"Sure I do," the other rejoined. "And I swim, pretty nearly as well as any of you young fellows. But I didn't start any cigarette business when I was a kid, the way lots of boys do now. It wasn't until I was in college that I smoked my first pipe."

"Then you think it's all right for a chap to smoke after he's grown up?"

"I wouldn't go as far as to say that," the doctor said, "but there's no doubt that the cases which have turned out worst are those in which the habit began early. Nature's a wise old scout, Eric, and you're apt to find that a man who's likely to be hurt by smoking won't develop a craving for it unless he started too young, or unless he forced himself to excess."

The boy wanted to question the doctor further, for he was thoroughly interested in finding out that smoking prevents an athletic manhood, when the speaker was interrupted by a cry from the half-conscious man.

"Jake!" he called.

The doctor was beside him in a second.

"What is it, son?" he said, bending his head down so that his grizzled mustache almost brushed the man's face.

"Jake! Where's Jake?"

A sudden silence swept over the station. Only the Eel moved. With that queer sliding step of his that was almost noiseless, he went to the door of the little house that faced the sea.

"Jake!" again the cry came. "Where's Jake?"

The man was relapsing into unconsciousness when the doctor quickly took a powerful restorative from his medicine bag, which lay beside the cot, and held it to the man's nose. The fumes roused him.

"Where did you leave him?" queried the doctor.

"I—I couldn't get him," gasped the rescued man, breathing heavily.

There was a general rustle, and every man half-turned to the door. In the silence a man's boot, being kicked off, clattered noisily on the floor.

"How do you mean you couldn't get him?" the doctor persisted. "Was he swimming with you?"

"He went down—sudden—" came the answer, weakly, "and when I tried . . . to help . . . he pulled at my legs."

The words were hardly out of his lips before the station-house was empty save for the doctor and the rescued swimmer. As the door slid back behind them, Eric heard the man cry in a quavering voice,

"I've drowned him! I've drowned him! I had to kick him free to save myself!"

Outside, not a word was said. The men knew their work and their places. The coxswains were ready and the three white boats were sliding down the beach, the big boat down the runway, as the men heard that cry again,

"I've drowned him! I've drowned him. I had to kick him free to save myself!"

The words rang hauntingly in Eric's ears as his boat hit the first incoming billow. The former rescue in the moonlight had held a quick thrill, but it had been nothing like this tense eager race in the darkness. Nearly a quarter of an hour had passed in the station-house before the rescued man had recovered consciousness, and the rescue had taken at least five minutes. Almost twenty-five minutes had elapsed, then, since the first cry of help had been heard.

The boats leapt forward like swift dogs released from leash. The oars were made to resist extreme strain, but they bent under the terrific strokes of the lifesavers. Over six thousand miles of sea, the Pacific rolled in with slow surges, and out in the darkness, somewhere, was a drowning man, probably beyond help, but with just the faintest shred of possibility for life if he could be found immediately.

With that uncanny intuition which made him so marvelous in the work, the coxswain of Eric's boat steered a course fifty feet away from that of the larger boat.

Not a word was spoken until, above the swish of the water and the rattle of the rowlocks, the Eel said quietly, "We picked him up a little to wind'ard of here!" Three men, among them Eric, slipped into the water. Almost at the same moment, five or six men plunged in from the other boats. The lieutenant stopped Eric's chum.

"You'd better stay aboard, Eel," he said; "you've already had quite a swim."

The Eel shrugged his shoulders disapprovingly, but, after all, orders were orders, and the captain of the Golden Gate station was a disciplinarian to his fingertips.

In the broken gleams of the moonlight flickering on the tumbled water, the forms of the dozen members of the corps could be seen. Over and again one would disappear from sight for a deep dive to try to find the body.

This was a part of the work in which Eric was particularly good. He had a strong leg-stroke and was compactly built, although large-boned for his age. Tired though he was from swimming ashore with the Eel on the first rescue, he went down as often as any of his comrades. Looking back at the boat, he saw the Eel wave his hand in a direction a little south of where he had dived before.

Following out the suggestion, Eric took a long breath and went down. It was a deep dive, and he thought he saw a gleam of white below him. The boy tried to swim down a foot or two farther, but his breath failed him, and he shot up, gasping, to the surface. Not wanting to give a false alarm, yet knowing well that every second counted, the boy merely stayed long enough to get his breath, then, putting every ounce of power he possessed into a supreme effort, he went down again. This time he got a foot nearer, but not near enough to be quite sure. Again he darted up to the surface.

"Here, fellows!" he shouted.

The boat shot up beside him.

"Found him, Eric?"

"I think so, sir," the boy answered, "but he was too far down for me."

The Eel had stripped. He stood up and looked pleadingly at the lieutenant.

"Sure you're not tired?"

The Eel smiled.

"Overboard with you, then!"

He dived.

Dozens of times though Eric had seen the Eel dive, and often as he had tried to imitate him, the boy never ceased to envy his comrade his extraordinary power of going into the water without the slightest splash. Powerful dive though it was, scarcely a drop of water seemed to be displaced as the Eel went down.

During the few seconds that passed while these sentences were being interchanged, three or four others of the lifesavers had rallied to Eric's call and were headed for the boat. One man, especially, a big, burly fellow who looked as though he would be too heavy to swim, but who possessed an astounding amount of endurance and who could hold his breath longer than anyone else in the station, followed the Eel to the bottom. Eric was game, and although he was beginning to feel thoroughly done up, he joined the quest in the depths of the sea.

Moonlight gives no reflections beneath the water, and the sea was dark. The Eel was already out of sight below him, but as the boy made his way down, the powerful figure of the heavy swimmer came past him like a shadow.

A few seconds later, the Eel shot up by him, bringing an unconscious man in his grasp. The other swimmer followed. By the time Eric reached the boat he was exhausted and had to be helped in. The rescued man had been lifted into the large boat, and before the boy was even aboard, the other craft was halfway to the shore, racing like mad. The other boats followed.

As soon as the surf-boat touched the beach, the big man jumped out, two other members of the corps threw the unconscious figure across his shoulders for the "fireman's carry," and while the keel of the boat was still grinding on the beach, the rescued man was well on the way toward the house.

The doctor was waiting. The victim of the drowning accident, apparently dead, was put into hot blankets. His arms and legs were stiff. The lips were quite blue and the whole of the face discolored. At the sight of him, and the little slimy ooze from his lips, the doctor looked grave. The big lifesaver who had carried the sufferer in was already at work in an attempt at resuscitation.

A moment or two later, the first man who had been rescued and who was feeling a little stronger, turned over on the stretcher. He saw the swollen and discolored face of his friend and sent up a piercing cry,

"He's dead!"

Then, after a pause and a silence broken only by the rhythmic beat of the regular motions of the process of causing artificial respiration, came the cry again,

"I've drowned him! I've drowned him! I had to kick him free to save myself!"

Although the house was kept empty save for the four men, the doctor beckoned to one of the officers standing outside—so that there should be as much air as possible in the station—to come in and try to quiet the frenzied man.

"Bromides, Doctor?" queried the lieutenant, who had come in.

"Yes. Give him just one of the triple. No, that won't hurt him," he continued in answer to a look; "it's excessive stimulation that a man with smokers' heart can't stand."

The lifesaver gave the required dose and succeeded in soothing the poor fellow, who was still terribly weak. The men sat on the steps outside, talking in low tones. Every one of them was keenly conscious of the strain. For twenty minutes there was no sound from within the station except the hard breathing of the man who was putting in all his strength to give the recumbent figure the motions of respiration.

"Ryan!" the doctor called suddenly.

A strapping young fellow jumped up like a shot and darted into the station to take the place of the exhausted worker. Wiping his forehead and breathing hard, the latter came out to his companions.

"Do you think there's any change, Jim?" one of them asked.

"Not so far as I can see," the other answered, shaking his head.

"How long do you suppose he was under?" queried another.

Close comparison of watches gave the actual time as between nineteen and twenty-one minutes.

"Has anyone ever been saved who has been underwater as long as that?" asked Eric.

"Eighteen minutes is the longest I've ever seen," answered Johnson, the veteran of the corps, "but of course there's the Mooney case."

The boy listened a moment, but no sound came from the station. It was less nerve-racking to talk than to listen, so he went on,

"What was the Mooney case?"

"That was a Coast Guard job, in the days when the United States Life-Saving Service was a separate bureau. It was quite a queer case in a good many ways."

"How long was Mooney underwater? Half an hour, wasn't it?" questioned another of the men.

"Thirty-one minutes, according to general reports," Johnson replied, "but to make sure that they weren't stretching it, the official report made it 'twenty minutes or over.' One of my pals worked on the man."

"How was it?" queried Eric. "In a storm?"

"Beautiful sunny Fourth of July," was the reply. "And, what's more, it was in shallow water, near shore, and the man could swim!"

"But how in the world—"

"That's exactly what I'm telling," Johnson continued, resenting the interruption. "It was during a boat race on Point Judith Pond in Rhode Island. My pal, who was a surfman, had been assigned to duty there. Naturally, he was watching the races. On the other side of the pond a small flat-bottomed skiff, carrying one sail, capsized. There were three men in her. Streeter, that's the fellow I know, saw the boat capsize, but he knew that the water was shallow and noted that it was near shore. Just the same, he kept an eye on the boat. As soon as he saw two men clinging to the sides of the skiff, he started for the scene of the accident. He was about a third of a mile away.

"What had happened was this. When the boat capsized, the swinging boom struck Mooney on the head, making him unconscious. He was swept under the sail and pinned down by it. The other two men, neither of whom could swim, managed to scramble on to the capsized skiff. They saw no sign of Mooney, and knowing that he was a swimmer, thought he had struck out for the shore. It wasn't until several minutes later that it occurred to one of them that their comrade might be pinned under the sail.

"With a good deal of personal risk, for his hold was insecure and he couldn't swim, this chap managed to get hold of the canvas and somehow—he said he didn't know how, himself—succeeded in getting Mooney out from under the sail. He gripped Mooney's collar, but could not lift his head above water. All that he could do was barely to hold on."

"Showed a good deal of grit to do even that, it seems to me," said one of the lifesavers. "It's an awful feeling to be nearly drowned."

"It did show grit," agreed Johnson. "If it had been a drowning woman with long hair, she could have been held up all right; but a grip on the collar, when the head is hanging forward, means a dead lift out of water. I don't wonder that the young fellow wasn't able to do it.

"When my pal reached there, he got Mooney aboard; the other two clambered in, and they started for the shore. Mooney was as purple as a grape, and his arms were so stiff that two men, one on each side, could barely move them. Nearly a quart of water was got out of him, and they had an awful job prying open his jaws.

"They worked over him for an hour and twenty minutes before there was the slightest sign of life. Not until twenty-five minutes more did the heart begin, and Mooney did not regain consciousness until nine hours later. As his watch had stopped at 4:20 p.m. and it was 4:53 when Streeter got ashore, that man's heart had stopped, his breathing had stopped, and he had been practically dead for more than two hours."

"Just goes to show," said one of the others, "that it isn't merely swallowing water that drowns a fellow."

"It isn't swallowing water at all, as I understand," rejoined another member of the group. "Drowning's a kind of poisoning of the blood because the lungs can't get oxygen. It's just like choking to death or being hanged."

There was a call from within.

"Murchison!"

The lifesaver who had just been speaking got up quickly and went in to relieve Ryan.

"Any luck?" Johnson asked, as the latter came out.

The Irishman shook his head.

"There's nothin' yet, but he moight come round anny minute," was his reply, with the invincible optimism of his race.

Eric had been thinking of Murchison's description of drowning.

"Why did they roll half-drowned people on a barrel in the old times?" he asked.

"Sure, they were ijits," Ryan answered cheerfully.

"But what was the idea? To get the water out?"

"Just that. They used to think the lungs were a tank."

"Murchison was saying that people drowned because they couldn't get oxygen. Isn't there oxygen in water?"

"Av coorse there is," the Irishman replied. "But ye've got to have the gills of a fish to use it. Annyhow, a man's got warm blood an' a fish has cold. It takes a lot of oxygen to get a man's blood warm. An' if he doesn't get it, he dies.

"Ye see, Eric," he continued, "that's why ye've got to go on workin' over a drowned man. Ye can't tell how badly he's poisoned. An' it's honest I am in tellin' ye that I think we've got a chance in there."

"You do?"

"I do that," was the cheery answer. "There's no tellin'."

Again came that cry from the station, a cry whose very repetition made it all the more nerve-racking,

"I've drowned him! I've drowned him! I had to kick him free to save myself!"

Eric shivered. There was something gruesome in the monotony of the same words over and over again. The noises on the beach died down. Several of the men, who did not live at the station-house, went to their cottages. The boy gave a jump when he heard a step behind him and saw the old doctor standing there.

The night was very still. Nothing could be heard but the roar of the surf on the beach. Eric, who was imaginative, thought that the surf seemed to be triumphing in having snatched another life. Feeling sure that the doctor would understand him, the boy turned and said,

"Doctor, shall we be able to beat out the sea?"

The Highland imagination of the doctor instantly caught the lad's meaning.

"You've heard it too!" he said. "Many and many's the time I've thought the sea was skreeling in triumph when a drowned man was brought ashore. But I've snatched a many back."

"Will you—" began the boy.

"Doctor!" came a cry from within.

"Well?" he answered eagerly, stepping to the door.

"I thought I caught a breath!"

The doctor's keen eyes glinted as he knelt beside the prostrate figure.

Nine, ten, eleven times the weight of the lifesaver was brought forward and released. At the twelfth, there was a slight respiration.

"Did you see, Doctor?" he cried, pausing in his work.

"What the mischief are you stopping for?" was the doctor's impatient answer. Then he added, "You're doing splendidly, Murchison; just keep it up!"

Five more minutes passed without a single sign. Both men had begun to feel that possibly they had been mistaken, when there was a definite flutter of an eyelid. The surfman would have given a triumphant shout but for the doctor's rebuke a moment or two before.

Quietly the old Scotchman began to promote circulation by rubbing the legs upward, so as to drive the venous blood to the heart and thus try to start its action. Almost ten minutes elapsed before the doctor's patience was rewarded with the faint throb of a heartbeat, then another. It was soft and irregular at first, but gradually the blood began to move through the arteries, and in a few minutes a pulse could be felt. The lips lost a little of their blue color, and breathing began.

"He's got a grand heart!" said the old doctor, ten minutes later, as the pulse-beats began to come with regularity. "I hardly believed that we could bring him round. It's a good thing it was this chap and not the other. We could never have saved yon man if he had been half as long submerged."

"You really think that we shall save him?" queried Eric, more to hear the doctor's assurance than because of any doubt of the result.

"We have saved him," was the reply. "In a day or two he'll be as well as he ever was. And, to my thinking, he'll be wiser than he was before, for he'll never do such a silly thing as to go out for a swim at nighttime after dinner with—well, after a heavy dinner."

"Seems too bad that we can't tell his friend," the boy suggested. "It's just awful to hear him accusing himself all through the night."

"If he's asleep," the doctor answered, "that's better for him than anything else. Oh, I don't know," he continued, "he seems to be stirring. Do you want to tell him?"

Eric flashed a grateful glance at the doctor.

"If I might?"

"Go ahead!"

"Mr. Willett," said the boy, coming close to the stretcher. "Mr. Willett!"

"Well?" said the rescued man, waking out of a remorse-haunted dream.

"Jake has been saved. He's all right."

In spite of his exhaustion and his sudden awakening from sleep, the first man who had been rescued sat up on the stretcher and craned his head forward to see his friend. In spite of the sufferer's bruised and swollen appearance, it was evident to the most inexperienced eye that life was not extinct. The convalescent looked at the doctor and tried to find words, but something in his throat choked him.

He reached out and grasped the boy's hand, holding it tightly. Then, looking around the station, he said softly,

"A man's world is a good world to live in!"

Figuring the Variables

H. Paul Jeffers

THE MESSAGE HAD GONE OUT, AND IT WAS SHOCKING:

Passenger ship Prinsendam
Position 57 degrees—38 minutes North
140 degrees—25 minutes West
Fire in the engine room
Carbon dioxide
Condition unknown
Passengers 320, Crew 190

In the sixty-eight years between the *Titanic's* iceberg collision and the cruise ship *Prinsendam's* engine room fire in the Gulf of Alaska, the cruise ship industry saw communication and navigation advances that could have saved the *Titanic*. Unlike her doomed predecessor, the *Prinsendam* had a public address system, telephones, radiotelephony, radiotelegraphy, a VHF radio direction finder, radar, echo sounding, an automatic pilot, a gyro compass, and plenty of walkie-talkies for the ship's crew and officers. Her course, which could be tracked by the Coast Guard's satellite rescue system, was within range of Coast Guard cutters and just barely within range of its rescue helicopters.

But the passenger- and crew-filled lifeboats—maybe 500 people—
were now in frigid waters off Alaska, and the *Prinsendam* continued to
burn. The question quickly became: Would there be enough time to save
them?

Nearby was the biggest supertanker ever built in the United States,
the *Williamsburgh*.

Coast Guard Commander Richard Schoel would have to coordinate
the most complicated rescue ever attempted.

It was October 1980.

——

Every Coastie who worked with or under Commander Richard Schoel
learned that he was not a second-guesser. Like all good leaders, he laid
out his plan and left it to those who had to implement it in the heat of
action to take it from there. His personal leadership maxim had been
expressed by General George S. Patton. "Never tell people *how* to do
things," advised "Old Blood and Guts" in a posthumous book, *War as
I Knew It*. "Tell them *what* to do and they will surprise you with their
ingenuity."

In recommending the hoisting of nearly five hundred survivors into
helicopters, Commander Schoel was calling for the largest, most daring
and dangerous air-sea rescue in the annals of the Coast Guard. In doing
so he was acting in the great tradition of the service. The first use of a
helicopter by the Coast Guard for a lifesaving mission had occurred
on January 3, 1944, when a Sikorsky helicopter based in Brooklyn was
used to fly blood plasma to an injured crewman of the USS *Turner* after
the destroyer exploded off Sandy Hook, New Jersey. Later that year, a
helicopter landed on a sandbar in Jamaica Bay, New York, to rescue a
teenager who had become marooned. On the other side of the world,
a chopper was used in combat rescue for the first time when an Army
lieutenant rescued the pilot and three passengers of a light plane that had
been forced down behind enemy lines in Burma.

Commander Schoel knew this rich history and made a quick decision. To save precious time and to keep the exposed occupants of the
lifeboats from suffering hypothermia, he would employ helicopters and

use them to hoist passengers from the lifeboats to the deck of the *Williamsburgh*.

While Commander Schoel ordered the rescue to begin, preparations had to be made to accommodate, care for, feed, and probably clothe them for a voyage of several hours to the closest port, Valdez.

The effort would require coordination. Each helicopter had space on board for eight to ten people, depending on their weight. How long it would take to lift one person would certainly vary widely. Elderly people who were already traumatized from the experience of abandoning the *Prinsendam* and drifting in cramped conditions for several hours would now be required to deal with being inserted into a basket and lifted, swinging from side to side, between twenty and thirty feet into the air. Once at the open door of the chopper, they would be helped inside in a swift moment that could rightfully be called a yank and a shove.

If that was successful, they could be ferried to the waiting deck of the *Williamsburgh*.

Such a monumental undertaking would be difficult in good weather, but meteorologists reported that with a cold front steadily closing from the west, the already unfavorable conditions were going to rapidly deteriorate. Helicopters and ships should anticipate sustained high winds with strong gusts, heavy rain, and waves of ten to fifteen feet. This raised the horrifying prospect of a lifeboat capsizing and pitching up to ninety people into the water.

— ✦ —

The operation would initially involve Coast Guard HH-3 Jolly Green Giants out of Sitka, and the Air Force HH-3 flown by Captain John Walters from Alaskan Air Command base at Elmendorf. On board were flight surgeon Don Hudson and pararescuers. En route were a pair of HH3s and two Hercules transports from Coast Guard RCC in Kodiak and two Canadian Air Force Labrador choppers of the 44s Squadron based at Comox, British Columbia. With all helicopters operating and each picking up twelve people at a time, he would have to execute eight round-trips between the lifeboats and the tanker. Flight times would be variable, according to distances to be covered, weather, sea conditions, and the time required for landings, unloadings, and takeoffs on the *Williamsburgh*. Because this unprecedented airlift involved more than five hundred mostly elderly people, there was no guide for estimating how long the process would take. Another variable to be figured in these time calculations was the need for the choppers to leave the scene and fly to the Hercules tanker at the vicinity of Yakutat to refuel and return. The hope was that this massive effort would be accomplished before sunset, giving the operations about nine hours of daylight.

Worse to contemplate was two or more, perhaps all, of the lifeboats being overturned, swamped, and sunk. Should that happen, people without life jackets would drown. Among those who had them, hypothermia certainly would claim many, possibly hundreds. The sun would go down with the frigid waters of the Gulf of Alaska littered with floating corpses to be retrieved by the Coast Guard cutters that were heading to the scene at top speed.

— ◆ ◆ —

All his life, Edwin Ziegfeld had been asked if he were related to the legendary theatrical producer Florenz "Flo" Ziegfeld. The most famous Broadway impresario in the Gay Nineties and through half of the twentieth century, he had presented extravagant variety shows and Follies that featured the world's most beautiful women decked out in lavish and revealing costumes. He had presented the biggest names in show business, from singers Anna Held and Lillian Russell to W. C. Fields, Fanny Brice, Eddie Cantor, Al Jolson, and Will Rogers. Perhaps because of his last name, or as a former patron of New York City's Lincoln Center, the Metropolitan Opera, and stage shows at Radio City Music Hall, Edwin Ziegfeld observed the sudden burst of activity of helicopters from the rear lifeboat number six and saw a "marvelous aerial ballet."

A low, slowly circling C-130 Hercules operating as the on-scene commander reminded him of a model airplane dangling in a clutter of whimsical and blatantly commercial decorations suspended from the ceiling of the barroom at the rear of an expensive and notoriously exclusive Manhattan restaurant. Named "21" because that was its address, just off Fifth Avenue on West Fifty-second Street, it was close to the

Museum of Modern Art, where he and John Courtney had occasionally dined following Sunday afternoons enjoying MOMA's masterpieces of painting, sculpture, and other works that were featured in their college lectures. Having agreed to retire together in sunny California, they had decided to splurge on a farewell-to-New York "21" dinner. During most of the meal, they'd talked about eventually taking a leisurely cruise to the Far East to acquire works of Oriental art to enhance the stylish decor of their Mont San Antonio Gardens apartment in Claremont. Peering up at the cutout-like plane and helicopters' aerial ballet, he felt that he and John Courtney would soon be reunited. By the grace of God, and age and health permitting, they would one day resume their Pacific odyssey.

While the helicopters were heard throughout the night, alternately close and far away, they were hard to see, except in the off-and-on glare of Aldis lamps and the small blinking red-and-green running lights. In the light of dawn, flitting here and there, they looked smaller than they'd sounded. Flying low in the full daylight, they had white fuselages and diagonal stripes of the Coast Guard red on their noses, and they seemed huge.

In the sudden activity of helicopters, Richard Steele found another motion picture analogy. "Everyone was looking up," he said of the people in number four. "We were like the war refugees gazing at the plane to Lisbon in *Casablanca*, all wishing they were on it."

Also in number four, Jeannie Gilmore was increasingly worried about her seventy-five-year-old mother. Although Jeannie had fashioned a blanket into a makeshift tent for her, Neva Hall's face was white as her hair and her hands felt like ice. "When we saw the helicopter," Jeannie recalled, "many of us raised our arms and waved at it. It looked so beautiful, with its twin rotors."

In lifeboat number six, Earl Andrews thought the blades of the propellers whirled so fast that they looked like big horizontal circular saws. Betty Milborn watched from number five and saw haloes of giant descending guardian angels. Senator Dickinson supposed that the flurry of activity in the air was the start of a rescue plan that had been worked out after the helicopters had surveyed the situation and located the lifeboats. He assumed their movements meant the imminent arrival of Coast

Guard cutters and that they would make the pickups from the lifeboats. When a door opened on the right side of a helicopter hovering low over number five, he realized the Coasties had something bolder in mind.

Strapped by a nylon belt in the opened doorway of Lieutenant Melnick's HH-3 Pelican, Petty Officer Michael Oliverson was able to lean out and look down at the lifeboats. He wore a communications headset. Because Melnick would not be able to see what was beneath the chopper as it descended to a hover position, Oliverson, as a hoist man, would have to talk the chopper down to between twenty and thirty feet above the ocean. A veteran of numerous rescues of individuals and small groups of people from decks of ships, out of lifeboats, and in the water, he had not dealt with anything near the scope of the scene below that he found during a flyover to survey and assess the situation.

Like daring, fledgling offspring of a swan testing their ability to swim, the white lifeboats had spread from the *Prinsendam* in every direction. They rose and fell on large waves like the horses that bobbed up and down on an amusement park carousel, lurched forward and back like rocking chairs, and rolled violently from side to side. These conditions were more challenging, because each of the wildly cavorting boats was so tightly packed from bow to stern that there appeared to be no space to accommodate the hoisting basket. With no way of communicating by radio or walkie-talkie with the lifeboats, and with no one on the Coast Guard choppers equipped with scuba suits and gear who could be lowered to help load the baskets, people in the lifeboats would have to find a way to do it themselves, assisted only by hand signals from hoist operators.

"It was like fishing," said one hoist man, "except that when you cast your line, you're in a helicopter and you're trying to hook people who are packed like sardines into a bouncing boat. You do this, hopefully, without cracking some elderly gent's noggin with the basket or giving a little old lady who looks like your grandmother a bump that knocks her head over heels into a bath of cold seawater."

As Oliverson anticipated the operation unfolding, the basket would be lowered into the lifeboat, "someone would somehow crawl in, hold on for dear life, and we'd hoist him or her into the copter. Then another crewmember would flip the basket over and carry the person back in the copter, where we would try to distribute the weight evenly. When we reached our limit, we would hustle over to the *Williamsburgh*, unload, and go back for more."

The plan rested on assumptions by the helicopter crews that the pick-ups from the boats, shuttling to the supertanker, unloading, and return-ing for the next load would proceed quickly. With clockwork precision, deliberate speed, and efficiency, the rescue operations would be over well ahead of dusk, before the arrival of the cold front's worsening weather, and possibly before the *Boutwell* showed up. This optimism was a result of the fortuitous presence and response of the *Williamsburgh*. Without its helicopter pads, the choppers would have to make lengthy round-trips to Sitka and perhaps other land bases. Instead of flying miles between pick-ups, the hops to and from the supertanker would take only a few minutes. Less time in the air for choppers meant quicker relief of men and women who'd been suffering in open lifeboats for many hours.

In such conditions, when a few minutes could be the difference between life and death, the first challenge for Captain John Walters in his Air Force HH-3 helicopter was placing flight surgeon Don Hudson onto the *Williamsburgh*, along with blankets and medical supplies. It was Walters's first sea landing. With two copper pads on a deck that was broader and longer than an aircraft carrier's, and with the guidance of *Williamsburgh* crewmen, Walters set the chopper down as easily as if he were making a routine landing at Elmendorf.

A few minutes after Dr. Hudson and the supplies were offloaded, the helicopter lifted off and headed out in search of a lifeboat. Farthest from *Prinsendam*, it was number six. "On the flyover," recalled Walters, "I was struck by the jam-packed conditions and the age of the people. I knew then that we better put our PJs [parajumpers] into the water, because those folks would have trouble with the hoist." The type used by the Air Force, primarily for picking people up on land, had a bullet-shaped casing. Called the "forest penetrator," it opened to reveal the lift basket.

As the chopper hovered about ten feet above number six, two PJs in scuba gear and carrying survival equipment, John Cassidy and Jose Rios, leapt into the sea and swam to the lifeboat.

———— ✦ ————

"It seemed like an impossible task," wrote Lois Berk. "At first, there was no space on the lifeboat [number three] where the basket could be lowered because we were so crowded. After a few passes, some people in the stern were able to make room and catch and firmly place the basket in the boat. One at a time, nine persons were raised into the helicopter and then flown to the *Williamsburgh*. The copter came back five times before I was lucky enough to be helped into the basket, hauled up, and quickly helped out of it on the tanker. I don't know how many more trips the copter made. I heard that the crewman who worked the basket was operating his first real rescue. I was among the forty-five he plucked from death. We were older people, stiff and frozen, many of them were terribly seasick, and we had to be lifted out of the basket. He must have had extraordinary strength."

Describing the hoisting to *Reader's Digest* writer Joseph Blank, Petty Officer Oliverson noted that once the basket was loaded, he started his winch just as the lifeboat was riding the top of a wave. The account continued, "The survivor suddenly found himself dangling in midair, ascending. Pulled into the aircraft, some passengers were so scared—eyes shut, hands clenched around the edges of the basket—that a third crewman had to work to get them out. It took a helicopter at least thirty minutes to hoist up a load, skip over to the *Williamsburgh*, and to unload it. It was a daisy-chain operation. As one chopper lifted off the helipad, the command ship overhead gave the next permission to land."

Not all the lifts went as smoothly. As one basket holding an elderly women rose, it swung out from the side of the boat and suddenly dipped into the icy water. Quickly jerked up, the dripping-wet woman glared toward the helicopter, shook a finger at the hoist operator, and yelled, "Young man, don't do that again."

When a helicopter hovered thirty feet over lifeboat number four late in the morning, Marjorie Czeikowitz watched anxiously as the basket slowly descended. Not fully recovered from a stroke, she had difficulty walking and had needed a wheelchair that was left on the ship. As the basket came down, she expressed doubts to her husband, Richard, about her ability to get into it. "I'm here to help you," he replied. "You'll do fine." As the basket reached the level of the boat, a wave slammed it against her head and knocked her unconscious. The only *Prinsendam* officer in number four, the second maître d'hôtel, assured Richard, "She'll be alright, but you go up in the basket first and tell the helicopter crew what the situation is and to get her to the tanker right away."

In the first hour of hoisting operations, 150 men and women were plucked from the lifeboats and transported to the *Williamsburgh*. During the shuttling the sea had grown rougher, reaching twenty-five-foot swells. The wind had increased to fifty knots. "When the water started washing over the sides of the boat," said John Gyorokos, "the cold water was almost unbearable." Lois Berk recalled that the wind was strong, and waves were very high. In the *Williamsburgh's* wireless room, Jim Pfister radioed, "We have very difficult sea conditions. We have two hundred and fifty survivors on board now, but more are still in the water."

Earl Andrews found himself fascinated by the obvious coordination of the helicopters. They circled and made careful approaches to the lifeboats at medium altitude. A slow descent had them at a hovering level. After completing the hoisting process, they made a fast straight rise and turned to head to the ship. After unloading, they flew back to pick up more passengers.

John Graham watched his daughter Malory "go spinning into space and into a helicopter" and worried about worsening weather. The combination of roughening seas and increasingly strong winds would not only present helicopter pilots and hoist operators with a severe maneuvering challenge, but it would also attack the stability of overloaded lifeboats. Capsizing meant rapid hypothermia and certain death. As Malory's chopper sped away, he wondered if he would ever see her again. With the crests of waves blowing off, the boat was hit with torrents of seawater so cold they took the breath away. As a mountain climber, he knew you didn't have to be in water to develop hypothermia. Looking around the boat, he watched for the symptoms. First a person felt cold and shivered. When the shaking stopped, there came a feeling of warmth. Then, a sleep from which there is no waking. He figured that if everyone weren't picked up soon, in three to four hours they would die where they sat, or be thrown into the sea and drowned.

Hearing that the people carried to the *Williamsburgh* on helicopters did not report deaths in the lifeboats was little comfort to Dr. Don Hudson. Observing the state of those who stepped from the choppers onto the tanker's deck, he knew that the helicopters were in a race against time and weather. "While obviously relieved to have gotten out of the lifeboats," he told magazine writer Josh Eppinger, "the survivors looked grim." They were suffering shock, nausea, and sometimes were unable to control their bladders. The noise of the hovering helicopters made communication almost impossible. He and the makeshift medical team of paramedics, assisted by Isabella Brex, faced "a staggering range of medical problems."

A woman reported that she had a brain tumor. One man had an epileptic seizure, another had terminal cancer, and one suffered from malaria. "Everyone was cold," Hudson noted, "and most were suffering severely from motion sickness. A few were already in advanced stages of hypothermia, and I was sure someone was going to die. We had three people that I would say had less than an hour before they were irreversible."

With the help of Isabella Brex and *Williamsburgh* crewmen, he began a triage system to find and separate the most critical cases. They organized a "buddy system" in which each person was told to keep an eye on another. Moving among the rescued on five decks, he examined each person every ten minutes. As more soaked and shivering passengers came on board, he said, "I need you." "Watch this guy's eyes." "Take her pulse." "Keep me posted." His purpose was "to get across the feeling that people were going to die" if they didn't help him. Hoping involvement with other passengers would take their minds off themselves, he found the age of many of the passengers contributed to a smooth and orderly operation. "If I had been dealing with people thirty-five or under," he said, "there would have been more panic."

For skipper Arthur Fertig, a ship on a routine passage from Valdez to Texas with full tanks of crude oil had become an emergency room and makeshift hotel for 250 civilians, with more to come, and a landing pad for the swarming whirlybirds. With astonishing speed, his crew had improvised an efficient system of handling the choppers and the dazed figures they brought to the ship. Of the journey from lifeboat to helicopter to supertanker, Betsy Price would write, "The three-man crew operating the basket worked so deftly, in no time I was out of the basket and helped to the rear of the helicopter. About three more passengers came aboard, and then we were off to the *Williamsburgh*. We had lost sight of the *Prinsendam* hours ago, but when we were in the helicopter we could see three ships in the area waiting to pick up survivors." Noting that the chopper had to make a second approach to the tanker, she continued, "We jumped into the arms of the crew and were ushered the length of the thousand-foot tanker to the quarters and the wheelhouse. We shed our life jackets and were whisked inside to warmth and a reunion with fellow passengers. Immediately, we started swapping tales."

By early afternoon, the crews on helicopters and at the landing pad were near exhaustion. With the continuous rubbing against steel cables, leather gloves of the hoist crews wore through. Muscles ached and cramped. Oliverson's chopper, piloted by Bruce Melnick, would eventually carry out dozens of sorties and rescue a hundred people. With the number of helicopters in the air at one time ranging from three to six, the crewman watching the radar screen aboard the on-scene commander C-130 that coordinated their movements also had to keep track of the lifeboats and rafts in what at times seemed more like a video game than the orchestration of the greatest air-sea operation ever to be carried out by the Coast Guard. In the five-plus hours since the C-130 located the *Prinsendam* around 4 a.m., the blips representing Coast Guard and USAF aircraft, the cruise ship, and the scattered lifeboats had multiplied to include the tankers *Williamsburgh*, *Greatland*, and *SOHIO Intrepid* and the freighter *Portland*. In time, the screen would mark the presence of the cutters *Boutwell*, *Mellon*, and *Woodrush*, along with two Canadian Air Force Labrador choppers.

After making two sorties to and from the *Williamsburgh* and lifeboat number four, Jeannie Gilmore's rescuing helicopter appeared in the late afternoon. Approximately twelve hours after she and her mother had wedged themselves into the lifeboat, she feared Neva Hall couldn't last much longer. "Her skin was blue, and she'd been out there a long time, but my mother was also a very headstrong lady. When I told her to get in the basket, she said, 'I'm going down with the ship!'"

Jeannie replied, "Mother, there's only so much fuel in these helicopters, and they can't wait. You have to get into the basket right now."

"I'm not going," said Mrs. Hall, removing her rings and handing them to Jeannie. "Give these to my sister Mary Lou."

"Well, I couldn't very well hit her, or use physical force on an old lady," Jeannie recalled with a laugh, "so I got the idea of tricking her by telling her that my son-in-law, John, whom she really loved, was up in the helicopter. I told her, 'He's doing search-and-rescue work and wants you to get into the basket.'"

After thinking a moment, Mrs. Hall threw off her blanket and said, "Well, if that's what John wants, I'll do it."

Relieved that her mother was strapped into the basket and being winched up, and in the expectation that other older passengers would be the next to go, Jeannie sat down to wait her turn. An elderly woman said to her, "You really should go with your mom. She doesn't look very good. I'm sure no one will object."

When no one did, Jeannie reluctantly agreed. Given a farewell kiss on the cheek by the young man who had operated the rowing mechanism with her, she climbed into the lowered basket to be hoisted. As the basket reached the helicopter door, it was caught by a gust of wind. She recalled later, "It hit the side of the helicopter and went sailing out like a kite. I found myself seeing more of the ocean than I ever wanted to see again."

Winched into the chopper and helped out of the basket, she sat on a bench with knees touching those of the woman opposite her. Looking around at "wet and bedraggled people, weak from throwing up and terribly scared," she exclaimed, "We're all going to be fine, and you can all come home with me."

Landing on the *Williamsburgh* in heavy rain, they were assisted from the helicopter by Indonesian crewmen of the *Prinsendam* who had been taken from the launch and other lifeboats, then escorted by *Williamsburgh* crew across the deck and into the warm superstructure that rose several stories at the rear end of the ship.

Richard Steele wrote admiringly of the men who carried out the rescue operation, "They fight winds and gigantic waves as they maintain a level curse over the lifeboats to complete their death-defying, lifesaving mission. After ten hours drifting in the frigid sea, my wife is hoisted aboard a Coast Guard helicopter. She flashes the 'V for victory salute.'"

Because the helicopter Louise boarded was low on fuel, she would be flown to Yakutat. Richard would be picked up by a Canadian Air Force helicopter and flown to the *Williamsburgh*. "Our rescuer is highly skilled and coolly competent," he wrote. "He responds to our effusive thanks with a shrug and a grin and says, 'That's what I'm paid for. Glad you made it.'"

There were flashes of humor. Watching the woman who was briefly dipped into the sea, comedian Roger Rays said to Jack and Beatrice Malon in lifeboat number three, "What the hell is this, Operation Granny Dunk?" Betty Milborn gasped with horror as an eighty-year-old man who had been lifted from boat number five slipped out of the basket and into the water. When a *Prinsendam* officer grabbed the man's arm and yanked him back into the lifeboat, everyone applauded at the quick retrieval. Grinning broadly, the old man shook himself like a wet dog and said, "I'm sure you'll all agree that I really needed a bath! Well, you don't smell like a bunch of fresh-picked daisies, either!" When asked by an interviewer for a Boston television station to describe the experience of being hoisted out of a lifeboat, Steele replied, "I don't know if I can do it justice. It's like the W. C. Fields joke in a movie when he's about to be hanged. When he's asked if he has any last requests, he replies, 'I'd like to see Paris before I die, but Philadelphia will do.'"

Storm of the Century

Martha LaGuardia Kotite

One never knows what he is going to do when he sits in the doorway of the helicopter.

IT WAS A FREAKISH THING. IT WAS ONLY MID-MARCH, YET A HURRICANE-like storm spun into the Gulf of Mexico. Its course was a direct hit on Florida's west coast before it moved up the eastern seaboard of the United States. The repercussions of this superstorm were swift, vast, and disastrous. By the time it was over, it would strike twenty-six states and have an impact on the lives of nearly 100 million people, according to a University of Illinois case study.

"I'd never seen anything like it before," said rescue swimmer ASM2 Dan Edwards of the storm's unusual power and path. Edwards, assigned to Coast Guard Air Station Clearwater in Florida, defined the system, "like a nor'easter, only they don't blow across the Gulf of Mexico. The air temperatures were mid- to high thirties and the water in the forties. Normally it would be closer to fifty to fifty-five degrees Fahrenheit." With this surprise package came wind speeds that gusted upward of ninety miles per hour, record low pressures, and snowfall amounts that "were more than enough for this storm to gain the status of 'Storm of the Century,' as documented by the University of Illinois. The storm was monumental, killing over 250 people and canceling 25 percent of the United States' flights for two days."

—◆ ◆—

"One never knows what he is going to do when he sits in the doorway of the helicopter," said Edwards of the situation he faced. He had been on a week's vacation in Tampa, Florida, when he received the late-afternoon phone call from the air station. It was Saturday, March 13, 1993. Recalled to help with what became the second day of catastrophic events in the Gulf of Mexico and for towns along Florida's west coast, he drove as quickly as possible to Air Station Clearwater.

Edwards would immediately fill in for the rescue swimmer who had already flown too many hours and was "bagged" from multiple rescue responses. Edwards's return was hampered by bridge closures and washed-out roads. He had to follow back roads and detours. In Tampa Bay, the storm created seas of such increased height it was too dangerous for motorists to traverse the low-level bridges.

—◆ ◆—

Growing up, Edwards had always been around the water, boats, and the Coast Guard. Before he enlisted, he knew he wanted to fly. Of the aviation rates, being a rescue swimmer seemed like a natural fit. He was willing to wait two years before going to the rescue swimmer school to be tested mentally and physically to see if he was capable to serve his country in this demanding profession. By the time he went to school, his heart and mind were resolute. He succeeded and was not washed out. He credited his family's support as part of why he achieved his quest.

Four years after he qualified, this quiet, self-described family man had perfected his skill as a swimmer. He was athletic, strong, and a force to be reckoned with at five feet eleven inches tall and one hundred ninety pounds. A fairly new guy at the air station, the brown-haired, brown-eyed swimmer did not know anyone he was assigned to fly with that night when they headed directly into the superstorm.

—◆ ◆—

They launched close to sunset, after Dan Edwards jumped aboard the Coast Guard HH-3F Pelican helicopter, tail number CG 1486. The pilot, Lieutenant Tom Maine, and copilot, Ensign Tim Tobiasz, flew the helicopter over the Gulf of Mexico toward their assigned area of operations. In the cabin, avionics man AT2 Ken Newbrough maintained the radios and kept up their communications guard with home base. He sat near the flight mechanic, AM2 Russ Jones.

"This was an all-hands situation," said Maine of the flurry to call Coast Guard men and women in the region into action. "Everybody was coming in to the air station to fly, and the orders given were like 'You're next, go!'" No one had time to develop flight schedules because of the fast pace of events. The operation required aircrews to quickly get on scene to help people in distress along the flooding shoreline and offshore in the churning waters of the Gulf of Mexico.

"It was like the wild, wild West. Confusion everywhere," said Maine. "Clearwater is a pretty pleasant place to fly generally, kind of fair weather flyers down there. The thing that struck me was that we had an old crusty lieutenant commander, Bill Kesnick, who had completed his second tour in Alaska. He was talking to us on the radio saying, 'This is just as bad as anything you'll see up in Alaska.'" Alaska, in the minds of many, was really the last frontier, especially compared to the Sunshine State.

Maine had flown as an HH-3F aircraft commander for less than a year, accumulating a grand total of one thousand flight hours in that command position. Before transitioning to aviation, he had been enlisted and worked as a Coast Guard corpsman.

"I was green," said Maine. "Dan did not have a very capable guy in front of him that he trusted with his life. We were a very junior crew up front." The copilot, twenty-three-year-old Tobiasz, had graduated from the Coast Guard's Officer Candidate School in 1992. He had served as a pilot in the U.S. Army for four years flying the UH-60 Black Hawk helicopter. "I had about twelve hundred hours of flight time and was brand new to the H-3," said Tobiasz. "Our experience levels were probably about the same, both fairly junior."

For Maine, this was his first really challenging case. In his words, "my first scary one."

The tremendous seas and strong winds were cause for multiple distress calls through the evening. Coast Guard helicopter crews were tasked with locating activated Emergency Position Indicator Radio Beacons (EPIRBs). These beacons, stored on boats in an upside-down position, would automatically broadcast a distress signal on 121.5 (VHF) or 243.0 (UHF) MHz via an antenna. The automatic signal was sent when the vessel overturned and the device rolled one hundred eighty degrees with the vessel, which was the beacon's upright or "on" position.

The Coast Guard correlated these distress indicators with all available information, including active search and rescue satellite tracking. When the satellite passed, the Coast Guard's Rescue Coordination Center (RCC) in Miami calculated a composite solution or general latitude and longitude. RCC Miami relayed the information to Coast Guard Group Saint Petersburg and Air Station Clearwater. These units and others in the region would then launch resources by air and sea to locate the source of the distress.

—◦—

By ten o'clock that evening, Edwards and the aircrew located four distress signals by using the helicopter's electronics to hone in on the devices. The direction-finding equipment could track the "aurl" or audio strength of the radio frequency and its associated bearing to determine in which direction the pilots should fly to locate the beacon. As they flew toward the signal and got closer, the "aurl" would strengthen.

In some cases, signals they tracked down were correlated by land-based SAR prosecution teams as left over from previous evacuations. Others signals were located, but no people were found in the vicinity.

"There were so many search and rescue cases. Our direction was that if we didn't see anybody, divert on to the next one," said Edwards.

The next one changed his life.

—◦—

Maine and Tobiasz, as it turned out, searched with the only available HH-3F in the region. Of the twelve helicopters assigned to the air station, eight or nine of them were either flying elsewhere or down for maintenance. "We flew the planes until they broke," recalled Edwards.

Suddenly, they were redirected. The aircrew received instructions to locate and rescue ten crewmen abandoning a sinking merchant vessel. The *Fantastico*, a two-hundred-foot Honduran ship, was in a reported position sixty nautical miles west of Fort Myers, Florida. It was an hour and a half flying time away. They entered the coordinates into the navigational equipment and made best speed toward its last known position.

From Friday into Saturday night the storm's force had magnified. Winds had continued to build and bellow from the west-northwest, driving the seas faster, larger, to heights exceeding thirty feet. Visibility was also restricted because of heavy rain showers.

"That's what caused the *Fantastico* to break up and what promoted severe flooding in the Clearwater region," said Edwards. "Many boats and people had trouble."

The helicopter was en route when a Coast Guard HU-25A Falcon jet flew over the *Fantastico*'s distress beacon. It provided an advance report of the exact location of the emergency locator transmitter (ELT) hits. The fixed-wing aircrew also reported seeing two white strobe lights nearby.

"We never saw the *Fantastico*," said Maine of their approach, "we were coming down from the north, fighting the severe winds and turbulence. I remember vividly, looking through night vision goggles. I saw to the south strobe lights on the water and our direction-finding needle pointed toward the distress beacon. I thought, *Oh my God, there really are people in the water here.*"

Maine circled the helicopter low over the area before establishing a hover. Edwards identified ten strobe lights attached to life jackets tossed up and down by the gigantic waves. He noticed that almost every second the strobes flashed white against the black seas and night sky.

"When the pilot asked that I get in the doorway and assess the situation, I pretty much knew I was going out," confessed Edwards. "I thought every person had a strobe light on them. All you could see was a bunch of blinking strobes."

Edwards felt that these helpless people were counting on him to get out there and rescue them. "I didn't even really think about it," said Edwards of his decision to go into the hurricane-force winds and seas. "I just gave the pilot the thumbs-up signal, which meant 'swimmer ready,' and started the rescue."

"Every swimmer has a choice about whether or not he's up for the task. A swimmer could say no, this is not something that I want to do," said Maine. "We talked about the situation. We knew this was something we had not done before, and I wanted to make sure Dan was up for it."

Dan Edwards was unhesitant.

"Put me in, coach," Maine recollected Edwards saying.

Maine confessed that, because he was himself a relatively inexperienced pilot, he was concerned. "It scared the hell out of me when he left the aircraft. I thought, *I'm not sure I can get him back*. These were times, before direct deployment, when the swimmer would not stay attached to the hoist cable. Now, he's just another person in the water, albeit a good PIW [person in water], but in heavy seas."

Wearing a back-straining swimmer's sling adopted from the U.S. Navy, Edwards was hoisted down. About ten feet below the hovering helicopter, a thirty-foot wave rolled underneath and slapped his dangling body. "I jumped out of the harness and fell into the water. I started swimming. These waves were so close together it was like swimming upwards," said Edwards, who didn't have time to think about anything else. "Swimming up the crest of the wave, the wave would break over your head, I'd pop out and fall down the back side of the wave. Then, it was time to start swimming again."

The waves continued to charge by, one after the other. Occasionally, Edwards would be met with a smaller wave that enabled him to break out on top of it just enough to see a strobe light in the distance. The giant waves pushed the strobe lights in his direction.

Several things added to the severity of the situation. The pilots were not authorized to fly using their night vision goggles during hoists, only on the approach. Keeping an eye on their swimmer was extremely difficult. The helicopter was not equipped with a powerful searchlight or nose light called the "night sun." The trainable, movable floodlights underneath the helicopter were burned out. With no time to replace them or install the night sun, crews just refueled the helicopters and sent them back out to sea. "We were just doing everything we could under the circumstances," said Edwards.

With the reduction in visibility, they relied heavily on the fixed hover lights as a primary light source. This diffused light only illuminated the area directly below the aircraft. The searchlight would normally be used to track the location of the rescue swimmer and his work with the survivors. Edwards would pop in and out of the illuminated area and frequently out of the pilots' view.

For the pilots and aircrew, maintaining the helicopter's position above the water and over Edwards was hazardous because of the severity of the circumstances. Edwards's hand signals, when they could see them, were all his teammates had to identify what assistance he needed while battling the rough waters below to find survivors.

The first member of the *Fantastico* crew Edwards reached was in pretty good shape. It became a monumental task for the flight mechanic and pilots to coordinate placing the basket close and low enough for Edwards to reach it. When it was placed near him, a split second later the water moved so fast it was jerked out of Edward's reach. For twenty minutes, the team struggled to get the survivor inside. "I didn't think it would be so hard," said Edwards later.

With one man in the helicopter, Edwards was hoisted by the rescue sling and repositioned near the next blinking strobe light. He reentered the seas and began the exhausting swim toward the light. As he approached, he guessed the man was deceased but checked him anyway. He was facedown in the water and not responsive to Edward's attempt to revive him by lifting his head and shaking him.

The pilots hovered the aircraft above Edwards. He was picked up and deposited close to a third blinking light. Edwards reached out for the man and held him. He tried to talk to him. With no response, he shook him and slapped him on the face as he was trained to elicit any sign of life. Nothing, the man was dead.

Edwards was positioned near another twinkling light. He found another deceased crewmember. "They must have been sleeping just before they abandoned ship," recalled Edwards. "They were dressed only in T-shirts and shorts. It was absolutely too cold to be out there in that."

Edwards was lifted by rescue basket to another light. This time the survivor was inside a swamped lifeboat. Edwards discovered that the man, who appeared to be in his late forties, did not speak English. Encircling his waist were no fewer than ten empty milk jugs for flotation. As Edwards encouraged the Honduran to leave the flooded little boat, he became combative. He did not want to be removed and fought to stay. "I kept motioning for him to come out of the boat. He refused," said Edwards, and they had a few words. "He didn't want to go, and I didn't want to stay. I was not going to go by myself."

Edwards was left with no choice. As he was taught to do, he took control of the situation. "I grabbed him by his life preserver, pushed him up and off the boat, and twisted him into the water. I put my feet on the side of the submerged boat to give me more leverage."

After about thirty minutes of "Herculean effort," Edwards was successful in maneuvering him into the rescue basket. "Once he was up in the helicopter, that's when I learned he had a steel spike or metal piece which went through his hip and out the other side," said Edwards. "At the time of his rescue, all I knew was that he was alive. I didn't see the spike."

"It was truly amazing that Dan was able to get this guy with his injury over to the basket and into it," commented Maine. "Truly amazing. We didn't know what he was going through down there. It was all I could do to keep the aircraft in a reasonably stable hover above the waves. I was working pretty hard just to do that."

Edwards admits he was scared and had asked himself, *What are you doing here?* "When your mind is in a kind of limbo, the repetitive training just kicks in. It works," recalled Edwards. For more than an hour Edwards searched and found people in the water, his state of mind conditioned by his training to not panic, but to do his job. Yet, he was doing it with a vigor enhanced by his pumping adrenaline.

Edwards was hoisted into the cabin. Standard rescue swimmer training was based on thirty minutes of effort. He had been in the water for over an hour. "I told them, give me five minutes to get my composure and I'll get back at it again." Edwards removed his helmet to attend to the two survivors. In doing so he was disconnected from the ICS used by the crew to communicate with each other over the loud noise of the helicopter and storm.

The flight mechanic relayed to the pilots that Edwards was puking up seawater while trying to attend to the survivor with a spike in his leg. "If he's asking for a break, I'm not going to put him back in the water," stated Maine, who had silently thanked God several times that he did get Dan back inside the aircraft.

The Coast Guard case summary described the ordeal: "Having spent nearly one hour in the water under the worst weather conditions imaginable, ASM2 Edwards was completely drained physically after rescuing the second survivor."

During that period of much needed rest, they searched for additional survivors. With the assistance of an HU-25A Falcon jet circling overhead, they located something. The pilots hovered the helicopter above two survivors and expedited the lowering of the rescue basket to them. It was a pretty difficult proposition. "We fought the basket for quite a while trying to get to them. The winds are blowing the helicopter around, the seas are blowing the survivors and the basket around, and we're trying to make it come together at the same time," said Maine. "The temperatures were pretty cold that night, and the survivors were getting hypothermic."

Jones, the flight mechanic, worked to control the hoist cable. He leaned out the door to better observe the basket below and control its violent movements. A wave crested and rolled underneath. As the basket rose with the wave top, its sudden elevation simultaneously created a loop in the hoist cable. This loop became a dangerous component of untamed cable. It snaked behind the flight mechanic's ear and became caught underneath his flight helmet.

In a breath, the wave dropped, released the basket. It toppled down into the seas. The hoist cable tightened. All slack was gone. Now taut, it jerked Jones headfirst right out the door.

His safety belt, hooked into the deck of the cabin, stopped his forward flight. Somehow, a few feet outside the door, Jones managed to keep his boots on the edge of the doorframe.

"I heard a scream," said Edwards, who had been working with the survivors and was not aware of the emergency situation. He had been disconnected from the ICS and was unable to hear the emergency shouted over the communication system. "When I looked up and turned around, all I could see was his boots. He was hanging there by his tippy toes!"

Newbrough, the avionics man, reached over and grabbed the tether attached to the flight mechanic's safety belt.

"We heard him yelling, 'Shear! Shear! Shear!'" said Edwards. "When I reached up to do it, the light had turned green, which meant it was. The copilot had sheared it."

Newbrough swiftly pulled the flight mechanic inside as the cable released from around his helmet and neck. He was bleeding. "It looked like he had broken his nose, split his lip, and had lacerations around his neck," recalled Edwards. "It very well could have killed him."

The helicopter's hoist capability was completely finished. The basket was gone. The only way to rescue anyone would be if they landed the amphibious aircraft. The pilots discussed this in earnest with the inbound relief helicopter pilots. The approaching helicopter, tail number CG 1431, also an amphibious HH-3F, would arrive on scene in minutes. Collectively the pilots decided not to attempt a landing in such terrible sea conditions. It was also important to transfer the rescued survivors to the nearest hospital for emergency care.

Edwards talked with his pilots over the ICS system. "They wanted to know if I wanted to help pre-stage, or set up, survivors in the water for the next helicopter's rescue," Edwards remembered. Because the hoist was broken, it would mean Edwards would have to free-fall at night into seas exceeding thirty feet. This was against rescue swimmer procedures. Even so, Edwards considered it. He was informed that there was another helicopter on its way with a rescue swimmer aboard. Edwards asked if anyone in his crew was trained as an emergency medical technician, a necessity for the proper treatment of two survivors who were hypothermic and one severely injured. No one spoke up. So Edwards elected to remain to treat them.

Released from the case once the relief helicopter was on scene, Maine and Tobiasz flew to Naples, Florida, with their survivors.

—◦—

"Needless to say, when the other helicopter arrived on scene, the rescue swimmer elected not to deploy," recalled Edwards, who learned of this after they departed for the Florida hospital. "I support the decision of the other rescue swimmer," explained Edwards. "Coast Guard policy supports a rescue swimmer not deploying if there is debris in the water, predators, or a dangerous sea state. We had two of the three, and if he was not comfortable deploying, then that's his call."

"The aircraft that relieved us worked for well over an hour trying to get the basket near two guys on an overturned life raft or piece of debris," recalled Maine. "They were getting too hypothermic to force themselves to reach out and grab the basket, which was almost on top of them."

Still, Edwards felt terrible. For weeks he second-guessed his decision to remain and care for his survivors instead of going back down. Even though the men he saved were in critical need of his skill as a trained EMT, Edwards believed he did not do enough.

"Of the four living people we saw, we were able to get two out," said Edwards. "We never saw ten."

The STAN Team, which critiqued the rescue, supported his decision and helped provide Edwards the closure he needed. Edwards learned that the rescue swimmer who arrived in the second aircraft had held a life raft and data marker buoy (DMB), a device that is normally dropped to search for a survivor. He planned to take it with him into the seas that night. "Normally, we're in the water before the DMB. He was psyched out and did not want to go in," concluded Edwards.

The conditions during the Storm of the Century were above and beyond what any rescue swimmer had trained to work in before. The Advanced Rescue Swimmer School, which was commissioned years later, would train swimmers, pilots, and crews for rescues in big surf and seas, as well as in caves, on cliffs, and in other risky environments.

ASM2 Dan Edwards was awarded the Distinguished Flying Cross for his extraordinary heroism the night of March 13, 1993. "It changed my life," said Edwards. "It helped me shape who I am now. The experience definitely strengthened my belief. I feel that I have nothing to fear, so I go and do what I've been trained to do. It takes a lot of stress off you knowing that." Edwards has since been promoted to AST1 and works at Coast Guard Aircraft Repair and Supply Center in Elizabeth City as the office manager for technical services. "We take care of all the life support equipment, tests and evaluations of new gear, and procurement," stated Edwards. "Basically, out in the field if they have questions about how to fix something, they'd call us, and we'd find the right answers for them."

Lieutenant Tom Maine was awarded the Coast Guard Air Medal. Promoted to commander, he is the operations officer at Air Station Cape Cod. After Hurricane Katrina devastated the Gulf Coast, he provided much needed relief to New Orleans–based aircrews for nine days. He flew missions and rescued people from the floodwaters and rooftops. Ironically, he filled in as the acting operations officer at Air Station New Orleans for Lieutenant Commander Tim Tobiasz, who needed to rotate out for rest.

Lieutenant Tim Tobiasz received the Coast Guard Commendation Medal. He is currently assigned as the operations officer for Air Station New Orleans. AM2 Russ Jones was awarded the Air Medal for his efforts during the rescue. He has since retired from the Coast Guard.

Admiral William P. Leahy, Coast Guard District 7 commander, summarized Air Station Clearwater's efforts in a report: "Throughout this ninety-six hour emergency, HH-3Fs and HC-130s flew 55 sorties totaling 165 flight hours, prosecuted 32 SAR cases, saved 62 lives, and assisted 27 others in extremely hazardous, hurricane-like weather conditions."

Air Station Clearwater was awarded a CG Unit Commendation. Dozens of aircrew personnel received individual awards for their meritorious actions.

On the subject of the nature of rescue swimmers, Maine added, "We think of these kids as being machines, just another piece of rescue equipment that jump out of the helicopter and do their superhero stuff. They are human beings, and they know their limitations better than anybody. For Dan, on this night with a couple of young knuckleheads up in the plane in front of him with his life in their hands, to say, 'Yeah, let's go,' is pretty significant.

"These guys are macho to a fault; they are kind of our Special Forces folks. It's a big deal for one of them to turn down a rescue. So for this next helicopter to come out, with more experienced pilots by the way, for that rescue swimmer to say 'No,' that is pretty impressive. To relay it back to what Dan did, it is pretty impressive.

"As a young guy who was seeing my first real challenging conditions for the first time, I don't think the magnitude of what Dan did hit me. I don't think I appreciated it until later on. I've told the story many times of what he did, went in the water with a couple of young knuckleheads and a flight mechanic he didn't know, trusted us with his life. There is no question in my mind, as the guy at the controls, that he was a fraction away from losing his life himself. There would not have been any other options. He put himself right in the face of death to rescue those two people. To me that is the most heroic thing I've seen in my twenty years in the Coast Guard."

Two Tankers Down

Robert Frump

February 12, 1952
Baton Rouge and Norco, Louisiana
Aboard the SS Pendleton *and the SS* Fort Mercer

THE BIG TANKER, NEARLY THE SIZE OF TWO FOOTBALL FIELDS STRETCHED end to end, lay at dockside, half-filled with 15,000 tons of heating oil and kerosene.

A slender stem of pipe and hose ran from her deck across a narrow slice of the Lower Mississippi River Basin and disappeared into a whole huge farm of silos and storage tanks in the Louisiana bayou country near Baton Rouge. It was through this straw that the SS *Pendleton*, 503 feet stem to stern, seemed to sip, feed, and sink, like a huge swollen tick, lower and lower into the water on a warm, summerlike night, February 12, 1952.

This was a time when any tanker captain got the jitters. Nervous little thoughts and fears bumped and sizzled the consciousness like the bugs buzzing about and banging into the lines of lights that lit the tanker decks. Captain John Fitzgerald of the *Pendleton* was not an exception. He had been through the war and seen it all. Yet seven years after the fighting stopped, any good tanker captain remained alert at a wartime level when the tankers were neither full nor empty.

There was good reason to be nervous. Fumes filled the big tanks of the tanker and mixed with oxygen. When the mixture of oil and air reached a certain critical point, it could explode. Even Daniel Ludwig, now the multi-millionaire owner of fleets of tankers, found out what could happen back in 1926, when he was a young captain in Boston on the tanker *Phoenix*.

He heard his crew calling for help from below. Fumes were overwhelming them. Ludwig rushed to the rescue and pounded down the ladder into the hold after them. Later, they figured the nails in his boots produced a spark on the steel ladder. For the men below, it was like a bomb. The crew died instantly.

For Ludwig, with his hands still on the ladder, the blast was like a rocket engine. He was propelled out of the hold, up the ladder, and into the air in an arc and landed 25 feet away.

Now, in 1952, Daniel Ludwig was the father of the supertanker and well on to being the richest man in the world. And the same problems still pained him, literally. Severe pain in his back from that explosion would accompany him the rest of his life. And on a larger scale, regarding the larger pain, platoons of Ludwig scientists and engineers never could wholly solve the problem of explosions. Tankers could be bombs. The smallest source of energy could spark the fuse.

So Captain Fitzgerald kept a close watch over the ship as she was loaded, and so did his chief mate, Martin Moe. It was close to eighty degrees in Baton Rouge, and Moe, in charge of loading, could see the wafts of the fumes of the cargo; he could smell them too. Kerosene had a light, sharper odor to it that could sting your nose. The heating oil had a danker smell, a bass note on the olfactory scale. Some inevitably spilled into the water and formed greasy rainbows. Fumes from both cargoes intermingled and provided a chemical-infused micro-atmosphere, a bit like the service bay of an auto mechanic's garage. It was muggy. Close.

Raymond Sybert was the chief engineer of the ship, and any engineer had to love the SS *Pendleton* and the modern miracle this ship was. The explosion problem was not solved, but technology had eased it. She was welded, for one thing. Ludwig always hated the old riveted ships and felt the explosion that hurt him was caused in part by leaks of fumes flowing through loose rivet fits. Welded ships did not leak—at least not like the riveted ships did.

In the old days, too, loading tankers involved laborious measurements in a series of tanks, each separately serviced from the outside. Load one tank to full and keep the others light and the ship could be dangerously out of balance. Fumes, sparks, cigarettes, cutting torches, oxygen, all could come together disastrously. Tanks billowed wavy lines of gases to the deck. A dropped set of car keys, a careless welder: Anything could set it off.

But on the *Pendleton*, Moe and Sybert could pump and dump oil wherever they wanted it. They could fill tank 1 and without much of a pause switch the incoming flow of oil to tank number 2. Or if the tanks already filled needed trimming, Moe could pump oil from tank number 5 to tank 2 and from there to 3, if he so chose. If the ship was 6 inches lower at the stern than it was at the bow, he could pump cargo forward and trim the ship. All of this was in a closed circuit, more or less, with far fewer fumes wafting anywhere more than they had to.

And below? In the engine room? It was an electrical engineer's dream. They had built these tankers during the war and designated them T-2s. Like most ships of the time, the T-2s relied on steam power. But unlike other ships, the steam did not directly turn turbines that turned the prop. On T-2s, the steam turned turbines that produced electricity, and the electricity drove huge electric engines.

The design was that rarest of commodities: a luxury born of necessity. Reduction gears used in conventional turbine drives were in short supply during the war, and the electrical engines were an elegant workaround. The even pull, the control, the smoothness Sybert could employ using these engines was extraordinary. He could move from full ahead to full astern if he wanted to. The T-2s were great wartime ships. When German bombers were reported en route to a port, the captains of regular ships needed to build up steam. The T-2 captains just put it in drive and did an electro-glide out of harm's way.

And the power? It was no exaggeration. It was no metaphor. T-2s had been used often in the post-war period in third world countries. The ships would dock and thick cords would be snaked ashore. The ships literally lit whole cities.

Now, post war, there were hundreds of them out there. And this was their coast—the tanker coast of Louisiana and Texas. America was booming, and all along the Gulf, the T-2s were tied up to docks outside tank farms and refineries and their long slender hoses and pipes sucked in oil. They would feed and when filled cast off and head to the Northeast coast.

Not far from the *Pendleton*, downriver at Norco, Louisiana, very close to New Orleans, the SS *Fort Mercer*, another T-2, was also taking on a cargo of heating oil and kerosene from the big Shell Oil facility there.

They were nearly identical ships, with just a few differences. The *Pendleton* was bound for Boston and carried more heating oil than kerosene. The *Fort Mercer* was heading slightly north of there to Portland in Maine and carried more kerosene than heating oil.

Also, the *Fort Mercer* loaded slightly light. On a normal trip, she would have exited Norco through Southwest Pass, but a ship was stranded there. So she needed to take an alternate route, a shallower route. She could not carry her normal full load because she would not clear the new passage.

So she loaded light—30 feet forward and 30 feet aft in freshwater—with the forward deep tanks essentially empty. Once she hit the salt water, her draft would rise slightly to about 29.5 feet. The *Pendleton* loaded about 1 foot deeper in fresh than salt water.

Aside from that, they were the same ship. They were 503 feet long and about 70 feet wide. Each produced around 6,600 horsepower. They both had nine cargo tanks. And they both departed on the same day: February 12.

At the helm of the *Fort Mercer*, Captain Frederick Paetzel had the hardened nerves of a wartime merchant officer. He was a large man, a bit overweight, and some of the crew thought him too harsh an officer, though this was by no means universally shared. Some did not know him, nor he them. The vessels each carried a crew of more than forty: forty-three for the *Fort Mercer*; forty-seven for the *Pendleton*. Men came, men went. Willard Fahrner, the second mate, thought Paetzel was just fine. Fine enough anyway, a steady guy. Fahrner, like most of the other men, was happy to be in the coastal trades, where they made runs to

Boston or Maine, six days up and six days back. America was booming, and the dreams put on hold by the war for men like Fahrner were now coming true.

There was a time and place he dreamed of little but surviving, after all: June 23, 1943, the tanker *Stanvac Manila*, in the southwest Pacific, not far from New Guinea. A Japanese torpedo had split the ship Fahrner served on, and he knew what true danger at sea could be. Merchant mariners, man for man, had suffered more war casualties than any branch of the service except the Marines.

But this duty? Well, tankers had their troubles. But the coastal run was a piece of cake. You did it so many times you could do it in your sleep. So when the ships headed to sea, they both followed a common route: down the dredged-out channel of the Lower Mississippi, across the well-worn sea lanes of the Gulf of Mexico, around Florida, and up the eastern seaboard. The bridge and officer quarters of both ships were located forward, atop a small housing that ran up three stories from the deck, a bit more than a third of the ship's length back from the bow. The engineers and crew stayed aft in a larger housing near the stern of the ship. A narrow, railed catwalk connected the two command centers.

All those things the two ships had in common one with each other: design, cargo, configuration, and destination. And then there was the other thing too—the thing all T-2s seemed to share, the part the men knew at some level but did not talk much about. These ships were built in wartime. They had done their job. But the builders had been rushed.

They had used that new welding technology.

How could you say it? Some of the ships weren't solid. But you didn't know which ones, really. The Coast Guard and the American Bureau of Shipping had acknowledged the problem and required that the ships be reinforced. On the decks of both ships, and below as well, ran thick steel belts, or "crack arrestors." The crack arrestors were a response to a question that no one had the answer to: What made the ships crack in the first place? Why were some fine and others catastrophes? All the inspectors really knew is that the ships cracked and the big metal bands might help stop the ships from splitting clean in two.

The men walked over these crack arrestors on the deck daily and had to be reminded by the thick riveted belts that there were some structural questions about the ships. But at another level, even those who were skittish did not spend a lot of time worrying about it. Risk was a given. There were so many war stories out there, you'd go crazy thinking about them all.

Besides, there were stories, too, on how tough a ship those T-2s were.

How about the SS *Ohio*? She'd left the River Clyde, Scotland, on August 8, 1942, for Malta, carrying 13,000 tons of kerosene and fuel oil desperately needed by the Allies. Malta was an island where the Allies staged air raids on the Axis ships out of Italy supplying Rommel's tanks in North Africa. Germany was close to taking Alexandria when Axis supplies ran low. Rommel ran out of diesel fuel for his tanks, and the war at this point boiled down to whether Germany could or could not resupply him via its own tankers sailing across the Mediterranean. The Allied bombers and fighters on Malta kept the supply line closed and shut the door on supplies to Rommel. But then the Allies ran out of gas on Malta. Only the SS *Ohio* could deliver the goods—the gas—in time.

The Junker 88s and Stuka dive-bombers caught up with her on August 11 near North Africa, and for three days she was strafed and bombed. An Italian submarine torpedoed her. Two Junker bombers crashed into her. She lost her rudder, and holes in her hull meant she had only 30 inches of freeboard—less than a yardstick, separating her deck from the water. Still, she made it, propped up on either side by destroyers, like two buddies aiding a drunken third. The Allies refueled their planes and kept the door shut on Rommel.

So you could be selective about the truth you wanted to hear: T-2, unsafe at any speed; T-2, indestructible warhorse, the ship that may have saved the Allies from defeat in North Africa. And besides, many of the crew and officers were war veterans who discounted risk at a steep rate. Hell, an assistant cook on the *Fort Mercer* had been a combat marine. They sailed aboard ships that were bombs—and they did this willingly.

Ask them if they were worried about the ship splitting in two at sea and survival in cold waters?

It was a trick question.

They were *tanker men*. It was the explosion that was going to kill them.

▬ ▬

February 16, 1952
Chatham Lifeboat Station, Chatham, Massachusetts

At the Coast Guard Lifeboat Station in Chatham on Cape Cod in Massachusetts, the men had settled into a winter routine. The summer crowd and the calls for sailboat and surf swimmer rescues were long gone. Almost all the jobs now were related to commercial fishing vessels or maintaining navigation aids, and most of those were run-of-the-mill.

This boat had broken loose from its moorings. That one was trapped by ice in the harbor. A channel buoy was ripped loose by a storm surge. The lighthouse boat needed provisions. Bernard C. Webber, a young lifeboat coxswain, had some slack time. He decided the new guys in command were growing on him, but he still dearly missed Frank Masachi and Alvin E. Newcomb, the old commander.

Masachi had saved Webber—not physically, not literally as in a water rescue. But if it had not been for Masachi and the discipline of the Coast Guard, Webber did not know where he would be. A kid in trouble was his guess.

Webber seemed to be someone who did not easily get the hang of things by himself. He needed rules. He needed things clear. He had been in trouble at age fifteen in 1943 in Boston, and it might have been a little thing had it not been for one very big thing. He was the son of a Protestant minister. The trouble was nothing that serious. He would acknowledge that he had been "easily led" by friends. That much he would say and no more.

Was it joyriding? A little drinking? Some close to him at that time said it was nothing that serious—just breaking a few street lights with rocks or rolling about in hedges until they broke. Pretty harmless Huck Finn stuff but a big deal when you were the son of a preacher man. Bigger stuff still when you hung with the Catholics in town, as Bernie did, and the lights and hedges were in the Protestant neighborhoods served by the Tremont Temple Baptist Church, where your father was associate pastor.

Worse still when you were undiplomatic enough to get caught.

Mostly, he and Stephen Holden, the kid down the block, were high on the war. It was intoxicating to young teenagers, and the adrenaline and the testosterone just could not be contained within wholly acceptable borders. Good lord, the country was at war. Friends of theirs just a few years older than they were heroes. Bernie's three older brothers all were in the fray, in the show. You only had to be sixteen to join the merchant marine, and already there were stories of glory. So if you could not get into the war, then you got into whatever you could, including trouble. His father and a well-meaning, well-to-do parishioner had the solution, and it was not sending Bernie to war. Instead, he was sent to a prestigious and expensive boarding school, and he would study for the ministry. His dad knew he was a good kid. Bernie had a good heart. He wanted to help people. He was just very affected by the war. The best schools, the best people would bring out the best in him.

And Webber was holding his own at prep school academically. But he felt out of place. He did not dress like the rich kids. The rich kids worked clearing tables; he worked in the fields and gardens. He'd walk in late to French class smelling like manure, and his instructor each time would remind him of that. He did not easily get the hang of things. And this "thing"—an East Coast elite prep school—was something he would never get.

So perhaps it was fate that when his old friend in mischief, Steve Holden, wrecked his father's car, Holden headed straight for Webber. They hid out for a few days in the school. Bernie sneaked food from his dinner to Steve. But it was not long before they got caught. His parents were called, but before the Reverend Webber could come and pick him up, Bernie and Steve Holden ran away, plodding through the cornfields outside Northfield, Massachusetts.

Being a fifteen-year-old on the lam got old quick, and Bernie slumped home. There, his father stewed and stewed and then finally relented. There were programs where sixteen-year-olds could join the merchant marine. Bernie Webber badly wanted to go. He made the case to his dad. Since age twelve, he'd been a Sea Scout, a water-going Boy Scout, with the Wollaston, Massachusetts, troop. He loved the sea. And his dad had to concede the sea was in the family blood. Each summer the Webber family went to a place on the Kennebec River just below Bath, Maine. Bernie's uncles worked at the Bath Iron Works building ships. He was just a small kid when they'd bring him in to watch the big ships being constructed. He'd watch them build the ships and then launch them into the river. Bernie saw those ships moving out to sea, and that's where he wanted to go. His dad *had* to let him go to sea, the young man said.

The Reverend Webber conceded the point. When Bernie turned sixteen, his father signed the papers. Webber was jubilant. He was on his own and filled with freedom. Bernie even started smoking. It seemed jaunty. Webber was on his way to the war. He joined his first ship in the Panama Canal, cocky as could be.

He scrambled up a Jacob's ladder to the deck with a lit cigarette dangling from his mouth, ready to take on the world. The ship was a tanker. The chief mate saw Bernie, saw the cigarette, and said nothing. Instead, the chief swung a roundhouse right at Webber that caught him on the cheek and knocked him cold. Bernie was out for a few minutes. He awoke. The cigarette was gone.

The chief mate stood over him and said:

"Did you *learn* anything?"

Webber silently shook his head yes.

"Because if you haven't learned anything, next time I will *personally* throw you over the side," the chief mate said.

The education of Bernie Webber had begun. He spent two years aboard the tanker—a T-2, as it turned out—during wartime, sailing the Caribbean. The ship was fitted out with antiaircraft cannon and machine guns. But by that time, the Caribbean was quiet, and the ship saw little action, just hours and hours of plowing through the blue-green waters of paradise. These were warm waters. His tanker, the *Sinclair Rubiline*, held up just fine as she ranged from Aruba and Curacao, moving fuel to the South Pacific.

The discipline was good for him, and here, it seemed, he had found the hang of something. When the war was over, he returned to Boston but steered clear of his old habits and friends. He wasn't even eighteen, and shipping was a bit slow. You hung out at the union hall and hoped your card would be called. His wasn't. He wondered if he would be drafted into the Army soon if he could not catch a ship, and on a whim one day, at lunchtime when the maritime union office was closed, he wandered over to Constitution Wharf in Boston.

He strolled about and saw a large sign that said, "The Coast Guard Wants You." He was curious and popped into the office. There, a petty officer second class was eating lunch with his feet propped up on his desk. He took one look at young Webber and said, "What the hell do you want?"

Bernie said he'd seen the sign that said the Coast Guard wanted him.

"Well, that doesn't necessarily mean you," the petty officer said.

"I'm a merchant seaman," Webber shot back, and the tone shifted there and then. The petty officer prepared papers. Bernie's father needed to sign them, as Bernie was still under age, but in the end it all worked and he was accepted.

What he found in the Coast Guard was a hard-core discipline beyond the merchant marine. Right from the beginning, the officers made this clear to the new recruits. "Hard jobs are routine in this service," read his letter of acceptance. "The Coast Guard is always at war; against all enemies of mankind at sea; fire, collision, lawlessness, gales, derelicts and many more. The Coast Guard, therefore, is no place for a quitter or for a crybaby, or for a four-flusher, or for anyone who cannot 'keep their eye on the ball. . . . .'"

It was tough, and basic training was the toughest thing Bernie had done. But it worked for him. In fact, it worked better than he could have ever expected. He had real physical strength. He was 6 foot 2 and you would have called him a big lug if it were not for the fact he was so lean—only about 170 pounds on that frame. And he was smart too. He'd held his own at the prep school academically. He learned fast. And he had a knack on the water for steering, for navigating, for reading the sea and the tides and currents, for knowing where he was when the seas and wind turned most people around.

He liked the idea of a military unit that rescued people, though he was yet to actively achieve that goal.

Once out of basic, he was driven by jeep to Chatham, Massachusetts, on Cape Cod and got a glance at one of the rescue boats as he passed the harbor. It was a strange-looking thing. Stubby with stubborn-looking lines. The boat had no name. CG 36500 was on the vessel in black letters and numerals; that and "Chatham" on the back.

"What's that?" Bernie asked.

"That's a 36-foot rescue boat," the driver said.

Webber was unimpressed at first. Soon, though, he noticed just in passing that the rescue boat coxswains—the helmsmen, the wheel-men—carried themselves with what could only be called pride. They were rescuers. There was something to them, an air of substance. He decided that's what he wanted to do, and as he was leaving Chatham, he got another glimpse of the CG 36500. She meant something different this time. He felt a real affection for the boat, as if she were special. He was disappointed when he caught a ride in a 38-foot picket boat, not the 36-footer. He wished it was the CG 36500. There were whole weeks when he wondered if he would ever ride in a rescue boat. He had spent the first few months of active duty as a seventeen-year-old locked in a lighthouse with a seventy-five-year-old veteran of the old Lifesaving Service. This guy was old line. He would die in the Coast Guard. The old guys never retired.

In fact, Webber was absorbing the culture of the Coast Guard, the social traits that "managed" the agency as much as any rule or regulation. Sometimes for the better, and sometimes for worse. Tradition had it that there was a culture of courage, a small community devoted to this selfless task of rescue. The job paid little except in a currency of the high regard of the community and self-esteem. But the men themselves seemed in some way rich.

There were other traditions too. Not all of them good. How could you put this? The Coast Guard revered its heroes. But the Coast Guard and the country could forget them as well. For example, the old guy in the lighthouse not too many years ago could not have afforded to retire.

Underfunded and forgotten once the romance of rescue faded, the old Lifesaving Service could not pay pensions. Men could not retire. Toward the end of its life, before the Lifesaving Service merged with the Coast Guard, many of the men who had started as young specimens of the species were rowing toward wrecks in their sixties and seventies, because they had to. Charles McCormack, who won five gold medals for lifesaving and was the most famous of all the old salts, stepped from a lifeboat at age seventy-five, looked toward the sea and said, "Tide is ebbing."

Then he dropped dead, leaving his wife and family penniless, with no help from the government. Webber was yet to see that side of the Coast Guard as a young man, and he was benefiting greatly from the good side of the culture. He spent weeks on Monomoy Island, just off Chatham, at a lifeboat station where he had to use rainwater to wash his clothes. It was about as close to the old Lifesaving Service duty as you could get. He paid his dues. And finally, within a year, he moved on to work the motorized lifeboats.

They just seemed to grow on him as he understood more about them and how to run them, and once he did, he could not remember why he ever thought them odd-looking. They were crafts of extraordinary grace and beauty, he believed, blessed with great design and function.

At the start, though, he knew little. Masachi drilled him and drilled him, tested and retested, sent the seventeen-year-old on hours of endless patrols. Now, where he was six years later seemed perfect: the Chatham Coast Guard Lifeboat Station at the elbow of Cape Cod in Massachusetts. Webber thought it the most beautiful and charmed place on Earth. It was blessed with harbors and a town that looked like a postcard. The Coast Guard unit itself was contained within its own small culture, almost like the old U.S. Lifesaving Service, with its surfmen who would live for weeks and weeks in isolated stretches of wild beach land.

Yet the station was also a part of the town. The men would be ten days on and two days off in the lifeboat station, but not all of that was in isolation. They would patrol the harbor and help the local fishermen secure astray boats. And it was not uncommon for them to aid in a rescue, particularly near the notorious Chatham Bar, where the big Atlantic rollers met shallower water.

Fishing vessels had to cross the Chatham Bar to reach the Atlantic. In foul weather it was impassable—a thunderous churning of white water on shallow sand. Even in fair weather, it was dicey. Frequently the returning boats, loaded with fish, would be pitch-poled, turned over and over, by the big rollers coming from behind. Webber and the other Coastguardsmen—the "Coasties"—would fish out the dead. And it was here, not in the war, that Webber hauled his first dead man over the thwart of a boat. The Chatham Bar took few prisoners.

It took none from the fishing vessel *Cachalot*. Two Chatham fishermen, Archie Nickerson and Elroy Larkin, had taken the *Cachalot* out the day before Halloween in 1950. Crossing the bar was always the most dangerous part of the trip. Outward bound, the trip was fine.

Coming in, all *seemed* fine. But as they approached the bar, one of those big ocean rollers came up from behind the *Cachalot* and upended her, end over end. The *Cachalot* tumbled forward and then came down with a thump upside down on the beach.

Bernie was among the first on the scene and recognized the body of Elroy Larkin. Nickerson was never found. It stunned Bernie. He knew the Chatham Bar could kill. But he had not seen firsthand the awesome strength of the ocean, the power of the waves on the bar to pitch-pole a 40-foot boat as if it were a tiddlywink flipped and spun by a thumb.

And this was not work done in anonymous commodities. This was personal. These dead men were friends. That's the way the Coasties felt about the town and the fishermen. The town felt the same about the Coast Guard. It was not uncommon for the men to marry local Cape Cod girls. It was not uncommon for Chatham lads to seek careers in the Coast Guard. Many times the sons of drowned fishermen would do just that—make rescue work their life work, in homage to their lost dads. Larkin's son, Murray, did just that, enlisting in the Coast Guard and working on a cutter out of Woods Hole. Larkin's daughter, Esther, married a Coastie. Beverly Nickerson's daughter, Betty, was also to marry a Coast Guardsman who worked with Bernie.

So that is how it was. All of them in the fishing village knew the Coast Guard was there for them, that the Coasties would go out to their men in trouble when the water got rough. They knew that from what Frank Masachi did two years earlier. Even if the Coast Guard brass did not know it sometimes, the town knew Masachi had done the right thing.

The Chatham Lifeboat Station had received the call on April 7, 1950, late at night as a seventy-mile-per-hour wind blew snow, sleet, and thunderous whitecaps into Cape Cod. Out there in the Atlantic, the fishing dragger *William J. Landry* was in big trouble with a boatload of fishermen onboard. The boat's wooden seams had opened to the sea in parts of her hull, and now the crew and captain were bailing madly to keep her afloat. The Coast Guard took two actions. The officer in charge directed the *Landry* to head for the *Pollock Rip* lightship—a floating lighthouse run by the Coast Guard. There, Guy V. Emro, the ship skipper, would try to pass the boat a hawser, make it fast to the lightship, and get some pumps aboard. The officer also dispatched a small motorized lifeboat, just in case the lightship gambit did not work. Masachi would skipper it. Webber and two others would serve as crew.

Of the two boats available for the rescue, one was much closer. But the obvious and only choice was CG 36383, in Stage Harbor. The close boat—CG 36500—was in Old Harbor, a much shorter run to the *Landry* as the crow flies. But they could not follow the crow to the *Landry* because nothing in the water could cross the thunderous waves crashing down on the Chatham Bar. The storm had sealed Old Harbor. Nothing could challenge the bar and live.

So Masachi, Webber, Melvin G. Gouthro, and Antonio Ballerini set out for the Stage Harbor boat. The lifeboats were 36-foot affairs with a ton of bronze in the keel to keep them stable. A ninety-horsepower gas engine powered them surely, if slowly, through almost any sea. But because every inch of Chatham wharves were devoted to fishing vessels, the rescue boats were moored in the harbors and not kept dockside. So to reach them, the men first had to row out in a 19-foot dory.

Webber looked out at the harbor. Normally, it was quiet and protected. Tonight, it was a foamy torrent of whitecaps and storm currents. They would be rowing directly into the wind and the waves, and it would not be easy. Bernie Webber and Gouthro grabbed the oars and strained toward the CG 36383. They seemed frozen in time and space, hardly moving at all. One stroke forward seemed to carry them two back, so fierce was the wind. Webber's arms were throbbing and seemed pulled from his sockets when they reached the CG 36383. Eagerly the men reached out for the lifeboat—just as the waves hit the little dory dead wrong.

The boat flipped, and the rescuers found themselves in peril. Suddenly, they were in freezing water, gasping in the cold. They reached out, all four of them, and grasped the overturned dory. No one was there to rescue them now, and the danger of hypothermia was upon them. Men sometimes died in just fifteen minutes immersed in such water. But they held on. They toed off their boots, which were heavy with water, and clung to the dory as they drifted in the blizzard. Soon they saw they were drifting not toward the mainland but toward Morris Island, a deserted piece of land with only an old boathouse. Numbed, with teeth chattering, they washed up on Morris Island. The men looked to the boathouse and were moving toward the shelter when Frank Masachi stopped them. Find the oars, he said. Right the boat. Let's carry it down the shore and try this again. The men mumbled in disbelief, but they ought to have expected it. Masachi was old school. He had worked with some of the old surfmen, and every one of them knew those stories. And they knew the motto.

Perhaps Patrick Etheridge represented the tradition the best. The legendary lifesaver—an African American of Pea Island, North Carolina, on the Outer Banks—asked one of his men what the situation was one stormy day in 1898 regarding progress toward the rescue of passengers on a wrecked ship. The man looked out at the wreck, looked at the storm, looked at the huge waves and the rip, and allowed as how, well, they could get out to the wreck fine, but they would never ever make it back.

Etheridge looked as if he was dealing with a dolt. "The Blue Book says we've got to go *out*," he snapped at the man. "It doesn't say a damn thing about having to come *back*." And in truth that is what the "book"— the manual for rescues—said. "The statement of the keeper that he did not try to use the boat because the sea or surf was too heavy will not be accepted unless attempts to launch it were actually made and failed. . . . If the device first selected fails . . . he will resort to one of the others, and if that fails, then to the remaining one, and he will not desist from his efforts until by actual trial the impossibility of effecting a rescue is demonstrated."

And in one of his most famous of rescues, Etheridge did exactly that. At first, Etheridge tried to shoot a line to a wreck. Then he and his men tried rowing. The winds were too strong, the seas too rough. So finally, Etheridge tied lines to his men. They swam out, grabbed the passengers, and swam back through towering seas to safety.

In 1952, the Blue Book passages were exactly the same. Etheridge's words on the beach had morphed through the decades so that a half century later the informal Coast Guard slogan was shorter and simpler.

It went: You have to go out. You don't have to come back. And so, in that cold gale of April 7, 1950, Frank Masachi was seen neither as a zealot nor seriously imbalanced. He was just Coast Guard. With no boots, barefooted, in soaking clothes, in a freezing blizzard, the men carried the dory 200 yards up the shore and set out again for the CG 36383.

Again, they strained against the oars. This time, they strained so hard that the thole pins, the holders of the oars, snapped. The dory veered in the high waves and strong currents and again overturned. The men were again submersed into frigid water and exposed again to hypothermia. They held on again to the dory and washed up again on Morris Island. This time, to the relief of the crew, Frank walked directly to the boathouse and kicked in the door. Thank God they were done, Webber thought.

But then Masachi fired up the gas generator in the boathouse and his bedraggled crew stared back at him in various states of exposure and hypothermia. How was he going to get them out of this, off the island and in front of a warm fire? Was he calling for the DUKW, the amphibious vehicle that motored on land and water?

"Here," Masachi said, or in words very close to these. He had tossed them an old broom. "Use your knives. Whittle new thole pins. We're going back out to the boat." Then he cranked up the magneto telephone and told the rescue operations leaders they were going to try again. Soon they were back at the dory, launching again. This time, the thole pins held. But the oars did not. The very oars themselves cracked and splintered. The boat wheeled wildly and sent the men into the drink again, into the freezing cold water. They took the same frigid commute to the shore and washed up near the boathouse. Again, they banged through the door. Masachi, shivering, cranked the magneto again and called in. He confirmed the fishing vessel was still in peril, and then told his men they needed to keep trying.

Now they were headed to the other lifeboat, the CG 36500, which could only go out over the Chatham Bar. It was a suicide run. They all knew it. Masachi walked his men a mile, barefoot through the snow, to a narrow channel the men could wade. They left Morris Island and on the mainland were picked up by jeep. They made it back to the station, changed to dry clothes, and began to recover from exposure that would have hospitalized a sane man.

Then Masachi gave the orders. They were taking the other boat. They were heading to the CG 36500 and were going to run the Chatham Bar. *He means to kill us,* Webber remembered thinking. *He is taking it personally, and he will aid the* Landry *even it means our lives in the try.* Bernie Webber wished with all his might that this would just go away, that he could run away from it. All of his Coast Guard training had not prepared him for this.

Then they all heard it on the radio and there was no time for thought. The *Landry* had rammed into the lighthouse boat and was damaged. The men on the fishing boat were exhausted. They had spent twenty-four hours fighting to stay alive and could no longer try to moor alongside the lightship. They would just wait for the lifeboat, for Masachi. The transmission propelled Masachi and crew toward the door, and Webber moved to the door too. They had no choice. They had to go out. There were fishermen out there waiting for them, and they lived in a town of fishermen. But then they heard Captain Emro on board the lightship.

"Oh, my God . . ." he said quietly over the radio.

A huge wave had seized the little fishing vessel and spun it around. The *Landry*'s captain came on the radio in a very tired voice. More water was coming on. The men were oh-so-tired. The engine room was flooding.

"Boys," he said at last, "we're going down below to pray and have something to eat. If we die out here, it will be with full stomachs; so long, thank you. God bless you all."

"God be with you," Emro said.

Just a few minutes later, another wave washed over the *Landry* and she and her crew sank quickly beneath the black, storm-tossed sea. There was a stunned silence in the Coast Guard rescue room in Chatham. All four of the rescuers were crushed. Webber could feel a deep ache in his heart. They had failed. He would have gone, he told himself. Wasn't he going when the boat sank?

But however you looked at it, they had failed.

They had failed, and the next day, a contingent of Coast Guard brass from Boston was there to investigate why. The men were questioned sharply, one by one. Then all the rescuers were assembled and the officers from Boston aggressively interrogated them as a group. The chiefs and the enlisted men took it silently without defending themselves. They simply said they were unable to get to the lifeboat, without explanation. They did not go into the repeated attempts. To a Coastie, it sounded like excuses. You have to go out. You *have* to go out.

It was Emro, the captain of the lightship, who finally intervened. A lieutenant was interrogating Masachi, and Emro could take it no more. "*Goddamn it!* Who do you think you are?" he demanded of the officers from Boston.

Emro was thirty years at sea. He wore an old-fashioned Coast Guard uniform with brass buttons turned green by salt spray. He strode into the center of the hearing hall and faced the three officers directly, with eyes flashing under shaggy black-and-gray eyebrows.

How long had they been at sea?

What were they doing that night?

Were they safe in Boston? Were they snug in bed?

Well, Emro wasn't. He was on a very large lightship just inches from the fishing vessel, and the seas were so strong he was lucky to stay afloat himself. And these men were not snug in bed either. They were floating in freezing water. Did the officers know, did the officers care, that the Coast

Guard ship *Hornbeam* also could not make it to the *Landry*? A 180-foot ship couldn't make it, and you're torturing these guys about swamping a 19-foot dory? They did their best.

They set out three times and would have gone four. They were going to shoot the Chatham Bar!

"God*damn* it," Emro said in closing. "Who do you think you are?"

And that was it. It corked the investigation. The officers left shortly after that confrontation. No critical word ever was heard. Except, of course, the words that the men heard in their own heads. Forget the fact that it was an impossible mission. They had failed. Fishermen had died. Each time they passed the *Pollock Rip* lightship, they felt a pang, a twinge of guilt.

And it was true, too, that each time the weather blew hard like it had that night in 1950, the heartache would return to Webber. Whenever, he saw the clouds move in hard and dark from the northeast like that—as they were now, in fact—Webber thought about the *Landry* and what they might have done differently. And how he admired Masachi and wished he could emulate him whenever he could. Webber did not want to have those thoughts about running, about hoping to avoid the dangerous rescues.

He wanted to be as good as Masachi. He wanted to be that brave. He wanted to be just like him.

———

Well, there was a storm moving in now, on this February day of 1952. Soon they would be doing some non-routine work, that was for sure. Masachi had moved on to another assignment aboard a cutter, so they would have to carry on without him. The new guys who came in—Daniel W. Cluff and Donald Bangs—were a little looser than Masachi, a little more laid-back, a little less disciplined. But Webber already had his model in Frank Masachi. He thought about the man a lot, particularly on days like this.

———

February 12–18, 1952
Aboard the Pendleton *and* Fort Mercer

All during the trip north, the *Pendleton* and the *Fort Mercer* steamed steadily in pace with one another, their officers not aware or caring particularly that the other ship was out there. They had no real meaning to each other. Just two ships out of hundreds.

Still, they were inextricably bound. For whether the crews knew it or not, whether the Coast Guard knew it or not, whether anyone cared or not, the two vessels were steaming toward a sort of "double blind" experiment of whether the American Bureau of Shipping was correct in stating that the crack arrestors would work.

The ships were nearly identical, with the same cargoes heading for the same general destination at the same speed. Across the Gulf of Mexico, they sailed in warm temperatures in the seventies, then rounded Florida and made the turn toward New England and colder weather. They were two huge floating containers accompanied by dozens of others in the coastal trade. They moved oil and kerosene that helped power the frigid Northeast during the winter months.

Paetzel, onboard the *Fort Mercer*, knew T-2s had troubles but had faith in the crack arresters. He could see two of them on deck and knew two more were below on the hull. The big steel belts were recommended in 1947 to attempt to stop cracks from spreading in the T-2s. The ships were among the first all-welded vessels produced en masse in the war, and mariners were suspicious of the welding process. Riveted ships with hulls of steel plating, each held together with steel pins, would suffer cracks but rarely casualties. The one plate might crack, but the crack would only run just through the plate, not the entire ship. The rivets would stop the crack, or the next plate over would hold firm.

Not so for the all-welded T-2s, with nary a rivet in place. Welds did not stop cracks as rivets and plate-ends did. Welds might even create cracks, some thought. And once started, the cracks did not stop. They shot around the ship at the speed of sound. The most dramatic example of what could go wrong was the *Schenectady*, a brand-new tanker that had been to sea trials in 1943 and was moored dockside. Without warning, in calm waters, she simply cracked in two. One crack raced through the girth of the ship in seconds and met itself in the middle. The *Schenectady* jackknifed down with her bow and stern pointing toward the sky, still moored dockside. Everyone thought bad welding was the problem. Everyone was pretty much wrong. Welding was visible and villainized, but at best played a bit role. The problem, discovered only years later, lay not in something so obvious or visible, but at the molecular level. In 1954, tests would show conclusively that the steel used in the wartime ships contained too much sulfur and behaved badly in cold water. The steel worked fine in riveted ships, but not in all-welded ships. Not at certain times, at least.

When it became too cold, the metal hulls began behaving differently. It was far less ductile. Normally, steel flexes. The whole ship bends and moves with the sea. But the ductility in this steel ("mild steel" it was called by some, "dirty steel" by others) changed with temperature. The colder it got, the more the steel took on the characteristics of crystal rather than a ductile, flexible metal. It became brittle. Taffy may stretch at room temperature; freeze it and it will shatter when hit with a hammer. In a sense, that is what was happening to the steel in the *Pendleton*'s hull.

At the time the *Pendleton* and the *Fort Mercer* sailed, officials mostly just knew when the ships were most likely to fracture, not why. Mostly those times were (a) when it got cold, and (b) when it got rough.

And now, the *Pendleton* and the *Fort Mercer*, far from the eighty degree weather of Louisiana, were going where it was both rough and cold. They were heading into colder water, and the nature of the steel of the hull was transformed from something that could give and take under the stress of waves to something that caved in and cracked. The two tankers first felt the brunt of the gale as they rounded Long Island on February 16. The storm was bad, but both ships had weathered far worse. Captain Fitzgerald onboard the *Pendleton* saw no need to alter course, nor did Captain Paetzel onboard the *Fort Mercer*. Miles apart, casually aware of each other on their radars, they both kept forward speed with the props rotating between forty-five and sixty-five revolutions per minute, depending on conditions.

They passed Nantucket and Martha's Vineyard and moved north on February 17 as the storm worsened. The two ships came even with Chatham and Bernie Webber's little outpost, noting the lightships that guarded Chatham Bar and Pollock Rip and marked the dangerous currents at the elbow of Cape Cod. There was a new experimental radar machine at the Coast Guard station, and it may have picked up the T-2s as they passed and headed for their ports of call. The new system was glitchy. A technician was there to tweak it, in fact. It worked, then didn't; worked, then didn't.

At Race Point, near the tip of the Cape, the paths of the two ships diverged finally, each heading to her port of call. But once there—the *Pendleton* outside Boston, the *Fort Mercer* outside Portland, Maine—visibility was next to nothing and the storm had worsened.

Independent of one another, each captain came to the same careful decision: Docking in this sort of weather was not worth the risk. It would be much easier to ride out the storm overnight in deep water and come into port on a sunnier day. Ships bumped into things in ports when visibility was so poor. Or they bumped bottom in shallow water if they missed channel markers.

In the deep waters off the Cape lay safety. The ships would pitch and buck in the waves there, but they would come to no harm, as there was nothing hard to hit. The *Fort Mercer* turned south from Maine and took up a position about twenty-five miles off Cape Cod. The *Pendleton* took a similar bearing from Boston and turned her bow into the waves, keeping just enough forward movement to maintain steering and stability. She was a bit farther north of the *Fort Mercer* and a bit closer to the Cape but under full control. Both ships turned slightly into the waves at an angle and kept up power so the bow split the waves. It was a big blow, but each ship had handled much bigger ones.

This was all routine, and the crews of both ships settled into the routine. The deck officers and able seamen stood watch on the forward bridge, four hours on, four hours off, as was the tradition. Farther back in the stern section, the engineers and oilers and wipers toiled deep belowdecks, keeping the boiler fires burning, the steam coming, and the smooth electrical drives turning the powerful props. Someone measured the ocean temperature. It varied between thirty-eight and forty-two degrees that night. The winds were fifty miles per hour, and the waves, some of them, crested at 30 to 45 feet.

Still, this was no big deal. Yes, in years past, thousands of sail vessels had crashed on that leeward shore in storms just like this. A dismasting, a loss of a rudder, a sudden failure of wooden seams, and a ship was quickly blown into the surf line. Running ashore was not salvation; it was ruin.

Ships would drag bottom hundreds of yards from safety, and the waves would pound the ship and the men into the sand.

But that was then and this was now—in the age of steam and power. The *Fort Mercer* and the *Pendleton* took the seas just fine. The strong and sturdy bows would plunge and be buried by the sea, then back into the air, buoyant, triumphant, pointing toward Boston, toward Maine—just waiting for the storm to clear a bit. Most of the crew expected to be on land in two hours. That's where their thoughts were: already on shore.

Chief Engineer Sybert in the engine compartment of the *Pendleton* kept the prop spinning just as Captain Fitzgerald had signaled him with a series of bells that were activated by wires that ran from the forward bridge to the engine room astern. Sometimes Fitzgerald would ring to speed up, sometimes to slow down. The bells told the engine room what the bridge desired. She was handling nicely, Sybert thought, but early in the morning, before 5 a.m., a heavy sea washed over the poop deck. It was nothing really, but notable enough to call to the bridge. If they changed watch and sent seamen back from the forward bridge to the stern quarters, they could be in real trouble. Sybert told Fitzgerald something like, "We've got seas over the poop deck; best not to send anyone back aft on the catwalk else they might get drenched."

Fitzgerald acknowledged the seas; he had already seen them. He told Sybert that he had sent the seamen down to get coffee in the forward salon. But thanks for the heads up. Thus did little decisions above the decks of the *Pendleton* affect the fate of the crew as, below the decks, in the hull itself, very small changes in the steel would have a profound impact upon them all.

The men may have been warm aboard the *Pendleton*, but the *Pendleton*'s steel was far too cold. And with 35-foot waves, that steel was most certainly being hammered and stressed. It was cold. It was rough. The two factors that accompanied most T-2 crack-ups weren't just present, they were prevalent.

At around 5:50 a.m., Sybert felt the ship take a heavy lurch. There was an explosive bang, very loud. Then Sybert felt an even heavier lurch, and the explosive sound this time was even louder than the first bang.

Others felt it more than heard it: a sound, a force, a pulse of energy. Another said it was a tearing sound. They were not sure what it was, only that "it" was not good.

"Did it take five minutes?" one of the men was asked later.

"Five seconds," he replied.

Sybert felt the ship roll heavily and take a list to port. Then she straightened. It was normal again. Thank God everything seemed okay. The one problem was he could not reach the captain to find out what Fitzgerald wanted done, to see what had happened. The signals were dead, and so were the phones. Had they run aground? Struck something? Sybert needed instructions now.

How fast? How slow? Forward? Reverse? What did Captain Fitzgerald want? There were no bells.

So Sybert dispatched oilier Tchuda W. Southerland to the deck to see if he could make his way forward to contact Fitzgerald. "Ask the captain what we should do," Sybert said, "but be careful on the catwalk moving forward." The waves had been breaking over the ship at times.

And when Southerland got topside, he was careful. He ran slowly forward toward the bridge against the ripping gale—and found there was not a forward there. He gaped out at the emptiness where the forward part of the ship had been and then was distracted. Another ship was close by them. Too close. He stood on the stern section of the *Pendleton* and looked at the bow of the second ship. Painted there clear as day was the word "Pendleton."

But *he* was on the *Pendleton*, and there was a split second before he understood that he was looking at the free-floating bow of his ship, and that the *Pendleton* had split in two at the number 7 and 8 tanks.

About the same time, pumpman James E. Young was awakened from sleep and thought the ship had just taken a heavy lurch. He went to the mess, where everyone else was. "The ship's split," they said. He did not believe it and rushed topside. Instantly, he was scared. The gale knocked him about, and the wind and ice and snow stung him. And there was the bow. Unmistakably. He rushed back down to confirm the bad news to Sybert.

Sybert already knew it. He had glanced out from his cabin through the porthole there and seen an odd sight. It was the bow of the *Pendleton*.

He could see Fitzgerald there. It was unmistakably the captain. He was fighting to keep his balance, grabbing for the rail as the bow pitched and bucked in the waves. Sybert took stock. The officers were stranded on the front part of the ship, the bow section. The engineers and most of the crew were in the stern section.

Circuit breakers had kicked out all electricity to the forward part of the vessel, while the machinery in the rear continued as if normal. The stern section resembled a hotel that had had one wall blown away. The cross section of the ship was exposed to the elements but still functioning and to an extent seaworthy, even in a gale.

Sybert kept up steam, ordered watertight hatches closed, and closed down the electrical power for a moment as a precaution. Then he summoned everyone to the mess room.

All of them waited for an explosion. Their kerosene and heating oil had sprung from the tanks when the ship halves separated. Hell, they were tanker men. Death by explosion was foreordained. But the fire never came. The wind was too strong. It whipped away the fumes. Or the break—so complete and large—dispelled the fumes quickly so no magical and deadly mixture of oxygen, gas vapors, and spark created the traditional tanker bomb. For these things the men on the stern could be thankful.

The officers on the bow, on the other hand, were in a different world—without time for an SOS, without time for anything. The men were stranded on the bridge of the ship with no way to life rafts or lifeboats. The bow pitched and bucked at a forty-five-degree angle to the sea. It was buffeted, swept and raked by heavy seas. What had been the command center of the ship was now more like a beach at storm tide. Breakers swept over it. The bow-half bobbed about, tilting evermore toward a vertical plane. On the stern, Sybert brought power back up. He discovered he could actually steer the ship—a bit. He had power. He had a rudder. She would buck and heave, but for brief moments he could control the ship.

The thought had to strike Sybert there and then. It was strange, but there it was. He was master of a ship, his half-ship. He had given a command, maneuvered her, and she responded. He was a master. He took command. But there was one problem with that—and he quickly confessed it. He gathered all the survivors in the mess and told it to them straight: "Boys, our officers are gone and you able-bodied seamen are going to have to pick up the slack. I know engines. Don't know much about navigation, lifeboats, and seamanship in general."

Quickly, he found that one able-bodied seaman, Jacob Hicks, and another, Ray Steele, would take leadership positions. He came to think of Hicks as a makeshift chief mate, the ranking deck officer.

Did Sybert want them to check the lifeboats? Yes, Sybert said, but he thought the best thing to do was remain on board the stern section of the ship if it seemed seaworthy. Others were dispatched to close all water-tight doors. Sybert and his engineers checked the salinity of the boilers to see if too much seawater had leaked in. Hicks and Steele scrambled up on the deck, and what they saw and felt there was disheartening. The gale was now a full-blown screeching storm with winds of fifty miles per hour and more. It would reach more than seventy before the night was through, reports said, sometimes clocked at eighty. You had to lean into a wind like that just to stand steady. They struggled to reach the lifeboats and, once there, prepared them for launch. But below them—sometimes over them—soared waves of 35 to 45 feet. Launching a lifeboat into such mountains of water would be fearsome work. It would be a miracle just to get a boat out there without the sea splintering it. Once launched, how long could a small lifeboat remain afloat?

They seemed stuck staying with the stern. They looked across the water toward the bow. The bow and all the deck officers on it were carried swiftly away from the stern by the mountainous waves. The bow section was still afloat, but increasingly it rose at an angle to the plane of the sea, lifting the bow to the sky, plunging the bridge and deckhouse down toward the bottom. In fifteen to twenty minutes, the bow disappeared from view, bobbing away into the rain and snow, invisible to the men on the stern now.

Sybert was certain they would get help soon. The radioman had almost certainly sent an SOS from the bridge. It took time for it to sink in that this was improbable and that no one on shore was aware any of this was happening. Slowly, they were understanding the fix they were in. The splitting of the ship was clear enough; the ramifications of the split less so. Yes, the captain and most deck officers were located toward the front of the ship in a structure that rose from the deck and gave them a clear view ahead. The engineers and engine room were located aft. So the officers were gone, but the clean fracture had wrought even worse chaos. The bow had the radio but no power; Sybert's new half-ship had the power but no radio.

Sybert did the math. The ship had split apart in about five seconds. There could not have been time, no time at all, to understand what was happening and send out a signal. Sybert thought they were close to shore. They had been nearly twenty-five miles offshore due east of northern Cape Cod, but their drift was south and west now, which would take them quickly toward the elbow of Cape Cod, toward Chatham. That fact had been a blessing initially and somehow comforting. But now? He could maneuver the stern section a bit, but he knew they were drifting *too* rapidly toward shore—the Cape Cod shore, where so many thousands of wrecks had washed up. If he attempted to steer and control too aggressively, the ship would pitch and lurch. There was little he could do other than go with the flow and steer to keep the stern section straight. He could not steam her farther out to sea, just keep her straight as she drifted.

Every time he attempted to steer and maneuver, he could, briefly, but the forward exposed part of the stern dipped down and got drenched. Above him, on deck, Hicks dug out a flare gun from the lifeboat. He pointed it skyward, and the flare arched out over the water into the darkness. Perhaps they would be spotted visually from shore. Perhaps the officers on the bow would respond with a flare back. He took out another flare cartridge and aimed it skyward. The cartridge fizzled and popped but did not fire. From the bow, no reply came at all. Hicks looked at the date stamped on the flares: July 1942. He threw the dud flare into the water after it had fizzled. He loaded another. No luck. No signals. He took smoke markers from the lifeboat and lit them, then tossed them overboard. They put out a pathetic smudge of smoke that was quickly whipped away to nothing in the gale.

No radio. No flares. No smoke. No blinker lights for sending code.

No one who could send or understand code, either.

No one knew they were out there. No one knew they were in trouble.

No one had any way of finding out.

Well, there was one way, one ancient way.

Aaron Powell, a wiper, rigged up a line to the steam whistle. Another wiper was too small a man to work the rig himself; it took some heft to pull the line. So Powell drafted George "Tiny" Myers, an OS, ordinary seaman. He weighed more than three hundred pounds, not much of it muscle, it had to be said, but Tiny had plenty of spirit and enough weight to heave that whistle lanyard.

They were not sure what the true navigational whistle signals were for their situation but kept blowing and blowing and blowing. The danger signal was all Powell knew . . . a series of short blasts. They would blast out four short signals and then pause to listen for any reply.

There was none. They were alone.

—◆—

February 18, 1952
With Webber—evening

Webber's little boat was heading straight down the wave and toward the bottom of the ocean when finally the propellers, thrown hard into reverse, caught and helped slow the boat. At the bottom of the wave, in the valley of the watery mountain, the bow broke through the water and was buried. But buoyancy brought the boat back up quickly. Webber slammed the gear into forward, and the CG 36500 now began to crawl slowly *up* the new mountain of a wave in front of her. *So now what?* Webber thought. They had survived the bar and were cruising up and down the huge storm rollers. But their compass was gone. They were in pitch darkness and blizzard whiteout simultaneously. Radio contact was spotty at best. Webber just pointed the boat where he thought the *Pollock Rip* lightship *might* be. He could get directions from there.

They were all shivering, all very cold and wet. Webber lost track of time. In the darkness, he peered out through his shattered windshield. At times he saw lights out there, and then realized light was playing off shards of glass stuck near his eyes, still embedded there in bone. He tried to pluck them out. Some came loose. Others broke off. Still others could not be budged.

His plan was to head for the *Pollock Rip* lightship, but he was having no luck finding it. He radioed in, but there was no reply. After a time, he saw a shadow that was darker than the darkness. It creeped him out at first; it was spooky and made him uncomfortable. He slowed the boat, nearly to a stop. "Turn on the spotlight," Webber told a crew member.

Someone scrambled out on the bow and switched the light on, but a wave caught the bow of the boat and the crewmember was tossed in the air, just gone. Then a second later, there was a large thump in the boat. When Webber looked, the crewmember was back, claimed by the sea but then spat back on the boat. Webber had no time to check on the man's condition.

He was in a world of spook and wonder, danger too for that matter. He motored slowly forward and saw what he took to be the entrance to a tunnel, a tunnel they were headed into. Broken and twisted steel and wires marked the entrance to this tunnel, and it rose up in the water with each wave and then settled back, exhaling masses of foam. Each time it rose, waterfalls cascaded from it. Each time it fell, Webber thought, the clang of loose steel sounded as if the "tunnel" were groaning in pain. It had to be the *Pendleton*.

Warily, Bernie maneuvered the CG 36500. He moved along the port side of the hulk. There were no signs of life. Up above, steel railings were bent like pipe cleaners. All this way they had come, and no one was left alive, Webber thought. His heart sank at the uselessness of their effort.

He turned the spotlight on the stern and confirmed what they had found. The word "Pendleton" was painted on the ship's hull. Then he rounded the hull and saw what looked like lights up there on the starboard side of the deck. Webber saw the lights, then one man. He looked as tiny as an ant. Webber said to himself, *Holy shit! The four of us came all this way for one man.*

Then the man left the rail, but why? Webber soon found out. Dozens of men crowded to the railing and yelled down to Webber, cheering. Webber looked up at the scene in absolute and utter awe. Men ringed the rail of the ship and sent up a weak cheer. The cheer swept over the Coast Guardsmen like warm rain. It made their spines tingle, and they all felt a surge of pride and adrenaline. Webber thought for a moment on how this all would work now. Now that they were here, how would they take them down? His answer came in the form of the Jacob's ladder fluttering and banging down the side of the hull as the ship pitched.

Bernie brought the boat in closer to the ladder. He peered up at the ship and could not help but think it. Guys, we should go *up* the ladder and wait for help. That half-ship seemed a lot sturdier than did the CG 36500.

But he said nothing. He did not have time to. Already, men were clambering down the ladder. The tanker men were coming home.

⌐✦⌐

February 18, 1952
The Pendleton *stern and the CG 36500—8:00 p.m.*

Steele and Hicks and James Young, the chief pumpman, tossed the Jacob's ladder over the side. It twisted and fouled and they had to hoist it back up. The second time, the ladder accordioned out down the side of the ship's hull and dangled into the waves below. Normally, the departure would be in terms of seniority, with the lowest rank going first and the officers staying behind. But this was a perilous venture—not an easy trip down a flight of stairs, but an unknown descent into fierce seas.

So Steele, it was decided, would go first. The able-bodied seaman was just that—as fit as anyone there. He would chart the way down. Over he went. He did not like the top of the ladder. It seemed rotten both in rope and wood. But he did not tarry at the top. Down he went, with 4-

to 5-foot gaps between the wooden plank steps. You had to have some upper body strength to do this. Hold on as you reached down with your foot almost an entire body length to the next plank. Slide down a bit with your hands, feet dangling for purchase on the next rung.

And the rock and the roll of the ship and the sea made it like no trip off a ship Steele had ever experienced. The ship listed to port, so at times the ladder was close in to the starboard side of the hull. Then the ship would rock and he would swing out then slam back into the hull. The waves were a force that changed like swirling clouds. One moment, Steele would look up and 20 feet above his head, he would see a wave curling like a house of liquid. Then it would drop with a *woomph* as the cycle moved past and he would look down into a valley, a hole really, that was now 20 feet *below* his head.

There was no fixed point if he looked out there. And there was nothing much he could do but keep going down. The last step was a tough one: two lengths down, for a plank was missing. But when he got to the bottom rung, there was the CG 36500. Webber had timed it perfectly. He had made his pass just as Steele hit the bottom, and the seaman, taken by the arms by the crew, stepped gingerly aboard the small boat.

Once onboard, Steele saw how bad it was. These were not so much "passes" that Webber was making at the ship. It was more like a bumper car. The wooden boat would slam into the hull, bounce off, and Webber would bring it around again.

Harnessed still to the wheel, the young coxswain needed three hands to run the CG 36500: one for the wheel, one for the throttle and speed, one for the direction and gearshift of the boat. He was in constant motion, and the shifting, the turning, none of it was on automatic power.

Each shift, turn, and gear change took real physical effort.

"Where are your fenders?" Steele yelled to the crewmen. Where are the padded protectors that boats carried to protect against damage when moored at dockside? "Below," one of the crewmembers said, and Steele scurried down, found them, fetched them topside, and rigged a few in place, hoping they would protect the CG 36500.

Above him, the rope was crowded with men descending. Hicks, still on deck, had seen Steele make his passage and decided that the older and weaker should go first now. They stood a better chance the sooner they were off and the fewer people were on the boat.

So down they came. And Webber, looking up, thought to himself, *My God, how many of them are there?* The CG 36500 was rated to carry twenty. There were a hell of a lot more than twenty. He would have to make two trips.

And he knew the futility of that thought. Even if he and his men and his boat could physically make the run, the *Pendleton* stern would not last. It was listing ever more precariously. Bernie had no desire to climb upon this hulk now. She was about to go over.

He made a decision then, a resolution and vow to himself: *Either we all make it out, or none of us do. If there are fifty men up there, we try for all fifty. No one gets left behind.* The men continued down the ladder. Some of them timed the boat just right. Above them, engineer Edward Gallagher and others would wait for the right synch of wave, boat, and man on the ladder and yell, "Jump!" Most times, this worked.

When it didn't, Bernie's crew was right there. If someone missed the boat, well, Livesey, Fitzgerald, and Maske were right there. They were filled with adrenaline. They would reach down, singly and together, and grab a man by his jacket, his arms, his belt, and give a mighty hoist.

Most were sent below. They needed to pack in passengers carefully now if they were to have any chance of handling everyone. The system was working methodically. Bernie would maneuver, be hurled toward the ship, back off in reverse, gun the engines, swerve in, swing the wheel, heave-to under the ladder—and the men jumped. The ladder swerved and banged and skipped about. It dunked them up and down in the ocean as if they were tea bags. But they all came down. For those who hit the water, it was tuna fishing time. They were hurled on board, then sent below.

Six men were left on top when Aaron Ponsel and Tiny Myers were next down the ladder. All night, they had been blowing the whistle. Now it was time to leave. Ponsel scampered down easily and ran to the stern of the ship, ready to go below. He turned to see Tiny cumbersomely ease down the ladder. He was very heavy and very tired, with little strength left. The 4 to 5 feet in between rungs were a struggle for him. Waves slammed against him, and it seemed as if he had lost his pants up there. The ladder would bow out with the sway of the half-ship, and then slam Tiny hard back against the steel hull. Webber thought he could hear the big man groan. It was a bizarre scene, this huge man, nearly naked, struggling down the ladder.

And then Myers came to the bottom rung of the ladder, the last rung. The one that was a double length away from the next one up because a rung was missing. Strength seemed to go out of the big man then, and he hit the last rung with his feet and then with his knees. He was kneeling on the last rung, but it all looked lined up. The boat was there. "Jump!" someone yelled. It was unclear whether Tiny jumped or slipped.

The boat was there. And then it was not. Wave action pulled it away and Tiny hit a part of the boat, then went into the water. Immediately, hands were on him. Not just the CG 36500 crew but the hands of the crew of the *Pendleton* as well. They had him. They could get him. But they could not get him into the boat. He could not lift his leg up over the gunnels; he had no strength or energy left. And when they reached down to grab him, they could get no good purchase. His pants and belt, a normal grasping point, were gone. His jacket let them lift him up, but not over. Water-soaked as he was, the men were attempting to deadlift four hundred pounds or so.

So they held him there. All the time, other men were coming down.

Some hit the boat. Some missed it. Bernie needed to maneuver to reach them. They were coming whether he wanted them to or not. Young, the pumpman, was one of the men grabbing Tiny when a wave picked up the boat and jammed it toward the hull.

"Watch out, you are going to hit your head on the ship!" Steele yelled out. Young kept hold of Tiny Myers, and Steele grabbed and pulled him back. Tiny slipped down as the boat rammed against the hull, and against Tiny. Richard Livesey, the CG 36500 crewmember, still had a hand on Tiny, and his hand was crushed between the boat and the hull. He let go.

The crew caught Tiny with their spotlight. They could still see him. He was floating. They were perilously close to the ship's hull. Men were still coming down and landing on the boat, landing in the water. Tiny drifted toward the propeller of the ship. Webber could see him; he was still alive, and their eyes locked. It was a look from Tiny, Webber thought, that said, "It's okay. It's okay."

There was only one way to get to Tiny, Webber thought, and that was to ease the bow to him and have the crew grab him. Myers was in a narrow area of the ship near the prop, and the CG 36500 could not approach him broadside.

So he turned the bow toward Tiny, eyes on his eyes the entire time. And then the sea caught the CG 36500 and pushed her forward against Myers's chest and crushed the big man against the stern of the *Fort Mercer*.

The impact on the crew was devastating. But they could not tarry. There were still men coming down, still live men in the water. The crew turned the searchlight away from Tiny Myers and toward the living.

David A. Brown, the first assistant engineer, was the last man down the ladder. He made a smooth descent. Sybert was already on board; along with Bernie and the others, they directed the men here and there, packing them into whatever spaces were available.

Webber confirmed there were no more men on board. He made a head count and confirmed it with Sybert. They had thirty-two men out of thirty-three on board.

Webber keyed the mike on his radio and made history with those simple words. This is the CG 36500, he said in effect, and we have thirty-two of thirty-three survivors from the stern of the *Pendleton*. We are heading home.

Behind them, before they left, just twenty minutes after the last man was down, the stern of the *Pendleton* took another list, creaked and groaned as tanks collapsed. Then it capsized and rolled sideward into the sea, its decks awash.

———

February 18, 1952
With Webber—late evening

There was exuberance and disbelief in the Chatham Coast Guard station when Webber's radio message came through. Impossible! They had figured Webber for dead.

But the glee was quickly replaced by rapid-fire questions, both from the Coast Guard station and the Coast Guard cutters attending to the *Fort Mercer*. "Send him out to sea and we will take the passengers off on a cutter," one officer said. Another disagreed, and there was an argument over jurisdiction, over rank, over anything.

Webber, twenty-four years old, was shivering and near exhaustion. These guys weren't helping. He did not have to think about it this time. There is a time to follow the book and a time to throw it away. They were going to guide him in? They didn't know where *he* was; he didn't know where *they* were. How was that supposed to work? One of the officers on the big cutters directed him to come alongside the cutter and transfer the seamen to the cutter. How was *that* going to work? He had just done the near-impossible getting these men *down* a ladder and *off* a ship. Many of them had fallen. How was he going to get them *up* a ladder in these waters? He did not think they would fall up.

They weren't here. He was. Bernie Webber, so easily led in his youth, was leading now. He reached to the radio and then simply flipped it off.

He knew where *he* was going. He was going home to Chatham. He was heading home to Miriam. But most of all he knew he was responsible for thirty-two souls saved from the sea. That's how he thought of it. He had thirty-two souls at sea to save, and no one else could make the right calls now. He raised his voice above the wind and said something close to this: "Fellas, here's what we're going to do. We got out here heading into the sea and we will get out of here with the seas on our butt. We will hit land sometime somewhere that way. If we have to beach, get ready to get out quickly."

The word was passed along throughout the boat to those who did not hear it. And from the packed mass of *Pendleton* crewmembers, someone said, "We're with you, Coxswain!" And then spontaneously a cheer arose from the rescued seamen.

They motored on for an hour. The engine would die at times; the gravity feed was too jostled to get gas to the engine, and Fitzgerald would crawl in, burn himself, and prime the pump. They would sputter and motor on in silence. Bernie figured the worst that could happen is they would hit land and a beach somewhere and he'd just run it aground. Or they would drift into Nantucket Channel and relative shelter, then know where they were.

Webber had no idea where he was. In deep water, the waves were steep but spaced far apart, with wide valleys in between the mountains of water. So he knew he was still at sea. The boat itself was silent. Men were packed everywhere. They shivered. They clung to the boat. But they did not talk. There was the low roar of the motor, the screech still of the wind, and the crash and slap of waves as they crested over the covered deck. Time passed and the scene was unchanged. Webber wondered what he had done and what he was doing. Had he made the right decisions?

Then he noticed that the waters had changed. The big waves and broad valleys of the ocean became rougher and the cycles shorter. The waves were not quite as big as the at-sea soaring rollers nor as rhythmic or patterned. The seas became "confused," in the parlance of mariners, and Bernie knew he was now heading into shallower water. They pitched and yawed, and it seemed to a few of the men onboard that they touched bottom at least twice. Definitely, they were in the shallows now. Livesey and some seamen were packed together like sardines at the back of the boat, and water kept washing over them, sometimes over their heads. Livesey was having trouble breathing. He hoped Bernie knew where he was. He didn't. Webber knew only that they had reached shallower water. But where? Bernie thought perhaps North Beach, an isolated area where they could find little shelter from this cold and little refuge for his cargo of frozen souls.

Then Bernie began hallucinating again, or he thought he was. He thought he saw a red light. But he had thought he had seen lights before, only to find out the shards of glass in his head were playing tricks of reflection on him.

Now this time? It was a flashing red light. Truly he was seeing things. For the light would be high above him at one moment. He'd look again and it was below him in the sea. It was in the sky, then it was in the sea. *It's the glass, the snow, the salt spray, all playing tricks on me*, he concluded. *I've got to stay calm here.*

But the red light persisted, and Bernie knew what it had to be. There was an aircraft warning light on the Chatham RCA radio station tower.

To be that high up in the sky, it had to be the RCA tower. The bad news was they seemed headed toward North Beach and isolation. What was the next step there? How could he give them shelter there?

Well, it was *something*, and Bernie steered toward the light. Up in the air he could see it one moment, then far below another. This was perplexing. The light was not behaving like a tower beacon at all. They seemed to be approaching the light in the water, and when they got a bit closer, Bernie told his crew to shine a searchlight toward the light. There was utter surprise, then elation. The searchlight caught a buoy. The light was on a buoy, and Bernie had enough time in these waters to know which buoy. It was the buoy on the *inside* of the Chatham Bar. That choppy water they crossed *was* the bar. The light in the sky and then down below was the buoy bobbing up with the monstrous waves then down into the valley of the waves.

Now they were in safe waters—or at least safer waters. They had somehow found their way back through the storm and retraced their rough course out. Now all Bernie had to do was navigate the twists and turns of the channel and he was home-free.

Once in this smoother water beyond the bar and inside the harbor, Bernie Webber keyed his radio and said: "This is CG 36500. We're inside the harbor heading to the Chatham Fish Pier."

There was shock and disbelief that the CG 36500 had reached the harbor. It lasted about two seconds before Webber again got a series of confusing instructions on the radio. He was to turn this way, then that way. Webber instinctively followed the first few commands, and then realized someone was trying to guide him in with the experimental radar. Everyone wanted to show that the expensive new equipment was of some help.

Webber did not try to be polite. He called the watchtower and said essentially that the only help he needed was when they got back to the fish pier. Perhaps someone could be there to help the survivors. Then he snapped the radio off again. He knew these waters. He was here; they weren't.

Steadily through the harbor, the CG 36500 parted through the calmer waves. The crew and the survivors could all see the lights of the

Chatham Fish Pier. Now the little boat came to life. Some of the survivors were thanking God aloud. Others were sobbing. Many more were talking with each other rapidly. Many of them were crammed together down below, knowing only that they were in calmer waters.

Bernie looked up at the pier as they motored in.

From a distance, it looked like the whole town was there.

For the first time in more than twelve hours, Webber felt warmth. It flooded over him. Warmth and a strange comfort.

Bandit

Gerald R. Hoover

THE NIGHT OF JANUARY 18, 1991, STARTED LIKE EVERY OTHER DUTY night, but was quickly seared into my memory because of a 63-foot shrimp boat named *Bandit*. I came on my duty at noon. My watch, and that of my fellow Coasties, would last for twenty-four hours. In the early afternoon, we might go on a training flight or perform scheduled inspections of the helicopters, keeping our skills sharp while waiting to be called upon.

Late that afternoon, the National Weather Service had issued a gale warning, and we could see from the low-slung clouds speeding by and shaking leaves on the trees that the report was true. The rain arrived later, creating a symphony of cymbals on the hangar's aluminum roof.

Like overprotective owners of fancy sports cars, we pamper our helicopters, knowing we must rely on them for our lives. We would surely do so that January day. Before the worst of the weather crossed our tarmac, we put the HH-65 Dolphin helicopters in the safety of the large hangar, closing the giant garage door. While all eighty persons assigned to Air Station New Orleans must report to work each day, only a small number of us stay the night. On this night, there were four enlisted men standing overnight duty: watch captain, flight mechanic, rescue swimmer, and line crewman.

Once the long day was done, we generally watched a movie, prepared for dinner, or shot the breeze. Most air stations operate like fire departments, providing single beds known as racks in sleeping quarters for the crews. At Air Station New Orleans, the bunkrooms were on the second deck over the hangar, with a kitchen and TV room downstairs. The quarters had recently been refurbished so that they looked like simple hotel rooms; the only thing missing was room service. The small single beds, two to a room, provided little more than a place to lay our heads while we waited to be called. That night, in view of the heavy rain and stout winds, I remember thinking I should turn in early, but the opportunity never came.

I had been standing duty for three years before *Bandit* entered my life. My unit usually responded to four hundred search and rescue (SAR) cases per year and each one I took part in transformed my helicopter into a classroom, the events becoming my teachers. Some cases became routine—mistaken flare sightings, prank calls, and the like—but others called for true grit. The weather wasn't the only cause for search and rescue. Thirty thousand oilrig workers made a living offshore, and we were often called on to be an ambulance service. On that particular January night, by the time the yellow tractor had rolled into the barn, I felt sure we would see some action. In fact, the events leading up to our launch were already beginning to take place just fifty miles away.

The captain of the *Bandit* was using the ship's wooden steering wheel to try and control the boat, whispering prayers as he struggled to keep his livelihood afloat. They were floundering in 15-foot seas created by fifty-five knot onshore winds. As they approached land, the waves piled close together, increasing the pounding effect. The uninhabited barrier island was about five miles off the Mississippi coast. These barrier islands are little more than sandbars with hearty, brushy growth of sea grapes and palm trees. The *Bandit* was heading for a cut of water known as Ship Island Pass, but more water was coming over the bow than the pumps could handle. The captain, John G. Crawford of Pearl River, Louisiana, broadcast a Mayday at about 7:50 p.m.

The radio watch stander at Coast Guard Station Gulfport, Mississippi, received the distress call over the open airwaves of Channel 16, the international hailing and distress frequency. The Coast Guard's main means of rescue was a 41-foot aluminum-hulled boat, powered by twin turbo-charged Cummins diesel engines. These boats are identified by their hull numbers, the first two of which indicate the length. Within the organization, they are called 41s. They are designed to respond to any mission in seas of eight feet or less and are the backbone of small boat stations across the country. Waves larger than eight feet place the crew in extreme danger, and the boat becomes unstable. The counterbalanced, lead-bottomed, and, therefore, self-righting 47-footers are used in heavier seas.

"We're taking waves over the bow. My pumps can't keep up," Crawford told Station Gulfport.

"What's the weather like where you are?" the watch stander's voice came back, and Crawford described the conditions as another voice from over the radioman's shoulder instructed, "Hit the SAR alarm and launch the 41." This voice belonged to the officer of the day (OOD), the enlisted man in charge of the small boat station. He then calculated the distance from the small boat station to the *Bandit*, in this case about twenty-five miles. He then factored in the weather and came to a troubling conclusion.

"I don't think the 41 will make it in time." He knew the 41 would take an hour to reach the boat at its top speed of twenty-six knots, but in the current conditions the coxswain (the enlisted person trained to operate the boat) would have to slow the boat to keep it afloat, stretching the time to several hours.

"Let me talk to the captain and get District on the horn. We're going to need a helicopter." The OOD keyed the microphone button and said, "Captain, we are getting our boat under way right now. Do you have lifejackets on board?"

"A hard foam ring with mesh net in the bottom," Crawford answered, knowing the Coast Guardsman was thinking that the *Bandit* would sink, and he and his crew would have to abandon ship. In other words, they were in deep trouble.

"I'm going to ask you to do something unorthodox," the OOD said. "If you feel it is safe to do so, I want you to beach your boat on Ship

Island." His wall-mounted chart showed this barrier island to the west of the cut they were trying to navigate.

"Uh, Coast Guard," Crawford said, "I think my wife Mattie is having a heart attack. Please hurry, she has a history of heart problems, and the stress is getting to her."

Meanwhile the radioman was calling the SAR coordinator at the Rescue Center at District headquarters in New Orleans. The SAR coordinator, buried deep in a room full of charts, radios, and monitors on the Coast Guard grounds near downtown, has an up-to-the-minute report on the status of every Coast Guard boat and aircraft within the District. It is his job to use those assets wisely. Each SAR case initiates a sequence of events, and it is the coordinator's job to take whatever steps he deems proper. In this case, one of his first steps was to request the launch-ready helicopter. That was us.

The air station is in Belle Chasse, just south of the greater New Orleans area, about twenty miles from the SAR coordinator's office. Until he called our operations desk, we were unaware of the events unfolding out at sea, but once that call came through, an alert over the public address system sent us jumping.

"Put the ready helo on the line. Shrimper taking on water off Ship Island."

The watch captain bellowed instructions as we launched the small tow tractor to the tow bar on the nose of the aircraft. The line crewman held the button that opened the hangar door as the pilots charted the position of the *Bandit*. The flight mechanic and I raced with our gear toward the helicopter's open door. The pilots followed closely behind us. The aircraft commander, as the person in charge, bears the responsibility for every man in the crew and for those below. The copilot, still learning the tricks of the flying trade, is also the primary navigator and troubleshooter, which allows the aircraft commander to concentrate on flying. The flight mechanic is the single most important position in the aircraft; they are the hoist operators. The rest of us could not complete our part of the mission without them.

The twin engine HH-65A is a French-built Aerospatiale helicopter originally designed as a corporate transport helicopter. It was a modified version of this aircraft that we were about to pile into. It replaced the aging single-engine Sikorsky H-52 Sea Guard, which had a top speed of eighty knots; the HH-65A can double that. The new aircraft was also very agile and almost able to complete a barrel roll. It was fun to fly. But the HH-65 was not necessarily the best aircraft for the many other duties. The Coast Guard had bought ninety-six of them when catching drug runners was our priority, and its limitations would make our job a little more difficult that night. The working space inside the aircraft is only about six feet long and a little over three feet wide, leaving little room for survivors. It's great with speed, but we needed that greater power to hoist multiple survivors. We could hoist two or three as long as the aircraft's tanks were not full of fuel, but we often had more survivors than we could hoist. The way I saw it, the Coast Guard had bought a sports car when what they really needed was a pickup.

The four of us jumped in, strapping the five-point harnesses around our bodies. Over the static of the internal communication system (ICS), I heard the pilot's metallic voices as they ticked off the items on the start-up checklist. Soon the whine of the engine and the thump of the blades became a steady beat. During start-up, I always tried to answer only direct questions so as to not create any distractions, taking this time to mentally complete my own checklist. "Did I forget my fins?" But once the blades started beating, my heart started pumping.

In the air, the aircraft commander briefed us, as much as he knew, on the mission at hand. As happens on many SAR cases, especially in severe weather conditions, the difference between what is reported and what is actually happening can be significant. We looked forward through the windshield as we sped towards the *Bandit*, and could see the rain reflecting the flashing position light on the aircraft—beyond that, nothing.

While we were bouncing through unstable air, buffeted by wind gusts and pelted by rain, the SAR coordinator completed another required step, an Urgent Marine Broadcast, which calls all ships in the area to help an endangered boat if they can. The captain of the gambling ship *Europa Jet* was just a few miles from the *Bandit* and made top speed toward the stricken fishing boat. Within minutes of answering the hail, Captain John M. Foretich, a mariner with thirty-three years of experience, was piloting his big ship as close as possible, but he could not follow the sinking boat into the shallows. Knowing that lives were in danger, he lowered a small boat with his ship's doctor on board; the waves crashed over the exposed boat and slammed into the side of the bigger ship. Fearing for the safety of his own crew, Captain Foretich gave up and ordered the boat back on board. Deciding the only other thing he could do was to block the relentless winds and sledgehammering seas, he turned his ship sideways. The ship took heavy rolls while attempting to provide a lee, and in the darkened night he hoped to provide some relief, while the gamblers played on.

We arrived overhead of the *Bandit* within an hour of receiving the call from the District SAR coordinator. On scene, we discovered the boat heeling to port about forty-five degrees, waves breaking over the stern, the deck and pilothouse awash. It was resting on the sandy bottom, but the rear of the boat was still being lifted and dropped by the breaking seas. The bow of the ship had been pushed hard aground, almost on the beach, raising it higher than the stern. The waves were ramming the stern of the boat like a wrecking ball, green and white water exploding in spray toward the bow.

"I'm going to make a low, slow pass overhead, I want everybody to take a good look," Lieutenant Tim Rourke ordered. He was the aircraft commander and sure of himself. "It looks like the only clear hoisting site is the bow."

The pounding waves obscured the aft portion of the *Bandit*. With the bow slightly raised, however, we agreed that the flight mechanic should lower me on the hoist cable down to the bow, where I was to release from the cable and prepare the survivors for the rescue.

"I can hit that, no problem," the flight mechanic said. "We just need to be careful of the steel cable running from the mast to the bow."

Rourke said, "Good call; I didn't even see it until you pointed it out," then turned his attention to me and said, "Jerry, the boat is tilting to port pretty good; I think we can keep you off the cable, but you'll have to fend for yourself if we get too close."

"No sweat. Let's do it. Do you want to hoist all four or what?"

"Let's get the heart-attack patient first and transport. We don't have the power or the room to get all four. And, Jerry, I want you to go with the patient during transport. The rest of the crew will have to wait until we get back."

"Understood."

The plan sounded so simple until I leaned into the open helicopter door, hearing the moan of the wind and feeling the sharp stinging rain on my face. The *Bandit* was making sounds like breakfast cereal—snap, crackle, pop. I yanked the ICS cord from my helmet and waited for the hand signal from the flight mechanic. The rotor's high-pitched scream assaulted my ears—for me, it's a comforting sound. The flight mechanic swept his arm toward the door, and I scuttled across the deck from my seat in the rear and sat in the open door, my feet dangling in the wind. I looked at the boat below, where I was to package the patient in a litter or basket. Can she sit upright? Does she need oxygen? How much fuel do we have, and will I have time to finish this? My mind raced through the questions without waiting for answers. I would simply have to react as the situation dictated.

The target landing area was a two-foot-square section of wood deck, somewhat protected from the breaking waves by the pilothouse. Slick with the windswept rain, the deck was leaning, and the *Bandit* was far from still as it was twisted and slammed by the incoming seas. Rourke pointed the nose of the aircraft into the wind, using it to create a lift and also placing the island behind and to the left of us. To an observer, had there been one, the boat and helicopter would have looked like a T, the aircraft being the horizontal and the boat the vertical. From this position the boat was outside our right door.

The hoist cable was taut and I was lifted from the deck. I lowered my mask to protect my eyes from the rain and began swinging back and forth on the end of the hoist hook. *Bandit*'s bow was bathed in the helicopter's floodlights. When I was about eight feet from my ever-moving landing spot, I had little choice but to snag the thick steel cable, the one the flight mechanic had noticed running from the bow to the main mast behind the pilothouse. Fortunately, I had learned to wear my wetsuit gloves during every rescue, regardless of the temperature. Several months earlier, I had grabbed another cable very similar to this one, only to find its strands burred out in all directions so that they ripped my bare palm into hamburger meat.

With the *Bandit* in my grip, but before my feet were on solid deck, the flight mechanic began rolling out hoist cable. I was on the wrong side of the boat from my intended landing mark and had to flip both legs over the steel cable. Once I gained footing on the lip of the anchor hatch, I skidded to my knees with the grace of a wooden duck. When I finally stopped sliding, I released the hoist hook and the flight mechanic retrieved it skyward. I was just ten feet in front of the pilothouse.

Everything was moving. The ship was swaying, and the metal net booms rocked back and forth. I had to squint up into the blinding hover lights as I waited for the weight bag and the trail line to be lowered to me. The trail line is a polypropylene line 105 feet long; on the delivery end, a small brass snap hook with a weight bag holding five pounds of lead shot keeps it from blowing in the wind and rotor wash. Out of the darkness, the bag swung into focus, fluttering in the beam of light. Now and then, I could see the big, white letters "USCG" on the bottom of the aircraft. The helicopter was preparing to deliver the basket with my emergency medical gear, so I gathered in the trail line hand over hand until I could retrieve the basket and unload my gear on deck.

The flight mechanic then hoisted the basket clear while I half-crawled, half-climbed down to the pilothouse and my patient. As I passed the windows of the pilothouse, I noticed my reflection, mask still on my face, and realized if I appeared out of the gloom like big orange alien I'd give the heart attack patient a fatal scare. I tilted the mask to my forehead.

With each step, my wetsuit booties slipped on the tilted, moving deck as if it were covered in fish guts. A time or two, I even looked down to make sure it was only wind, rain, and waves as I slid down toward the port side of the pilothouse and the open cabin door, feet spread wide and hands gripping the rails. I spun around the open door to be greeted by the panic-stricken crewmen. Mattie sat on deck next to the wheel, with Captain Crawford just inside the door, as the other two crewmen braced themselves in the shadows of the dimly lit cabin. Like most shrimpers working the Gulf, the pilothouse of the *Bandit* had a long, narrow path from one door to the other with chart tables behind the wheel, radios mounted overhead, and flat, vertical windows facing forward.

Captain Crawford said, "She was feeling weak and said it feels like another heart attack."

I knelt to talk to her. "What does the pain feel like? Is it only in your chest or elsewhere too?"

"My chest feels squeezed, and I can feel the pain all the way down to my hands," she said. "I also take nitro tabs for angina, but I didn't bring any for this trip."

"When was the last time you took the nitro?"

"I can't remember."

"How long have these symptoms been going on this time?"

"About an hour, but they're worse than usual."

Warning bells were ringing in my head. This might be a real heart attack and not just stress, but to make a definitive diagnosis was not my job. That would happen in a hospital, not on a shrimp boat being torn apart by the surf. It was up to me to make the best and quickest decision possible and provide the correct treatment that would keep Mattie alive long enough for a doctor to care for her.

"Captain," I said, "we need to get your wife out of here now," frantically considering the best way to transport my patient. I thought a semi-sitting position would be more comfortable for her than laying her flat and quickly discarded the idea of trying to hoist her in the litter. With the tilt of the boat, wind, and waves, I didn't think we could pull it off.

"You're not going to leave us here are you?" one of Crawford's crewmen pleaded, his eyes bulging with fear.

"I have to, but I'll be back; you've got my word on it," I said. I could tell it was not a comfort. After Crawford shot the man a look that silenced him, the man turned away. One of the many lessons I had learned from other cases was the tension in such an environment is often thick, like a crowd on the edge of a riot. My bullish confidence and actions might make the difference between success and mayhem.

I leaned down and checked Mattie's pulse as I spoke to her about what we needed to do. Her every action—how fast she was breathing, what she said—were signs, giving me clues to her true condition.

"Mattie, I'm going to put you in a basket. It will seem scary, but I need you to trust me. We know what we're doing, and this is like a ride at Disney World," I said, though I doubted she had ridden any roller coasters for years.

"I'm going to have the helicopter hoist down a basket and bring it to the door. We'll place you in it and carry you onto the deck." Reluctantly, she agreed to let us hoist her off with a soft, "Okay." I stood and radioed the hovering helicopter fifty feet above my head, explaining what I wanted to do.

While I was on the *Bandit* the District SAR Coordinator was requesting a second helicopter from Belle Chasse, knowing our limited cabin space might prevent a timely rescue. Each air station is required to maintain one fully qualified crew twenty-four hours a day. In most instances, if a second crew is needed, they must be recalled from home. There is no guarantee that a full complement can be reached, despite the public's faith that when you call on the Coast Guard, they will come. That night the officer manning the desk back at the air station was able to recall a pilot, a copilot, and a flight mechanic, but unable to reach another rescue swimmer. The second aircrew launched and would arrive at the *Bandit* about ten minutes after we were scheduled to return from our rendezvous with the ambulance. At about the same time, the OOD at Station Gulfport had arranged for an ambulance to meet us at the local airport.

Many miles from all those players helping to ensure our success, I keyed the mike of my radio: "I'm ready for the basket." Our rescue basket was welded from polished stainless steel and floats with the aid of two round rolls of foam covered by red Cordura material.

I climbed out of the crowded pilothouse, trying to find footholds wherever I could. With the *Bandit*'s nose shoved onto the sand and the stern being lifted and dropped by the breaking surf and the heavy leftward lean, I had to move downward to port then upward to starboard. The rain was still coming down in steady sheets, leaving the deck as slick as wet glass. I gripped the handrail of the front of the pilothouse with care and pulled myself up to my earlier landing spot on the anchor-hold hatch. I then slung one loose arm around the cable handrail that encompassed the ship and turned my eyes skyward. As the basket came screaming by my head, I snagged it and had slammed it to the deck, leaving the cable attached, then carried it close to the door of the pilothouse.

"Mattie, get it," I yelled over the noise of the hovering helicopter. "You guys grab the other side. We can't hoist it from this spot; we need to be in the clear."

Crawford and the upset crewmen grasped the sides of the basket; Mattie was a petite woman, and we were able to traverse the slippery deck quickly. The helicopter began creeping sideways; the open door where the flight mechanic knelt was getting closer. Before I even gave the thumbs-up signal to indicate Mattie and I were ready for the pickup, the screaming aircraft crept down closer to us, hovering thirty feet directly overhead. The cable went tight, and, despite the rain, wind, moving boat, and obstacles, Mattie was gingerly lifted from the deck. Once the basket was clear, I signaled I was ready for pickup as well.

In a blur, I was back in the helicopter and we were on our way to shore. I momentarily connected to the aircraft's ICS in order to pass Mattie's condition to the pilots. "We've got an ambulance waiting at an airport ten minutes from here, Jerry," Rourke replied. With the strong tailwinds, we landed in eight.

Once we were on deck we moved on fast forward, fearing there might be nothing left of the *Bandit*. Though not in direct communication with the small-boat crew during our brief stay on the tarmac, we believed they were still making their way toward the *Bandit*. I was concentrating so hard on caring for Mattie, I didn't remember the pilot telling me about the second aircraft, but by the time we were airborne again they were well on their way too.

Thirty minutes had passed while we delivered our patient, got fuel, and returned. The boat was still there, but we couldn't see any crewmen on deck. We hoped they had hunkered down in the pilothouse hiding from the storm and tried hailing them on the radio—no answer. What had gone wrong? Were they washed overboard, or did a brave civilian rescue them? We were anxious and quick to investigate.

When I hit the deck—hard—I noticed the difference immediately. The boat felt spongy, less sturdy, and sat much lower in the waves. From my landing spot on the deck, I saw no survivors, and the ship had gone dark. I unclasped the hoist hook and held my open palm toward the sky, the signal for "I'm all right." I slid across the deck and caught the pilothouse door, thankful to see three wide-eyed faces expressing fear and wordless relief at seeing me again.

John Crawford said, "I didn't think you guys could make it back in time. The radio's dead, and she's coming apart." Constant pounding by the heavy breakers had finally broken the keel, and water had raced through the hull, filling the engine spaces, killing power and the radio.

My own radio crackled to life. Rourke asked, "Are they all right?"

"Roger that, three wet survivors ready for the basket. But we need to hurry; the boat is not doing so well."

"The Coast Guard small boat had turned back, it's just us for now," he said. I realized the heavy weather had made it too dangerous for them to continue. There would be no rescue boat as a backup.

Crouching in the pilothouse, I felt the boat rise from the rear as a steep, especially vicious wave pushed toward the beach. The bow punched the sand with a thud; a shuddering vibration shot through the deck, and we heard wood cracking and splintering. The boat quivered for a second as the wave passed the bow, then settled back onto the bottom.

"Time to go," I said into the radio. With my mind still calculating all the angles of this rescue, I worried about the helicopter's ability to hoist all four of us. I knew we had neither the power nor the room. Had I known about the possibility that my survivors and I might be going for a swim, I might have worried. Rourke and the rest of my crew, meanwhile, thought I knew about the second aircraft.

I shouted instructions to each crewman and told them to come out onto the deck one at a time when I waved my hand. Then I clambered back to the hoisting site and again wrapped my right arm around the steel handrail cable. My right shoulder was almost touching the deck. If the boat had been level, I would have been lying down. Though it would have been much easier to control the basket with both hands, there was no way I could let go of that cable. I surely would have been tossed overboard by the waves, because they were, by that point, crashing over the length of the boat.

When I waved to the man watching from the pilothouse window, he nearly sprinted across the deck and jumped into the basked. I held it until it cleared the bow cable and was on its way up. In seconds the empty basket came back, and the second hoist went up just as smoothly. Captain Crawford's crewmen were safe, but I watched with mounting anxiety as my helicopter, my lifeline and ride home, slowly hover-taxied forward and disappeared into sheets of rain.

Before I could grab my radio and—politely—ask for a new course of action, the second aircraft crept out of the dark skies like an angel shrouded in light, illuminated by its floodlight. I gave the ready signal immediately, for I was indeed ready. I should have been cold, but I was sweating as Crawford and I anxiously waited our turns. With each passing minute, the deck became softer; boards were shifting and cracking under my weight. The lights of the hovering helicopter lit up debris that moments earlier had been at the bottom of the boat but was now scattered outward in the breaking waves. I thought we might end up going for a swim at any second. If the *Bandit* failed to hold together for a few more minutes, that swim would be our last, the waves too powerful for our feeble human bodies.

The last planks of the deck were coming apart as I watched Captain Crawford disappear above my head. The flight mechanic hurriedly dropped the basket with Crawford still inside onto the helicopter deck, then sent the bare hook right back down even sooner than I expected.

A bare-hook recovery is considered an emergency; no communication is necessary between helicopter crew and swimmer. If a hook is lowered, the swimmer gets on it no matter what. I grabbed the hook without waiting for it to hit the deck. As a rule, we tried to let the hoist hook contact the water or some other grounding point, such as a boat, to discharge its built-up static electricity. This time, however, I didn't wait. Even though my neoprene gloves blocked the full charge, I felt as if I had stuck my finger into light socket.

I yanked the D-ring from its slot in the harness wrapped around my chest and snapped it on the hook. Looking upward, I gave my trademark two thumbs up, but before the flight mechanic could lift me, the rear of the boat rose like a shark lunging for its meal—I was that meal. The deck buckled but held long enough for the slack in the hoist cable to be taken up. I was hoisted clear, with the boat still coming at me; a wave was shoving it toward the beach as the pilot simultaneously backed the aircraft in the same direction. To compound the problem, the boat climbed skyward, canceling my sensation of moving up. Even though the flight mechanic was reeling in hoist cable like an excited fisherman with the catch of a lifetime, I couldn't clear the deck by more than two feet.

It was as if the *Bandit*, cheated of her victims, was determined to take me in their place. The aircrew could see what was happening and attempted to gain clearance for me by moving shoreward, toward the bow. I began sailing with great speed through the air and, from the corner of my eyes, glimpsed the forward stanchion on the bow. Its steel arms welded to a heavy post jutted up and out from the deck and stood in my path. Reacting automatically, grunting and heaving, I brought my knees and legs into the tightest sit-up of my life, almost touching my face. Still, I could see I wasn't going to make it. Hanging from the hoist hook with my knees touching my chin, my backside was the lowest part of my body, and in a split second was about to slam into the post. At sixty knots of airspeed I was about to create an explosion of blood and tissue. I closed my eyes and braced for the impact; instead, I only felt air rushing by me. I gave a twisting backward glance in time to see the boat disappear into the blackness.

The captain of the *Europa Jet* said, "It broke into a million pieces." He later reported finding debris scattered for miles.

I was greeted at the door of the helicopter by the toothy grin of one of the best flight mechanics in the Coast Guard, John "Flash" Gordon. When I began the wild ride off the boat, I had no idea who was working the hoist on the second helicopter, but I was immensely glad to see his friendly face. He saved my butt, literally.

About a week later, I called the hospital where Mattie had been taken, trying to learn of her condition. Like all non-relatives, I was given just the information that was considered public. She had been admitted and was receiving treatment. As least I had the satisfaction of knowing she survived.

Sources

"The Falls" from *So Others May Live: Coast Guard's Rescue Swimmers: Saving Lives, Defying Death*. Martha LaGuardia Kotite. Guilford, CT: Lyons Press, 2006.

"Superstorm: Inside Hurricane Sandy" from *Superstorm: Nine Days Inside Hurricane Sandy*. Kathryn Miles. New York: Dutton/Penguin, 2014.

"Saving New York Harbor." William H. Thiesen, PhD. US Coast Guard Department of Public Affairs, Fifth District. 2014.

"The Worst Days of a Bad Fall" from *Rescue, True Stories of the U.S. Life-Saving Service* (edited by John Galluzzo). Eric C. Hartlep. Hull, MA: Avery Color Studios and the United States Life-Saving Service Heritage Foundation, 2011.

"A Long Good Night" from *Brotherhood of the Fin: A Coast Guard Rescue Swimmer's Story*. Gerald R. Hoover. Tucson, AZ: Wheatmark, 2007.

"The U.S. Coast Guard in World War II" from *The U.S. Coast Guard in World War II*. Malcolm F. Willoughby. Annapolis, MD: Naval Institute Press, 1957, 1989, 2016.

"Ordeal in the Ice" from *Rescue, True Stories of the U.S. Life-Saving Service* (edited by John Galluzzo). Geoffrey Reynolds. Hull, MA: Avery Color Studios and the United States Life-Saving Service Heritage Foundation, 2011.

"Man Down" from *Deadliest Sea: The Untold Story Behind the Greatest Rescue in Coast Guard History*. Kalee Thompson. New York: William Morrow/Harper Collins, 2010.

"With the U.S. Life-savers: Rescue by Moonlight" from *The Boy with the U.S. Life-Savers*. Francis Rolt-Wheeler. Norwood, MA: Lothrop, Lee & Shepard Co., 1915.

"Figuring the Variables" from *Burning Cold*. H. Paul Jeffers. Minneapolis: Quarto Publishing Group/Motorbooks, 2006.

"Storm of the Century" from *So Others May Live: Coast Guard's Rescue Swimmers: Saving Lives, Defying Death*. Martha LaGuardia Kotite. Guilford, CT: Lyons Press, 2006.

"Two Tankers Down" from *Two Tankers Down: The Greatest Small-Boat Rescue in U.S. Coast Guard History*. Robert Frump. Guilford, CT: Lyons Press, 2008.

"*Bandit*" from *Brotherhood of the Fin: A Coast Guard Rescue Swimmer's Story*. Gerald R. Hoover. Tucson, AZ: Wheatmark, 2007.